UNITED STATES
MAGISTRATES
IN THE
FEDERAL COURTS

United States Magistrates in the Federal Courts

SUBORDINATE JUDGES

Christopher E. Smith

New York
Westport, Connecticut
London

Library of Congress Cataloging-in-Publication Data

Smith, Christopher E.
    United States magistrates in the federal courts : subordinate
judges / Christopher E. Smith.
        p. cm.
    Includes bibliographical references.
    ISBN 0–275–93396–2 (alk. paper)
    1. United States magistrates.   I. Title.
KF8792.S65   1990
347.73'2034—dc20   89-16214
[347.307234]

Library of Congress Catalog Card Number: 89–16214
ISBN: 0–275–93396–2

First published in 1990

Praeger Publishers, One Madison Avenue, New York, NY 10010
A division of Greenwood Press, Inc.

Printed in the United States of America

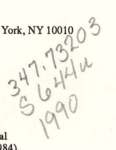

The paper used in this book complies with the
Permanent Paper Standard issued by the National
Information Standards Organization (Z39.48–1984).

10 9 8 7 6 5 4 3 2 1

For Charlotte and Alicia

Contents

Acknowledgments

I am grateful for the kind permission of publishers to incorporate material that previously appeared in altered form: Portions of Chapter 3 previously appeared in a slightly altered version as "Merit Selection Committees and the Politics of Appointing U.S. Magistrates," *The Justice System Journal* 12 (1987): 210–231. Copyright 1987 by The Institute for Court Management of the National Center for State Courts. Reprinted by permission. Portions of Chapters 9 and 10 appeared in an altered version as "Assessing the Consequences of Judicial Innovation: U.S. Magistrates' Trials and Related Tribulations," *Wake Forest Law Review* 23 (1988): 455–490. Copyright 1988 by the Wake Forest Law Review Association. Reprinted by permission. In addition, a portion of Chapter 3 previously appeared in altered form as "Who Are the U.S. Magistrates?", *Judicature* 71 (1987): 143–150. Copyright 1987 by Christopher E. Smith. Portions of Chapters 9 and 10 previously appeared in altered form as "United States Magistrates and the Processing of Prisoner Litigation," *Federal Probation* 52 (December 1988): 13–18.

This project would never have been possible without the generous assistance of U.S. magistrates and district judges who, contrary to the predictions of other social scientists, permitted me to observe the usually hidden details of their working lives within several federal courthouses. I will always be deeply grateful for these special opportunities to see the behind-the-scenes interactions of actors within the federal judiciary not only because they provided the basis for the analysis and conclusions in this study, but also because they contributed immeasurably to my personal education about judicial institutions. In addition, numerous judges, lawyers, and other officials involved with the federal judiciary were very helpful in answering my questions and providing useful documents and information.

I am indebted to George Cole for his advice and encouragement throughout this project. I also received helpful comments at various stages from Fred Kort, Robert Gilmour, and C. Neal Tate. A number of friends and relatives provided assistance on various matters: Frances Payne, Donald Vereen, Lisa Zimmer, and Peggy and Ernie Zimmer. I

x Acknowledgments

am grateful to Bonnie Ralston and Mari Bell Nolan for helping to prepare the manuscript.

My parents, Robert Lee Smith and Carol Payne Smith, both of Western Michigan University, provided inspiration, encouragement, and assistance.

Most of all, I must acknowledge both the research assistance and innumerable supportive contributions of my wife, Charlotte, and the pleasant distractions provided by my daughter, Alicia.

Part 1

Introduction

The Federal Courts' Subordinate Judges

How do court systems deal with increasing demands upon their scarce resources? The federal courts have experienced a well-documented increase in case filings. For example, between 1970 and 1986 there was a 192 percent increase in civil case filings while the number of authorized judgeships to process these cases increased only 43 percent.[1] Although some scholars dispute whether all court systems have experienced an actual "litigation explosion,"[2] this steady growth in the workload burdening the federal judiciary is a persistent source of concern for federal judges[3] and outside observers.[4] As with other governmental institutions, the identification of specific problems can spur the introduction of reforms and innovations designed either to increase institutional resources and efficiency or reduce the burden of demands upon that component of the political system. The documented increase in case pressures upon the federal courts has fostered reform and experimentation in court structures and procedures intended to reduce case backlogs and increase case-processing efficiency. Increased demands upon judicial resources led to the introduction of new actors from outside the judiciary, including mediators[5] and arbitrators,[6] the creation of new actors within the judicial branch,[7] and the implementation of new case-settlement procedures, such as summary jury trials.[8]

One little-noticed development in the federal courts was the creation of a new judicial office, United States Magistrate, in 1968. The magistrates were introduced into the federal judiciary in response to the growing caseload pressures of the 1960s. The creation and utilization of U.S. magistrates represents one particular kind of reform intended to expand the federal courts' resources, namely the introduction of an innovative, flexible judicial officer. By analyzing the magistrates' roles and behavior in the federal courts, the details and consequences of this type of judicial innovation can be better understood and evaluated.

Federal magistrates, working under the supervision of district judges, possess significant judicial authority. There are 292 full-time and 169 part-time magistrates working in federal district courts throughout the country.[9] In 1987 magistrates handled 466,078 matters for the federal courts, including the supervision of 962 actual civil trials.[10] Judicial authority is exercised by these congressionally created subordinate judges, despite the fact that they lack the protections of secure tenure and undiminishable salaries that insure the independence of federal district and appellate judges through the provisions of Article III of the U.S. Constitution. Unlike the Article III judges, whose constitutionally mandated term of "good Behaviour" can effectively keep them in office for life, full-time magistrates are appointed to eight-year renewable terms by judges within a district court; part-time magistrates serve for similar four-year terms.

Magistrates are federal judicial officers whose utilization and authority are open to flexible application by the supervising judges in individual districts. Over their brief history, the roles and authority of magistrates expanded from that of primarily hearing petty criminal matters and handling simple arraignments to reviewing civil rights cases, supervising case settlements, and even presiding over full civil jury trials with the consent of litigants. Without the published opinions and high public profiles of district judges, magistrates are relatively unnoticed and invisible as they carry out their work within the federal courts. Despite this anonymity, magistrates decide civil cases, incarcerate suspects, sentence misdemeanants to imprisonment, identify civil rights violations, and determine who is entitled to Social Security disability benefits. These are important decisions, both in human terms for individual litigants and for the policy outcomes produced by courts. Although magistrates are increasingly influential in deciding cases within the federal courts, their roles and behavior, unlike those of federal district and appellate judges, have not received thorough attention from scholars and legal commentators. In an attempt to describe and analyze comprehensively the consequences of introducing authoritative yet invisible subordinate judges into the federal courts, this study presents the findings and conclusions of an empirical examination of both the intricate details and broad, systemic ramifications of the magistrates' roles and behavior.

The introduction of judicial reforms has prompted warnings that the federal courts have become so "bureaucratized" that cases are improperly screened and terminated by subordinate judicial officers, law clerks, and staff attorneys.[11] The fact that judges and legal scholars feel they must warn the legal community and public about the problem of bureaucratization indicates that internal reforms affecting the judiciary possess a very low level of visibility. Although recent reform initiatives are not noticed or understood by the public, these changes raise important questions concerning the proper operation of the judicial branch within the framework of the United States Constitution's governing system. Most notably, the alleged "bureaucratization problem" raises the specter of litigants regularly denied access to the recognized federal judges in whom Article III of the Constitution exclusively vests the "judicial power of the United States."[12] In a larger sense, changes that are instituted within the judicial branch risk fundamental alteration of that branch's purposes and functions. Although reforms within the federal judiciary tend to be adaptations rather than basic changes, due to the political power of federal judges and low visibility of court reform,[13] some commentators believe that court reforms have been very damaging. For example, Judith Resnik has warned that judges' traditional adjudicatory responsibilities become subsumed by their managerial role in fostering case settlements and other aspects of modern litigation management and court administration.[14] In addition, she argues that congressional or judicial creation of decision makers within the courts who lack the narrow definition, constitutional protections, and adjudicatory traditions of judges under Article III fundamentally alters the nature of the courts' role within the American constitutional system.[15]

Although individuals' divergent conceptions of the judiciary's proper role in American society influence assessments of judicial innovation, most conclusions about the consequences of planned changes are based upon perceptions about the effects of reforms upon individual judicial actors and litigants. For example, Resnik and others assert that the proliferation of new, non-Article III judicial decision makers improperly places actual decision-making power and determination of case outcomes within the hands of the subordinate officials rather than under the control of the judges who supervise those officials.[16] This argument presumes that either supervising judges are not called upon to review subordinates' decisions (e.g., no appeal was presented by litigants) or that subsequent review of subordinates' decisions by judges does not effectively guide, alter, or otherwise determine the outcomes of cases. Although research within courts tends to validate this perception about the inherent risks of delegating decision-making authority,[17] a concrete assessment of the effects of any court reform can best be obtained through a careful empirical examination of the actual consequences of a particular innovation introduced within the judiciary.

FRAMEWORK AND METHODS

The examination of any subject through modern social science methods of empirical analysis requires the researcher to make choices about the questions to be explored and the investigative methods best suited to accomplish the study's objectives. Many contemporary social science studies of judicial institutions and processes utilize sophisticated quantitative techniques to measure the effects of specific, narrowly focused variables upon judicial decision making.[18] Topics such as sentencing[19] and appellate decision making[20] receive an inordinate share of scholarly attention. These studies make significant contributions to knowledge about human behavior within the judicial branch by building upon a substantial body of literature derived from previous studies on these topics. When confronted with a still-developing judicial innovation that has received relatively little systematic scholarly attention, however, the researcher is faced with myriad choices concerning topical foci and appropriate methods because of the limited number of preceding studies. The choices made in the design of this study were influenced by the opportunity to provide undiscovered details about the consequences of a young, evolving judicial innovation through observational research within the federal courts. Moreover, as with any study, the approaches selected for investigating this particular court reform derive from the presuppositions that underlie political science research on the judicial branch.

Political science research has focused on judicial actors, processes, and institutions as components of the political system.[21] For example, in his well-known study of the federal appellate courts, J. Woodford Howard described the federal judiciary as "an interlocking network of relations linking circuit judges to district judges, federal agencies, and the Supreme Court, and thence to other appellate courts, branches of government, and a wide array of individuals and interest groups who compose their chief constituencies."[22] Political influences affect the structure and composition of the judicial branch and subsequently determine the case decisions, policies, and other value-allocative outcomes produced by the "Third Branch." As newly created judicial officials, such as magistrates, become influential, albeit relatively invisible, actors within the courts, their activities and effects can be analyzed in light of prior political science research on the judiciary. Chapter 9 will discuss more completely how these premises inform the analysis of the magistrates' effects upon the judicial system.

This study examines the magistrates through the analytic framework of role theory, which has provided the basis for important studies of judges on state supreme courts,[23] state trial courts,[24] federal courts of appeals,[25] and the U.S. Supreme Court.[26] The basic premise of role theory is that individuals act differently within their institutional context than they do when acting in relative isolation. According to a leading theorist, a role consists of "behaviors that are characteristic of persons in a context."[27] Thus a judicial actor's role is a pattern of behavior that is determined by his expectations, the normative expectations that others have for him, and other factors which inform the actor's conception of his function in the judicial system.[28] Magistrates have expectations about how they should behave toward others, particularly district judges, lawyers, and parties appearing in judicial proceedings. In addition, judges, attorneys, legislative actors, and litigants have expectations concerning what magistrates should do.

The specific institutional contexts in which magistrates work affect aspects of their roles. There are generally both informal and explicit formal expectations about role behavior within institutions that are reinforced through incentive and sanction mechanisms. These expectations serve to limit the choice and discretion, and thereby define the roles and behavior, of the members of the institution.[29] For magistrates, their subordinate position and reliance upon district judges for delegated tasks and authority mean that the district judges substantially define the boundaries of the magistrates' role behavior. While federal magistrates share common positions and identical powers under the federal statutes, the institutional settings and organizational characteristics of the courts in which they work vary according to physical setting, geographic location, caseload characteristics, judicial traditions, and intra-court relationships between judicial actors. These diverse contexts and influences affect the magistrates' synthesis of expectations and lead to the formation of differing role conceptions and behaviors within different district courts. The diversity of magistrates' roles, while complicating the task of describing and analyzing the effects of these subordinate judges, underscores the importance of seeking an understanding of influential actors who are not only relatively invisible to the public, but also defy simple, standardized characterizations.

For this study, the roles of magistrates were examined through the use of two primary research methods: elite interviews and participant observation. In addition, the responses to limited surveys on specific topics supplemented information gained from the interviews and observations.

Between March 1986 and October 1987, interviews were conducted with twenty-one magistrates in thirteen courthouses within nine Midwestern and Northeastern districts. Interviews were also conducted with seventeen district judges, three appellate judges, members of merit selection committees responsible for nominating magistrate appointees—including practicing lawyers, and officials at the Administrative Office of the U.S. Courts.[30] Under the elite interview format, the magistrates, judges, and other interviewees were questioned using unstructured or semi-structured interview items to elicit a wide range of perceptions about court structures, processes, and norms affecting the magistrates' roles.[31]

Observation studies ranging in length from one day to six weeks were conducted for a total of twelve weeks with nine different magistrates in 1987. Magistrates were observed in two large court-houses containing at least ten district judges and four magistrates each. Additional observation research was undertaken with magis-trates in four smaller courthouses containing no more than two magistrates and four judges. The settings were selected to represent different, general institutional contexts in which magistrates work that would vary by size, caseload composition, complexity of court organization, and intra-court contact and communication between judicial actors. In each setting, magistrates were observed engaging in normal daily activities including conversations with their staffs, hear-ings, settlement conferences, and civil trials. The author literally shadowed the magistrates during all of their activities and interac-tions at the various courthouses.[32]

In settlement conferences and other private, closed-door situations, the author's presence was readily noticed by the attorneys and litigants. Some magistrates chose to introduce the author prior to the start of such conferences. Although these situations invited the pos-sibility of researcher-induced effects upon all of the actors present, the author's presence in the corner of the room did not discernibly affect the behavior of the lawyers whose adversarial responsibilities neces-sarily focused their attention upon the proceedings at hand. In most cases, the attorneys and their clients presumed that the author was the magistrates' law clerk when the magistrates chose not to introduce the author prior to private conferences. As a result, the findings and conclusions of this study benefit from unrestricted exposure to the intricate yet frequently mundane details of the daily lives of judicial actors.

The participant observation methodology utilized for this study is consistent with arguments by leading political scientists advocating field research emphasizing firsthand observation of political phenomena within their proper context.[33] The methodology has been used effectively for several important studies in political science,[34] including studies of judges.[35] Although observation is rightly criticized for a potential lack of reproducibility of findings,[36] the methodology possesses a special value for topics in their initial stage of examination.[37] Because there have been only limited studies of U.S. magistrates through surveys[38] and selected interviews,[39] specific details of magistrates' behavior were not previously available.

Like other judicial officers, magistrates work within the protective walls of the judicial system beyond the purview of the public. Because their legitimacy within the American governing system is dependent upon the maintenance of the "judicial myth" that judges act without political motivations by adhering to neutral principles of law,[40] judges have a great incentive to protect their discretionary actions from external scrutiny and evaluation. Opportunities for observation of the behind-the-scenes behavior and interactions of judicial officers are relatively rare. The author hopes that this study effectively exploits the unique opportunity presented to observe the intimate details of life for these subordinate judges in order to gain firmer understandings about judicial processes generally and this type of court reform in particular.

In order to present a comprehensive examination of the U.S. magistrates within the federal courts, the initial chapters provide background information on the creation and implementation of the system of subordinate judges. Chapter 2 describes the historical development of magistrates' authority and Chapter 3 presents findings and conclusions concerning the selection and composition of the magistrates nationally. The middle chapters, 4 through 7, describe the details of magistrates' roles and behaviors in representative court contexts based upon observations and interviews. Chapters 8 through 10 analyze the development of magistrates' roles and the subordinate judges' consequences for the judicial system and for American society.

NOTES

1. Bureau of Justice Statistics, "The Federal Civil Justice System," *Bureau of Justice Statistics Bulletin*,(July 1987), 4.

2. Marc Galanter, "Reading the Landscape of Disputes: What We Know and Don't Know (and Think We Know) About Our Allegedly Contentious and Litigious Society," *U.C.L.A. Law Review* 31 (1983): 4–71.

3. Committee on the Judicial Branch, *Simple Fairness: The Case for Equitable Compensation of the Nation's Federal Judges*, (Washington, D.C.: Judicial Conference of the United States, 1988), 16–20; Richard A. Posner, *The Federal Courts: Crisis and Reform*, (Cambridge, MA: Harvard University Press, 1985), 59–93.

4. Lawrence Baum, *American Courts: Process and Policy*, (Boston: Houghton Mifflin, 1986), 225.

5. Kathy L. Shuart, *The Wayne County Mediation Program in the Eastern District of Michigan* (Washington, D.C.: Federal Judicial Center, 1984).

6. E. Allan Lind and John E. Shepard, *Evaluation of Court-Annexed Arbitration in Three Federal District Courts* (Washington, D.C.: Federal Judicial Center, 1983).

7. The federal courts of appeals utilize staff attorneys to screen cases and some district courts have special "pro se law clerks" who evaluate the complaints

filed by indigent and unrepresented claimants, usually prisoners. Wade H. McCree, Jr., "Bureaucratic Justice: An Early Warning," *University of Pennsylvania Law Review* 129 (1981): 777, 785.

8.   Summary trials are one-day nonbinding trials in which attorneys present arguments before a real jury. The nonbinding verdict serves to inform attorneys about the strength of their cases and thus lead to a more realistic willingness to settle. M. Daniel Jacoubovitch and Carl M. Moore, *Summary Jury Trials in the Northern District of Ohio* (Washington, D.C.: Federal Judicial Center, 1982).

9.   Carroll Seron, "The Professional Project of Parajudges: The Case of U.S. Magistrates," *Law and Society Review* 22 (1988): 558 n. 2.

10.   Administrative Office of the U.S. Courts, *Annual Report of the Director of the Administrative Office of the United States Courts,* (Washington, D.C.: U.S. Government Printing Office, 1987), 34, 37.

11.   Owen Fiss, "The Bureaucratization of the Judiciary," *Yale Law Journal* 92 (1983): 1442–1468; McCree, "Bureaucratic Justice," 777–797.

12.   U.S. Const., Art. III, Sec. 1.

13.   Peter G. Fish, *The Politics of Federal Judicial Administration,* (Princeton: Princeton University Press, 1973), 432–433.

14.   Judith Resnik, "Managerial Judges," *Harvard Law Review* 96 (1982): 374–448.

15.   Judith Resnik, "The Mythic Meaning of Article III Courts," *University of Colorado Law Review* 56 (1985): 581–617.

16.   McCree, "Bureaucratic Justice," 789; Resnik, "The Mythic Meaning," 615–617.

17.   For example, because law clerks for Supreme Court justices bear primary responsibility for reviewing petitions for certiorari, there are inevitable risks that the clerks will exclude important cases. Howard Ball, *Courts and Politics: The Federal Judicial System,* (Englewood Cliffs, NJ: Prentice-Hall, 1987), 273.

18.   For example, Gregory A. Caldeira and John R. Wright, "Organized Interests and Agenda Setting in the U.S. Supreme Court," *American Political Science Review* 82 (1988): 1109–1127; C. K. Rowland, Donald Songer, and Robert A. Carp, "Presidential Effects on Criminal Justice Policy in the Lower Federal Courts: The Reagan Judges," *Law and Society Review* 22 (1988): 191–200.

19.   For example, Cassia Spohn, Susan Welch, and John Gruhl, "Women Defendants in Court: The Interaction Between Sex and Race in Convicting and Sentencing," *Social Science Quarterly* 66 (1985): 178–185.

20.   For example, Philip L. DuBois, "The Illusion of Judicial Consensus Revisited: Partisan Conflict on an Intermediate State Court of Appeals," *American Journal of Political Science* 32 (1988): 946–967.

21.   Henry R. Glick, *Courts, Politics, and Justice,* 2nd. ed., (New York: McGraw-Hill, 1988); Harry P. Stumpf, *American Judicial Politics,* (New York: Harcourt Brace Jovanovich, 1988).

22.   J. Woodford Howard, *Courts of Appeals in the Federal Judicial System,* (Princeton: Princeton University Press, 1981), xxi.

23.   John T. Wold, "Political Orientations, Social Backgrounds, and Role Perceptions of State Supreme Court Judges," *Western Political Quarterly* 27 (1974): 239–248.

24. James L. Gibson, "Judges' Role Orientations, Attitudes and Decisions: An Interactive Model," *American Political Science Review* 72 (1978): 911–924.

25. Howard, *Courts of Appeals*, xxii–xxiv.

26. Joel B. Grossman, "Role Playing and the Analysis of Judicial Behavior: The Case of Mr. Justice Frankfurter," *Journal of Public Law* 11 (1962): 285–309.

27. Bruce J. Biddle, *Role Theory*, (New York: Academic Press, 1979), 56.

28. Grossman, "Role Playing," 294.

29. James L. Gibson, "From Simplicity to Complexity: The Development of Theory in the Study of Judicial Behavior," *Political Behavior* 5 (1983): 17.

30. Interviews ranged in length from fifteen minutes to three and one-half hours, with the average interview lasting approximately fifty minutes. Two interviews were conducted over the telephone when personal visits could not be arranged. Follow-up questions were asked of some interviewees via subsequent telephone conversations. In addition to the formal interviews, numerous lawyers, litigants, and other court officials provided information in the course of informal conversations during the various observation studies.

31. An elite interview refers to interviewing "people in important or exposed positions [who] may require VIP interviewing treatment." Lewis A. Dexter, *Elite and Specialized Interviewing*, (Evanston: Northwestern University Press, 1970), 5. In a standardized interview or "focused interview," in its pure form, the researcher defines the questions and problems. By contrast, in the elite interview the investigator is "willing, and often eager to let the interviewee teach him what the problem, the question, the situation, is." Ibid. As described by Jarol Manheim and Richard Rich, "[t]he purpose of elite interviewing is generally not the collection of prespecified data but the gathering of information which will assist in reconstructing some event or discerning a pattern in specific behaviors." Jarol B. Manheim and Richard C. Rich, *Empirical Political Analysis*, (White Plains, NY: Longman, 1986), 132.

The interviews were conducted with assurances that no quotations would be attributed to specific individuals without explicit permission and that confidential information about specific cases would be protected.

32. The opportunity to undertake participant observation research in the judiciary and elsewhere involves the establishment of negotiated understandings between the researcher and court personnel. For this study, as with other judicial studies, "[o]rganizational access for field research on the courts must at some point be negotiated." George J. McCall, *Observing the Law: Applications of Field Methods to the Study of the Criminal Justice System*, (Rockville, MD: National Institute of Mental Health, 1975), 115. The magistrates who agreed to permit and facilitate observation of their roles in the federal courts were generally careful to gain a complete understanding of the author's goals and methods. In two courthouses, as part of negotiated understandings that would permit long-term access to the courts, the author agreed to spend some time assisting in legal research tasks. The agreement was partially a quid pro quo for permitting the author to take up so much of the magistrates' time and attention. In addition, the assignments enabled the author to gain genuine first-hand exposure to the types of legal research and writing tasks that absorb magistrates' time. Although this study is not based upon any premise requiring empathic experience as a basis

for learning, knowledge, or understanding, the research experiences provided valuable exposure to the nature of claims addressed by magistrates. The assistance was provided during time periods when the magistrates themselves were doing research and writing on other cases. This participation, although quite limited, poses additional risks that the author's perceptions were biased through participation. However, both the author and the magistrates were well aware of the author's goals and interests. This shared understanding, cooperation, and recognition of possible problems reduced the potential role conflicts for the author.

Furthermore, the vast majority of studies of judicial personnel are limited to interviews, surveys, and statistical analyses. Opportunities for direct observation "behind the purple curtain" of the judiciary are so exceptional that such negotiated understandings are a small price to pay for the new descriptions and analyses which result from closer study of the judicial branch.

33. For example, Richard F. Fenno, "Observation, Context, and Sequence in the Study of Politics," *American Political Science Review* 80 (1986): 3–15.

34. For example, Raymond Wolfinger, *The Politics of Progress* (Englewood Cliffs, NJ: Prentice-Hall, 1974).

35. For example, John Paul Ryan, Allan Ashman, Bruce D. Sales, and Sandra Shane-DuBow, *American Trial Judges*, (New York: The Free Press, 1980).

36. James L. Gibson, "The Science and Ideology of Judicial Politics," paper presented at the 1983 annual meeting of the American Political Science Association, 4.

37. Ibid., 5.

38. Carroll Seron, *The Roles of Magistrates in Federal District Courts*, (Washington, D.C.: Federal Judicial Center, 1983).

39. Carroll Seron, *The Roles of Magistrates: Nine Case Studies* (Washington, D.C.: Federal Judicial Center, 1985); Steven Puro, Roger L. Goldman, and Alice M. Padawer-Singer, "The Evolving Role of U.S. Magistrates in the District Courts," *Judicature* 64 (1981): 436–449.

40. Stumpf, *American Judicial Politics*, 32–36.

Part 2

The U.S. Magistrates: Historical Background and Selection Procedures

2

A Brief History of the U.S. Magistrates and Their Powers

Any understanding of the development of the role of United States magistrates requires familiarity with the historical, statutory, and case law elements underlying the establishment and evolution of the magistrate system. Although the office of United States Magistrate has a relatively brief history, the historical antecedents and political factors underlying the creation of the magistrate system have had a profound effect upon the design of that system and, consequently, the evolution of the magistrate role. In addition, a series of legislative and judicial decisions regarding the appropriate authority for these subordinate judges has further defined the roles of magistrates in the district courts.

THE ORIGINS OF THE MAGISTRATES ACT

The predecessors to the federal magistrates were the United States Commissioners. In an act passed in 1793, Congress provided that certain individuals "learned in law" could have responsibility for taking bail in federal criminal cases.[1] These individuals were officially designated as "commissioners" in 1817. During the next century, Congress gradually expanded the duties of the commissioners. Commissioners were appointed directly by district courts and were given responsibility for issuing warrants and fining persons convicted of petty offenses on federal land, including national parks and military installations. The commissioners, who were not required to be lawyers, were paid through a fee schedule that compensated them according to the number cases that they handled.[2]

As a result of a study conducted by the Administrative Office of the United States Courts (Administrative Office) in the 1940s, minor changes in the commissioner system, including a simplified fee schedule, were recommended by the Judicial Conference of the United States (Judicial Conference) and adopted by Congress. In the late 1950s, the chairman of the House Judiciary Committee recommended that the commissioner system be evaluated to determine if some alternative means might better assist the administration of justice in the federal courts. A few reform bills were proposed in Congress, but no legislation was passed.[3]

In 1965, Democratic Senator Joseph Tydings of Maryland, the chairman of the Senate Judiciary Subcommittee on Improvements in Judicial Machinery, initiated hearings to examine the commissioner system and to consider reform proposals. Those hearings illuminated a number of defects in the existing system, including irregularities in practices and procedures utilized by commissioners, the lack of any legal training or qualifications for many commissioners, and deficiencies in the fee system and other administrative matters.[4] As a result of the hearings, a bill was introduced in the Senate to eliminate the commissioner system and create the new office of United States Magistrate. The individuals appointed as federal magistrates, who needed to possess specific legal education and bar membership qualifications, were expected to fulfill the commissioners' duties in a more professional, systematic fashion as well as undertake additional, more complicated judicial tasks assigned by district judges.

Hearings were conducted by the Senate Judiciary Committee during 1966 and 1967 on the proposed legislation. When the bill came before the full Senate, the members unanimously approved the legislation without debate.

A House Judiciary Subcommittee conducted hearings on similar legislation the following year. After quick approval by the Judiciary Committee, the proposed legislation met opposition from several representatives on constitutional grounds. The opposition could not generate enough votes to stop the legislation and President Johnson signed the Magistrates Act[5] into law on October 17, 1968.[6]

The impetus for the reforms embodied in the creation of the office of United States Magistrate derived from the substantial increases in the number of cases filed in the federal courts during the 1960s. This increased caseload quickly exacerbated the extensive backlog problems with pending cases. For example, the federal courts had a backlog of 2,200 pending cases in 1960, but by 1966 the backlog had grown to 5,387.[7] During that same period, civil appeals increased by 50 percent; administrative agency review appeals increased by 96 percent; criminal appeals increased by 130 percent; and actions filed by prisoners increased by 280 percent.[8] Because of the increase in litigation, members of Congress recognized that the federal courts were overburdened and in need of additional resources.

The dramatic increase in prisoner cases received special attention in the hearings as one federal judge noted that "these particular matters take up an inordinate amount of time."[9] The Act envisioned that magistrates could handle the review of prisoners' petitions in order to ease the burden on judges. Subsequent developments indicate that magistrates have indeed assumed substantial responsibility for the ever-growing number of prisoner cases.

The substantial increase in caseload for the federal judiciary was an influential factor in creating a "policy window" for court reforms during the 1960s.[10] The caseload increases necessitated some type of reform, but the creation of a new subordinate judicial officer was only one of several possible options. Some judges and members of Congress advocated the creation of new federal judgeships.[11] Certain factors in the 1960s, however, combined with the caseload increases to generate the creation of the office of United States Magistrate instead.

One important factor underlying the Magistrates Act involved the political considerations that pervade the process of selecting and appointing federal judges. Federal judges are nominated by the president, usually in consultation with the senators from the relevant state if they are from the president's party. Thus there is a political patronage aspect to federal judicial appointments. In 1959, because of rising caseloads, the Judicial Conference requested creation of forty-three new federal judgeships, and President Eisenhower advocated creation of forty-five new judgeships. Eisenhower went so far as to pledge that he would fill half of the new judgeships with Democrats in order to induce Congress to act on the requested authorization for new positions.[12] Despite nearly universal, and apparently earnest, concerns over the state of the federal judiciary, partisan conflicts in Congress prevented the creation of the requested judgeships. Democrats were wary of introducing new judgeships during a Republican presidency. This record of political conflict over the creation of new life-tenure judgeships, with their concomitant policy-making capabilities lasting beyond the tenure of the appointing president, led many members of Congress to advocate the creation of limited-term magistrates who would be subordinate to the district judges.

Magistrates were also favored over new judgeships because subordinate judicial officers would be less expensive. Magistrates received lower salaries and, more importantly, required significantly lower expenditures for staff support. Judges need larger secretarial, clerical, legal, and security support staffs. New judgeships also create the possibility of significant capital outlays for construction of new courtroom facilities. In addition, magistrates, unlike district judges, could be assigned a limited range of tasks and be placed in remote areas such as national parks. Thus, some magistrates could be utilized inexpensively to continue the duties of the old commissioners in hearing charges pertaining to petty offenses on federal land.[13]

The Magistrates Act received additional support when it was exploited for publicity purposes as a "crime control" measure by Republican members of the House of Representatives.[14] The legislation benefited from this politicization during the year prior to the 1968 elections despite the fact that the so-called "crime problem" perceived by the public primarily involved violent crimes (e.g., robbery, assault, burglary, etc.) that are normally under state rather than federal jurisdiction. In actuality, the testimony and other legislative history underlying the act's purposes focused on the growth in civil case filings and prisoner petitions rather than increases in federal criminal cases.

Not surprisingly, the media and the public paid little attention to the reforms occurring within the federal judiciary. A review of all *New York Times* articles relevant to the Magistrates Act for the years 1965 through 1968, the years from the beginning of the first exploratory hearings through the passage and signing of the legislation, indicates that brief articles buried in the newspaper merely noted various steps in the legislative process.[15] As with other internal judicial reforms, the planning and discussion underlying the Magistrates Act remained strictly the province of lawyers and judges.

The primary opposition to the Magistrates Act of 1968 came from Representative William Cahill, a Republican from New Jersey, who conducted a crusade against the statute in the House. Cahill's opposition served as a precursor to stronger, more vocal opposition that would emerge when the Magistrates Act was amended in subsequent years to expand the authority of the subordinate judges. Cahill favored the creation of new judgeships rather than implementation of a new, subordinate judicial position. His concerns focused on the potential constitutional problem of conferring judicial authority on individuals who lack the protections of secure tenure and undiminishable salary provided by Article III of the Constitution for federal judicial officers. Cahill also feared that federal judges would become involved in political patronage through their power to appoint magistrates. He felt so strongly about the Magistrates Act that he attached a detailed five-page dissent to the House Report on the legislation.[16] Although the magistrates subsequently became accepted and incorporated into the district courts, controversy continued regarding the appropriate limits upon their status and authority as federal judicial officers.

THE DEVELOPMENT OF MAGISTRATES' AUTHORITY

The Magistrates Act of 1968 provided the new subordinate judges with power over three primary categories of judicial duties: (1) all duties and powers formerly exercised by the commissioners; (2) responsibility for minor criminal offenses; and (3) "additional duties" to assist the district court judges.[17] Although the "additional duties" authority included a number of specific examples, such as conducting pretrial and discovery matters in civil cases and reviewing habeas corpus petitions, this inherently ambiguous phrase eventually led to disagreements about which "additional duties" were legislatively intended and, moreover, which were constitutionally permissible. For example, the Seventh Circuit U.S. Court of Appeals ruled that a district judge improperly referred preliminary motion decisions to magistrates.[18] Yet the Second Circuit Court of Appeals and several district courts approved procedural rules within their jurisdictions which permitted precisely the same referrals that the Seventh Circuit found improper under the statute.[19] Various districts and circuits not only adopted different practices for utilization of magistrates, they also disagreed on the statutory and constitutional permissibility of such practices.

The Supreme Court was drawn into the controversy in a case in which the justices held, seven to two, that the Habeas Corpus Act prevented district judges from delegating evidentiary hearings in prisoners' habeas corpus cases to magistrates.[20] The Court did not discuss the constitutional limits of magistrates' authority, although Chief Justice Warren Burger, in his dissent, stated forthrightly that Article III of the Constitution posed no barriers to empowering the magistrates.[21] Burger concluded his dissent with an unusually explicit invitation to Congress to amend the Magistrates Act in order to enable magistrates to provide more assistance to the district courts.[22]

Although the Supreme Court broadly interpreted the magistrates' authority to conduct evidentiary hearings in Social Security cases,[23] the limited interpretation of authority in habeas corpus cases spurred Congress to reform the Magistrates Act. The push for legislative reform was helped by reports prepared by the General Accounting Office and the Federal Judicial Center which encouraged the use of subordinate judicial officers. Increased caseload pressures caused by the passage of the Speedy Trial Act, which imposed strict deadlines on district judges for handling criminal cases,[24] accelerated efforts to expand the magistrates' authority.

The Magistrates Act of 1976 expressly superceded the Supreme Court's decision by authorizing magistrates to handle evidentiary hearings in habeas corpus cases. In addition, the statute specified the tasks which could be assigned to magistrates and the procedures for appealing the subordinate judges' decisions. For example, magistrates may hear and decide any pretrial matter except for several specific dispositive motions.[25] A district court judge will review magistrates' findings on appeal according to the "clearly erroneous" or "contrary to law" standards, limited reviews which clearly vest magistrates with significant judicial decision-making authority because the judges are not second-guessing the magistrates' judgments. The judges merely look for patent errors in the magistrates' recognition of facts or application of law. For dispositive motions which would dismiss or otherwise terminate a case, a magistrate will file a report and recommendation on findings of fact and a recommended decision that will be reviewed *de novo*, or in its entirety, by a district judge if a party appeals within ten days. Overall, as one official at the Administrative Office commented, "the 1976 legislation placed the jurisdiction of magistrates on a much firmer and more uniform basis nationally."[26] The 1976 act served to codify and encourage uniformity for the practices that had grown up in district courts throughout the country. District courts retained freedom and flexibility for determining how to utilize magistrates, but the 1976 act gave judges more concrete parameters on the scope of their subordinates' permissible authority.

Prior to and since the 1976 act, many magistrates have found their working lives primarily consumed by what one magistrate described as "the big three," namely Social Security disability appeals, habeas corpus petitions, and civil rights suits by prisoners. These specific categories of cases, which are delegated to magistrates because district judges find them routine and repetitive, place a burden upon nearly all magistrates, even those who are permitted to perform a variety of other tasks.

Social Security appeals reach magistrates when claimants bring their cases to federal court after being denied disability benefits by the Department of Health and Human Services and by an administrative law judge. District judges frequently refer such cases to magistrates who review the findings and conclusions of the administrative law judges and then submit reports and recommendations to the district judges. The magistrate is, in essence, providing a very limited review to see if there is "substantial evidence" to support the administrative law judges' findings and to ensure that appropriate legal standards were applied. This is not a complete review of the evidence, but is merely a determination that the previous decision was supportable by the evidence and according to proper procedures. The parties have ten days to object to the magistrates' reports before the district judges enter final judgments. Such decisions may then be appealed to a circuit court of appeals.

Prisoners may contest their incarceration in jails or prisons through the habeas corpus procedures in two federal statutes.[27] Under these statutes, prisoners file petitions in federal court to mount collateral attacks upon the basis for their incarceration rather than contesting their convictions through the normal hierarchical appeals process, which is frequently more limited in its scope of review. Although district judges enter the final decisions, magistrates are frequently the officials who examine the briefs and records in order to produce reports and recommendations. Magistrates can often decide such cases without holding hearings, because the prisoners fail to meet all procedural requirements in bringing the case or their claims are based upon allegations, such as faulty jury instructions, which can be examined by reading court transcripts. Parties have ten days to object to magistrates' decisions before a final order is issued and parties may be precluded from appealing the district judges' orders if they do not submit timely objections to the magistrates' reports and recommendations.[28]

Prisoners can sue state officials under a civil rights statute for violations of their constitutional rights.[29] These claims, like habeas corpus petitions, are often presented pro se namely by the prisoners themselves because they do not have legal representation.[30] As with the other categories of cases, magistrates submit reports and recommendations to the district judges, sometimes based upon hearings but usually based only upon reviews of the complaints and briefs filed. Again, the parties have ten days to enter objections to the magistrates' findings before the district judges enter final judgments.

In each of these categories of cases, the parties are entitled to a complete or de novo review of the magistrates' determinations when objections are submitted to the supervising district judges. Because these large categories[31] of claims are often routine, repetitive, and only infrequently successful, especially when brought without the assistance of attorneys, there is a risk that district judges rubber-stamp the decisions of magistrates without providing adequate supervision and review. This risk has been exacerbated by a Supreme Court decision declaring that in cases contesting the veracity of witnesses presenting oral testimony, judges provide complete review of the magistrates' determinations about the believability of contradictory witnesses by merely reading the court transcript and not hearing the actual testimony.[32] Because of the limited requirements for supervision and review by the district judges, the magistrates, who often conduct the only complete review of the record, are very important decision makers in determining case outcomes for many claimants. Although the magistrates are relatively unknown and invisible to outsiders, discretionary judgments by these subordinate judges significantly affect district court decisions.

Magistrates may be assigned any or all of the tasks involved in preparing civil cases for trial. Magistrates decide motions submitted by the parties on evidentiary and other matters, hold scheduling conferences to plan discovery deadlines, and supervise pretrial conferences to finalize procedural matters before trial. Under their authorizing statute, the magistrates may submit only reports and recommendations to the district judges for dispositive motions that would determine the outcomes of cases. For nondispositive motions, such as evidentiary and discovery matters, the subordinate judicial officers may make the final determinations which are then reviewable by the judges according to the limited "clearly erroneous" or "contrary to law" standards.[33]

MAGISTRATES' TRIAL AUTHORITY

The "additional duties" authorizing language of the 1968 act enabled district courts to experiment creatively in the utilization of magistrates. Congress intended to permit judges to utilize their new subordinates flexibly according to the needs of their individual districts. The 1976 legislation did not authorize all of the practices that continued to be applied, most notably the referral of entire civil cases to magistrates for trial and decision. At least thirty-six districts referred civil cases to magistrates for trial before Congress authorized the practice in 1979.[34] In one 1974 case contesting the practice, a man sued a television network for allegedly stealing a character he had created. Both parties agreed that certain claims would be heard and decided by a magistrate, but the losing party subsequently objected to the procedure as exceeding the scope of the magistrate's authority. The court of appeals upheld the reference to the magistrate because the parties had freely waived their access to an Article III district judge.[35] This case helped to illuminate the controversy over the constitutional and statutory permissibility of referring complete civil cases to magistrates.

The Carter administration subsequently made a push for further reforms in the magistrate system by seeking to broaden magistrates' authority, including codification of the controversial practice of referring complete civil cases for hearing and decision by magistrates. During the 1970s, although many districts utilized magistrates to handle civil cases, it was not until reformers sought to enshrine the practice in legislation that full-blown political and legal battles developed concerning the constitutional propriety of referring cases to non-Article III, subordinate judicial officers. Because magistrates lack the tenure and salary protections provided to federal judges in Article III of the Constitution, it was feared that they would be subject to political influence in making decisions. The attempt to broaden the authority of magistrates called into question basic issues regarding the meaning of Article III and proper role of the judiciary in the American constitutional system and subsequently led members of Congress to oppose expansion of magistrates' powers.

Under the 1979 amendments to the Magistrates Act, district court judges may designate magistrates to hear complete civil cases, including jury trials, when the parties consent to have their cases heard by a magistrate. Prior to having the magistrate preside over the trial, the parties must agree on whether the appeal will go to a district judge or directly to a court of appeals. In either instance, the parties can appeal the magistrate's decision just as they may appeal a decision made by a district judge.[36] In every respect, the magistrate performs precisely as a district judge does in presiding over civil trials. A person entering a federal courtroom during a civil trial would have no way of knowing through observation whether the robed figure on the bench is a district judge or magistrate.

Strong opposition emerged in Congress to the provision for consensual reference of civil cases to magistrates. The primary objection concerned the constitutionality of the provision. In the words of two congressional opponents of the provision, "this measure should not be approved . . . [because of] the questionable constitutionality of . . . Federal judicial power by officers who are not appointed by the President, with the advice and consent of the Senate, who do not have life tenure, and whose salaries are not protected from diminution."[37] The critics further argued that magistrates would have the ability to exercise the awesome power of judicial review over legislative and executive actions. By empowering inferior judicial officers without Article III status to exercise this power, the Magistrates Act would effectively demean all of the branches of government and harm the balance of the constitutional governing system.[38]

Another critic ridiculed the Magistrates Act by comparing it to "authorizing a legislative assistant to vote on the House floor . . . or authorizing a White House aide to sign or veto bills."[39] In addition, questions were raised about whether consent to magistrate-supervised trials would be truly voluntary and whether the magistrate system would create a two-tiered system of justice in which poor litigants would be pushed away from access to real district judges.[40] Additional concerns focused on the lack of precedential value that magistrates' decisions would have within the federal courts, the lack of publication outlets for magistrates' opinions in civil cases, and the contradictory nature of magistrates' roles within the federal courts when they simultaneously act as independent decision makers on some matters, but subordinates to the district judges on many others.[41] Although the fundamental constitutional issues are a matter of principled interpretation, the other concerns about the effects of magistrates' expanded authority are based upon speculative predictions concerning difficulties emanating from magistrates' expanded roles. Subsequent chapters of this empirical study will discuss some of these practical effects and difficulties after nearly ten years of experience with the subordinate judges' expanded authority under the 1979 act.

The Judiciary Committee dealt with the serious constitutional questions through reliance upon "three pillars," each of which individually, *standing alone, would be sufficient"* to ensure the constitutionality of magistrates' authority over civil cases by the consent of the parties.[42] These "three pillars" were described in the Committee's report as:

> First, the magistrate is an adjunct of the United States District Court, appointed by the court and subject to the court's direction and control. When the magistrate tries a case, jurisdiction remains in the district court and is simply exercised through the medium of the magistrate.
>
> Second, both parties must consent to trial before a magistrate and must consent to entry of final judgment by the magistrate for the district court.
>
> Third, in all instances an appeal from a magistrate's decision lies in an Article III court.[43]

The legal literature relied upon by the Judiciary Committee argued that federal courts have long accepted delegation to non-Article III judges provided that the delegation maintained some elements of district court control, litigant consent, and appeal to an Article III judge.[44] Ultimately, with the passage of the 1979 act, Congress expressed the view that the expanded authority for magistrates passed constitutional muster.

Although one legal commentator envisioned the magistrates as constituting a new lower federal court in which "parties ... [with] relatively simple problems could be induced to consent to a reference [to a magistrate],"[45] Congress carefully insured the voluntariness of litigants' consent. The statutory language in the Magistrates Act explicitly forbids district judges or magistrates from pressuring litigants to consent to have their cases heard before a magistrate.[46]

The magistrates' expanded authority came under scrutiny in the aftermath of a Supreme Court decision invalidating the Bankruptcy Act of 1978 for unconstitutionally delegating too much authority to the non-Article III bankruptcy judges.[47] The factors relied upon by the Supreme Court in finding this unconstitutional delegation of authority could arguably be applied to the magistrate system which also involves delegation of judicial power to non-Article III officials.[48] In contrast to the bankruptcy case, however, the circuit courts of appeals have found the magistrates' authority under the 1979 Act to be constitutional. In the leading case, the Ninth Circuit, sitting en banc, reversed one of its own panels and found the reference of trials to magistrates to be permissible because of the voluntary consent of litigants, the control by district judges, and the avenues for appeal.[49] The Supreme Court subsequently declined an opportunity to review the issue of the magistrates' trial authority.[50]

Because of the 1979 congressional authorization for civil trials conducted by magistrates and the subsequent endorsement of these consent proceedings by the courts of appeals, magistrates may undertake virtually any task performed by district judges, except for felony trials and sentencing. The magistrates do not control which tasks they will perform because they must rely upon delegation from the judges and, in some instances, consent of the litigants. Moreover, some magistrates are confined to limited tasks by their supervising judges, so they do not actually supervise trials and exercise the breadth of their authority under the statute. Despite these limitations, however, the potential exists for these unknown, invisible subordinate judges to perform most tasks within the district courts and exercise their discretionary judgment to determine outcomes for claimants.

OTHER LEGISLATIVE ENACTMENTS AFFECTING MAGISTRATES' ROLES

In addition to the Magistrates Act and its subsequent amendments, other acts of Congress concerning the federal courts affect the magistrates' tasks and roles within the district courts. For example, the 1974 Speedy Trial Act and 1979 Speedy Trial Act amendments set time limits for processing criminal cases.[51] Thus criminal trials must frequently leap ahead of other cases on the district judges' trial dockets. As a result, civil trials can be delayed indefinitely if a judge gets several criminal cases. This extra pressure on judges can make magistrates particularly attractive as a resource for processing civil cases. Litigants may recognize that because magistrates' time is not absorbed by felony cases, definite dates for civil trials may be secured by consenting to have cases heard by these subordinate judicial officers.

The Bail Reform Act of 1984 created new procedures and criteria for setting bail.[52] The Act authorized detention hearings to determine if defendants fit criteria for "dangerousness" or likelihood of flight so that they should be incarcerated pending trial and not granted bail.

The detention hearings, with their opportunity for testimony from witnesses and cross-examination, create an additional set of tasks for magistrates to handle. Although magistrates are not permitted to preside over felony trials, in many districts they bear exclusive responsibility for preliminary criminal proceedings. The detention hearings under the Bail Reform Act provide a highly visible example of the subordinate judges' power as authoritative judicial officers, because it is the magistrates who make decisions about whether defendants should be deprived of their liberty and held in jail for weeks or months prior to trial.

JUDICIAL AUTHORITY AND THE DEVELOPMENT OF MAGISTRATES' ROLES

The statutory and case law developments that defined the magistrates' judicial authority also served to establish the basic framework for the magistrates' roles within the various district courts. Although magistrates are governed by the same authorizing legislation, the expectations of relevant actors within different districts have led to differences in the ways in which the magistrates' roles have developed. For example, some district judges expect their magistrates to act as limited, subordinate assistants, while other judges regard magistrates as judicial colleagues capable of handling broad responsibilities. As subsequent chapters will discuss, these differences in expectations about magistrates' roles are manifested in the selection process for magistrates, as well as in the daily tasks, relationships, and interactions occurring in districts throughout the federal court system.

NOTES

1.   Joseph F. Spaniol, Jr., "The Federal Magistrate Act: History and Development," *Arizona State Law Journal* (1974): 566.

2.   Peter G. McCabe, "The Federal Magistrate Act of 1979," *Harvard Journal on Legislation* 16 (1979): 343.

3.   Spaniol, "Federal Magistrate Act," 566–567.

4.   Statement of Senator Joseph Tydings, U.S. Congress, Senate Committee on the Judiciary, *Federal Magistrates Act: Hearings Before the Subcommittee on Improvements in Judicial Machinery on S.3475 and S.945*, 89th Cong., 2d Sess., and 90th Cong., 1st Sess., 1966 and 1967, 4–9.

5.   Federal Magistrates Act, Pub. L. No. 90–578, 82 Stat. 1107 (codified as amended at 28 U.S.C. sections 604, 631–639 and 18 U.S.C. sections 3060, 3401–3402).

6.   "Johnson Decries Stress on Crime," *New York Times*, 18 Oct. 1968.

7.   Testimony of the Hon. Harvey M. Johnsen, U.S. Court of Appeals, Eighth Circuit, U.S. Congress, Senate Committee on the Judiciary, *Crisis in the Federal*

Courts: Hearings Before the Senate Judiciary Committee on S.915 and H.R. 6111, 90th Cong., 1st Sess., 1976, 49.

8. Ibid.

9. Testimony of the Hon. Edward S. Northrup, U.S. District Court, District of Maryland, *Federal Magistrates Act: Hearings*, Senate, 52.

10. A "policy window" has been described as "a short time when conditions to push a given subject ... on the policy agenda are right." John W. Kingdon, *Agendas, Alternatives, and Public Policies*, (Boston: Little, Brown & Co., 1984), 94.

11. Testimony of the Hon. Theodore Levin, Chief Judge, U.S. District Court, Eastern District of Michigan, *Federal Magistrates Act: Hearings*, Senate, 58–77.

12. *New York Times*, 21 May 1959, p. 20; 28 Aug. 1959.

13. U.S. Congress, House Report No. 1629, Federal Magistrates Act, *U.S. Code Congressional and Administrative News*, 1968, 4257.

14. "House G.O.P. Group Backs Measure to Speed Justice," *New York Times*, 6 Nov. 1967.

15. "Modernizing the Federal Courts," *New York Times*, 11 July 1966; "Bill Would Upgrade U.S. Commissioners," *New York Times*, 12 July 1966; "Court Commissioner Urges End to Job," *New York Times*, 12 Feb. 1967; "Senate Approves U.S. Magistrates," *New York Times*, 30 June 1967; "House G.O.P. Group Backs Measure to Speed Justice," *New York Times*, 6 Nov. 1967; "Senate Passes Bill on U.S. Magistrates," *New York Times*, 4 Oct. 1968; "Johnson Decries Stress on Crime," *New York Times*, 18 Oct. 1968.

16. U.S. Congress, House Report No. 1629, 4266–4270.

17. McCabe, "Federal Magistrate Act of 1979," 349–350.

18. TPO, Inc. v. McMillen, 460 F.2d 348 (7th Cir. 1972).

19. Linda J. Silberman, "Masters and Magistrates Part II: The American Analogue," *New York University Law Review* 50 (1975): 1303.

20. Wingo v. Wedding, 418 U.S. 461 (1974).

21. Mark Tushnet, "Invitation to a *Wedding*: Some Thoughts on Article III and a Problem of Statutory Interpretation," *Iowa Law Review* 60 (1975): 937.

22. Burger wrote: "In any event, now that the Court has construed the Magistrates Act contrary to a clear legislative intent, it is for the Congress to act to restate its intentions if its declared objectives are to be carried out." Wingo v. Wedding, 418 U.S. at 487 (1974) (Burger, C.J., dissenting).

23. Mathews v. Weber, 423 U.S. 261 (1976).

24. McCabe, "Federal Magistrate Act of 1979," 353.

25. The specified motions include motions for injunctive relief, judgment on the pleadings, summary judgment, suppress evidence, dismiss or maintain a class action, dismiss for failure to state a claim, and dismiss action voluntarily. Ibid., 354–355 n. 62.

26. Ibid., 354.

27. One statute governs persons incarcerated in state institutions (28 U.S.C. section 2254) and the other governs federal institutions (28 U.S.C. section 2255).

28. Kent Sinclair, Jr., *Practice Before Federal Magistrates*, (New York: Matthew Bender, 1987), section 17.09a.

29. 42 U.S.C. section 1983.

30. A discussion of the problems associated with prisoners representing themselves in court is contained in Christopher E. Smith, "Examining the Boundaries of *Bounds*: Prison Law Libraries and Access to the Courts," *Howard Law Journal* 30 (1987): 27–44.

31. In 1987, magistrates handled 6,714 matters related to Social Security cases; over 9,700 related to habeas corpus cases; and 17,229 related to prisoners' civil rights cases. Administrative Office of the U.S. Courts, *Annual Report of the Director of the Administrative Office of the United States Courts,* (Washington, D.C.: U.S. Government Printing Office, 1987), 34.

32. United States v. Raddatz, 447 U.S. 667 (1980).

33. Sinclair, *Practice Before Federal Magistrates*, section 16.07.

34. U.S. Congress, House Report No. 1364, Magistrate Act of 1978, 95th Cong., 2d Sess., 1978, 4.

35. DeCosta v. Columbia Broadcasting System, Inc., 520 F.2d 499 (1st Cir. 1975) *rev'g in part* 383 F.Supp. 326 (D.R.I. 1974).

36. 28 U.S.C. section 636(c).

37. Dissenting Views of Representatives Robert F. Drinan and Thomas N. Kindness to S.1613, U.S. Congress, House Report No. 1364, 35–36.

38. Ibid., 37–38.

39. Dissenting Views of Representative John F. Seiberling, U.S. Congress, House Report No. 1364, 40–41.

40. Dissenting Views of the Hon. Elizabeth Holtzman, U.S. Congress, House Report No. 1364, 42.

41. Note, "Article III Constraints and the Expanding Civil Jurisdiction of Federal Magistrates: A Dissenting View," *Yale Law Journal* 88 (1979): 1023–1061.

42. U.S. Congress, House Report No. 1364, 11.

43. Ibid.

44. Silberman, "Masters and Magistrates," 1297–1372.

45. Comment, "An Adjudicative Role for Federal Magistrates in Civil Cases," *University of Chicago Law Review* 40 (1973): 599.

46. 28 U.S.C. section 636(c)(2) states: " . . . neither the district judge nor the magistrate shall attempt to persuade or induce any party to consent to reference of any civil matter to a magistrate. Rules of court for the reference of civil matters to magistrates shall include procedures to protect the voluntariness of the parties' consent."

47. Northern Pipeline Construction Co. v. Marathon Pipeline Co., 458 U.S. 50 (1982).

48. Comment, "Is the Federal Magistrate Act Constitutional After *Northern Pipeline*?" *Arizona State Law Journal* (1985): 195.

49. Pacemaker Diagnostic Clinic v. Instromedix Inc., 725 F.2d 537 (9th Cir. 1984) (en banc).

50. The Supreme Court denied a petition for certiorari in Pacemaker Diagnostic Clinic v. Instromedix Inc., 469 U.S. 824 (1984).

51. 18 U.S.C. section 3161.

52. 18 U.S.C. section 3142.

3

Who Are the U.S. Magistrates?
Selection and Background Characteristics

The passage of the Magistrates Act in 1968 created the new judicial office and provided the first formal description and authorization of duties and powers for magistrates. The legislation provided the initial basis for the subsequent development of magistrates' roles, but the statute could not, and indeed did not even intend to, define the precise contours of the magistrates' responsibilities within the various district courts. Congressional concerns about separation of powers and independence of the judiciary caused the legislators to leave the definition and development of magistrates' tasks to the district court judges. The first of the "three pillars," relied upon by Congress for the constitutionality of the magistrates system under the 1979 act illustrates the Congressional deference to the judiciary for actualization of the magistrates' roles: "First, the magistrate is an adjunct of the United States District Court, appointed by the court and subject to the court's direction and control."[1] Because the district judges control appointments, the selection process provides the first opportunity for judges to define magistrates' roles through the recruitment of appointees who possess the qualities necessary to fulfill the judges' conceptions of magistrates' duties.

INITIAL SELECTION PROCEDURES

When Congress first created the subordinate judicial office in 1968, the selection of magistrates was left completely to the discretion of the judges within each district court. The only statutorily mandated qualifications for appointment were that the appointee be a member of the bar of the highest court of the state; be determined by the appointing district court to be competent to perform as a magistrate; and not be related to the district judges by blood or marriage.[2] With no statutory requirements for a search process, judges were free to select nearly any interested lawyer who suited their perceived needs for the magistrate position. Although a district's judges would normally agree by consensus on the individual to be appointed, some districts rotated among their individual judges the prerogative of recommending an individual for appointment as vacancies occurred or new positions were authorized.

Because magistrates were new judicial officers whose authority was broadly defined by statute but whose task assignments were left to the discretion of the judges within the individual district courts, many judges lacked a clear conception of the magistrate's role. Because they did not have a definition of the qualities, experiences, and skills required for the magistrate position, many judges appointed familiar lawyers, such as former law clerks and assistant U.S. attorneys, with whom the judges had already established working relationships. For example, in districts examined for this study, one former assistant U.S. attorney was recruited by the district's chief judge; another magistrate was tapped by the judge with whom he had co-authored a book; a former law clerk was appointed when his mentor outmaneuvered another judge seeking the position for a different law clerk; and another former assistant U.S. attorney was asked to take the position by two district judges with whom he had long been acquainted.

The appointment of former law clerks, in particular, both reflected and reinforced judges' conceptions of a limited role for the new judicial officers. Without any experience with subordinate judicial officers, judges frequently applied their own customary experience, namely working with subordinate law clerks, to define their conception of the magistrates' roles. This resulted in the development of a magistrate role in many districts which perpetuated the task assignments and relationships between district judges and law clerks, except that under the magistrate system the subordinate helper had a new title, higher pay, and longer tenure. Some judges solidified their view of magistrates as extended-term law clerks by actually appointing the law clerk who happened to be working for them at the time the district received authorization for a magistrate position. In this instance, there was no immediate incentive to redefine and broaden the magistrate role because the relationship between the two individuals involved was already firmly established from the one or two years they had spent working closely together as supervisor and subordinate. The law clerk, now magistrate, lacked any other professional legal experience upon which to base an attempt to persuade the judge directly or by example that magistrates can assume the statutorily authorized broader role as a federal judicial officer. Most commonly, in the districts in which the judges characterized the magistrates' role as similar to that of a law clerk, the magistrates assumed primary responsibility for reviewing prisoner petitions and Social Security appeals—and little else. Magistrates in some districts continue substantially to fulfill this role, despite legislative actions to expand magistrates' authority and encourage broader use of the subordinate judges.

The direct selection method fostered several problems in addition to the appointment of some inexperienced law clerks and the reinforcement of a limited role for the new judicial officer. Direct appointment by district judges created the appearance and possibility of impropriety in granting judges an opportunity to make political patronage appointments. Although judges would clearly do themselves a disservice by appointing unqualified individuals, in the districts examined for this study several judges referred to specific magistrates as "political hack[s]" who were appointed for their political or family connections to influential people. In one district, it was generally believed by the lawyers and magistrates that the United States senators from that state had become involved in lobbying the district judges for the appointment of particular individuals to the full-time magistrate positions. Because many of the judges had received their positions through the sponsorship of the senators, the senators apparently felt they could influence the judges to appoint political supporters to the magistrate vacancies within the court.

In addition to the possibility of political patronage in appointments, another criticism of direct selection focused on the lack of women and minority group members appointed as magistrates. In 1979, women comprised less than 9 percent of the full-time magistrates and minority group members constituted only 5 percent.[3] Although these percentages exceeded the representation figures for federal judges, with the exception of appointees during the Carter era,[4] Congress viewed the magistrate system as an opportunity to redress the persistent fact that "women and minorities are underrepresented in the Federal Judiciary relative to the population at large."[5]

REFORM OF SELECTION PROCEDURES

According to a Senate report on proposed amendments to the magistrate statute, Congress recognized that "not all [magistrate] appointees have evidenced the same high quality" because judges "did not fully appreciate the full range of duties that a magistrate could perform."[6] Moreover, in the late 1970s, Congressional concerns about the appearance of patronage in direct selection by district judges and the lack of representativeness in appointments coincided with the Carter administration's efforts to institute merit selection procedures for the appointment of federal district and circuit court judges. These concerns led to a legislative effort, with the support of the Carter administration, to revamp the selection procedures for magistrates.

In the 1979 amendments to the magistrate statute, which authorized magistrates to oversee full civil trials with the consent of litigants, Congress mandated the creation of a new appointment procedure requiring the use of merit selection committees. District judges appoint citizen selection panels, "composed of residents of the individual judicial districts, to assist the courts in identifying and recommending persons who are best qualified to fill such [magistrate] positions."[7] The new procedure, as established in rules promulgated by the Judicial Conference, instructed the merit committees to advertise vacant magistrate positions, solicit applications, evaluate candidates, and submit a list of five nominees to the district judges. The regulations specifically instruct committee members to "make an affirmative effort to identify and give due consideration to all qualified candidates including women and members of minority groups."[8]

Although the merit selection process is designed to upgrade and diversify magistrate appointments by opening the selection procedures to all interested, qualified applicants, the district judges remain the focal point of the magistrate appointment process. Unlike state judicial selection systems, in which the key political decisions often involve the question of who will be appointed to the selection committees,[9] in the magistrate appointment process, the judges both appoint the selection panel *and* make the ultimate determination of which lawyer will be appointed to the magistrate vacancy. The judges can even reject the entire slate of nominees presented by the merit panel and force the committee to produce a new list of nominees.[10]

The power to appoint magistrates remained in the hands of district judges because of the concern about the constitutionality of magistrates' judicial authority. By retaining judges' appointment power as one of the "three pillars" underlying the constitutionality of the system, judicial independence within the American system of separation of powers could be protected. As the Ninth Circuit Court of Appeals noted in a subsequent case contesting magistrates' authority, by vesting appointment power in the judges, the magistrates are prevented from being "directly dependent upon loyalty to officers in either of the political branches [of government],"[11] namely the executive and legislative branches.

At the same time that the merit selection process was established, the 1979 legislation also upgraded the qualifications for magistrates by requiring five years of legal experience in addition to bar membership. This requirement did not preclude the appointment of former law clerks, but it halted the previous practice of elevating inexperienced law clerks directly to the magistrate position.

THE MERIT SELECTION PROCESS

The role of merit committees in the politics of judicial selection received its greatest attention in studies of state procedures, particularly in regard to the power of bar groups.[12] The merit selection procedures for federal judges created during the Carter era generated analyses focusing on several areas, including selection panel composition,[13] panelists' opinions of the merit process,[14] senators' influence over panel composition and selection deliberations,[15] and manipulation of nominations by officials in the executive branch.[16] These analyses noted the importance of partisan political affiliations in composing nominating commissions and selecting judicial appointees. The descriptions and analyses of the processes undertaken by the merit selection committees in evaluating potential nominees are primarily limited to first-person or personal experience-based accounts of the work of specific panels.[17]

The magistrate selection process is different from the merit nominating process utilized in the Carter years for appointing federal judges. Previous work on merit selection in other contexts has demonstrated that, in Elliott Slotnick's words, "[j]udicial selection processes have always been and will continue to be 'political' in nature—barring a change in our constitutional system which removes judicial selection from the political domain."[18] The magistrate selection process has been removed from the overtly partisan political domain of elected officials and instead involves the less visible political processes within the federal judiciary. The "political" nature of the magistrate selection process relates primarily to the power struggles and value conflicts between judges within individual districts, rather than the partisan affiliation and executive branch influence that infused the Carter-era nominating commissions and judicial appointments.

This study's examination of merit selection procedures for U.S. Magistrates draws upon interviews with judges, magistrates, and merit selection committee members. Surveys concerning the merit selection process were sent to chief judges in non-interview districts that had utilized the merit selection process for a full-time vacancy. The information from the surveys and interviews provides at least some data on 71 percent of the districts that had utilized the merit process for appointing full-time magistrates at the time of the study.[19] Virtually all of the merit panel members who were interviewed exhibited a desire to honor carefully their obligation to keep the panels' deliberations confidential. However, several members took a broad view of what information need not remain confidential so that many aspects of their decisional processes became apparent without revealing details concerning specific, identifiable candidates for the magistrate positions. By contrast, several judges were quite open in discussing the details of the merit selection process, especially when they were unhappy about the procedures within their districts. The interviews and survey provide a detailed picture of the use of merit selection procedures for appointing magistrates by exploring the process from the perspectives of both the committee members and the ultimate decision makers, the district judges.

A Typology of Merit Selection Panels

The Judicial Conference did not specifically instruct the district judges on how to choose merit committee members for the selection of federal magistrates. The regulations require only that "[t]he panel shall be composed of a chairman and other members appointed by majority vote of the active judges of the district court. The panel shall have not fewer than six members [and] . . . shall consist of lawyers and other members of the community."[20] In addition, the Administrative Office recommends that the selection board contain an odd number of members and include at least two nonlawyers.[21] The district judges can either maintain the same panel for all appointment and reappointment procedures or constitute a new committee for each occasion the process is needed.

The lack of regulations specifically dictating how merit board members are to be selected has resulted in the creation of panels that reflect judges' diverse conceptions of the merit process. The appointment and composition of merit selection committees also reflect the political and personal relationships between judges within districts. For example, a powerful or persuasive chief judge who effectively guides administrative policy within a district may take the lead in determining appointments to the selection panel. Conflicts between judges are manifested not only in constituting the committees, but also in the deliberation processes that occur within the committees.

The interviews and surveys conducted for this study indicate that merit committees can be placed into general categories—Blue Ribbon, Representative, and Proxy—based upon a rough assessment of several discernible factors (see Table 1). The first factor was the actual composition of the committees, judged in terms of gender and racial composition as well as chief judges' characterizations of members as representing particular groups within the district (e.g., women lawyers' association) or holding elite positions (e.g., law school dean). Another factor was whether the panelists were selected by one judge (usually the chief judge) or by several district judges, and whether or not all of the judges had to approve the selection committee members.

Table 1 Types of Magistrate Merit Selection Committees

Committee Type	Districts	
	(%)	[N]
Blue Ribbon	24.5	[12]

1. Composed of elite members, especially from legal community, who are well-known to the district judges

2. Relationships between judges and panel members facilitate shared values and communication

3. Homogeneous membership, predominantly white, male attorneys

----

Representative	67.3	[33]

1. Members characterized by judges as representing diverse groups

2. Representational basis for committee composition hinders communication between panelists and judges

3. Selection criteria emphasize qualities of "best" magistrate rather than particular role conceptions possessed by judges

----

Proxy	8.2	[4]

1. Each judge selects one or more members

2. Potential for interjudge conflict within committee deliberations as members represent the competing interests of their respective constituent judges

An additional factor was the acknowledged existence of communication between judges and panelists concerning selection criteria either before or during the selection process. Because of the availability of detailed information, the districts in which interviews were conducted could be readily categorized according to the typology. The information gained about various districts from the surveys, however, was not always consistent and complete. Thus, judgments were made about each district according to the characterizing criteria although the various districts within each category are not equally distinguishable from the districts in other categories. The typology serves as a useful tool for illuminating the merit selection process, but it is clear that boundaries between categories are imprecise.

Blue Ribbon Panel. Blue Ribbon panels are composed of leading lawyers and other prominent individuals whom the judges decline to characterize as representing particular groups and interests within the district. The panels are generally homogeneous in terms of race and gender. The interviews in two districts with Blue Ribbon panels indicate the existence of a collegial atmosphere in which judges cooperated with each other in matters affecting court administration. Collegiality is not a prerequisite for the formation of a Blue Ribbon-type committee, but there must be sufficient agreement among the judges to facilitate the appointment of a panel containing universally respected lawyers and lay members. Blue Ribbon committees result when the district's judges rely upon the reputations and abilities of a set of well-known individuals rather than seek broad community representation from across the district.

In one district, the chief judge selected the committee members based upon suggestions from the other judges. The panel included the chief judge of the state circuit court, the dean of a local law school, a bank president, the publisher of a local newspaper, and the chairman of a local utility company. The district judges explicitly instructed the panelists on the desired qualities for magistrate nominees. Apparently, relationships between the judges and Blue Ribbon panelists can be close, based upon mutual familiarity and shared values as local elites.

In another district with a Blue Ribbon panel, the board members were selected by the outgoing chief judge and then were presented to the other district judges for approval. The incoming chief judge ultimately suggested two additional members for subsequent appointment and reappointment procedures, but the board was primarily composed of the five individuals selected by the previous chief judge. This panel was composed of five lawyers who litigate regularly in the federal district court, including three former law clerks to the former chief judge and a long-time acquaintance of the current chief judge. The two lay members were a retired businessman and a retired clerk of the district court, both long-time acquaintances of at least one of the chief judges. The inclusion of three former law clerks can significantly affect the committee's decisions, as can the inclusion of any prominent people on other Blue Ribbon selection panels who are personally acquainted with the judges. The former law clerks' previous affiliation with the chief judge and contacts with the district court as litigators had the effect of not only familiarizing them with the values and goals of the district judges, but also enabling the judges to feel comfortable in predicting, if not influencing, the types of nominations that resulted from the selection panel's deliberations. The mutual familiarity between judges and panel members provided a common basis for shared values, or at least reciprocally recognized values, to be applied in evaluating candidates for the magistrate vacancy. The judges create a Blue Ribbon committee because they expect the members to have an appropriate conceptualization of the role that the magistrate will fulfill in the district and to understand the expectations that the judges have for a new magistrate appointee.

In this illustrative district, the composition of the Blue Ribbon panel distinguishes it from other types of committees, in part, because this panel obviously was not intended to represent diverse interests within the district. This committee, like many other Blue Ribbon panels, was entirely white, elite, and with the exception of one female attorney, all male. "Blue Ribbon" implies that the panel is composed of "the best and the brightest" of a local community. In the illustrative Blue Ribbon committee, unlike in Proxy committees, the judges did not select the panel members with a conscious intention to control the panel's deliberations. Although lawyers and other panel members all had connections to the federal court, they appeared to the judges (and, perhaps, to the public as well) as representing "the best qualified" in the district.

Representative Panel. A Representative panel contains members who represent various segments of the legal community and society in general. The idea of selecting board members representing various constituencies within the district comes closest to the House Judiciary Committee's original intention that "judges of the district court must secure representation on the panel of a cross section of the legal and non-legal community. This will insure that women and minority group members are considered for appointment to the selection panels."[22] This representational goal was a component of the Carter administration's overall push for implementing merit selection in order to increase diversity in the federal judiciary. However, the Judicial Conference did not specifically require or explicitly encourage the creation of diverse selection boards representing various segments of the district courts' respective local communities.

A Representative panel, especially one whose members are not personally acquainted with the district judges, is less likely to receive communication from the judges and less likely to base decisions upon a recognition of the judges' conceptualization of the magistrate role. Unlike the case of the Blue Ribbon panel, the creation of a Representative panel does not indicate that the judges have specific expectations for the decisions of the panel. Instead, the judges have gathered together a relatively diverse group of citizens, primarily lawyers, with the expectation that they will nominate the "best qualified" candidates according to the high-minded, but essentially subjective and ambiguous, criteria (e.g., "demeanor and temperament," "reasonableness and objectivity," etc.) supplied to the panel members by the Administrative Office.[23]

In the survey, the chief judges from Representative panel districts characterized the board members as being representatives from specific groups and interests. For example, one panel was composed of representatives from the large law firms, the women's bar association, the black lawyers' association, a rural county, and other constituencies within the district.

Proxy Panel. The distinguishing feature of a Proxy panel is that the committee members are chosen through a process in which each district judge is permitted to appoint one or more members to the selection board. This method of appointment for panel members creates an opportunity for the magistrate selection process to reflect the divisions and conflicts between the district's judges. On the Proxy panel, the selection of magistrate nominees may emerge from the advocacy of competing interests and magistrate role definitions espoused by individual judges through their respective representatives on the selection board. This process, which can occur in (but is not an inevitable result of) a Proxy-type selection panel, differs greatly from the processes which characterize the deliberations of Blue Ribbon panels, with communications and shared understandings between committee members and judges, and Representative panels, with application of generalized criteria for selection of the "best" candidate.

A magistrate vacancy can easily be viewed by judges as a potential personal resource. Magistrates assist judges in a wide range of tasks, so judges may want to influence the selection of a particular individual who will be most helpful to them. Because districts may assign tasks to magistrates through myriad organizational designs,[24] a judge might attempt to influence the selection of a particular individual in order to change the manner in which magistrates may serve as resources to the judges. For example, methods of assigning cases to magistrates include pairing individual magistrates and judges, specific assignments by an administrative official, and rotating assignments.[25] The selection of a particularly attractive magistrate may lead the judges to move away from a pairing system and toward a system that enables all of the judges to utilize the coveted magistrate's skills. In addition, judges may seek to guide a reformulation of the magistrate role within a district. For example, if one judge sought to expand the utilization of magistrates to the complete range of authorized tasks, including presiding over civil trials with the consent of litigants, the judge might seek to appoint an experienced, capable former state judge who can immediately handle complex civil litigation. Thus, even if the other judges in the district view the magistrate's role as that of a specialist in Social Security appeals, the introduction of a new magistrate obviously possessing the ability to handle full civil trials may help to alter the other judges' limited views of the magistrate's role within the district. Judges may also wish to influence the selection of magistrates in order to have a particular protégé appointed or insure the appointment of a magistrate from a specific political party, demographic group, or geographic constituency. The committee screening process operating within the district will ultimately help to determine which judge's (or judges') personal goals and views of the magistrate's role will prevail and be put into practice.

Although judges may desire to determine the outcome of the magistrate selection process for the foregoing reasons with any type of merit panel, the Proxy panel presents a special opportunity for the intentions of judges to be manifested in overt political conflict within the committee.

The interviews documented one specific instance of conflict within a Proxy panel during the selection process for a full-time magistrate vacancy. The panel reflected a continuing series of conflicts between judges which caused disagreements on virtually every administrative matter within the district, including the role definition and utilization of magistrates. The Proxy panel members remained in close contact with their constituent judges. In discussing the Proxy committee's work, one panel member continually referred to "my judge" as he described his role as a representative for the judge in the selection process. Similarly, two judges in the same district spoke repeatedly of "my member" or "my representative" and both judges indicated that their information about the merit board's procedures and discussions came through detailed, personal briefings with their respective representatives.

In this Proxy panel district, coalitions formed within the board to maneuver and push for certain candidates based upon preferences communicated to members by their individual constituent judges. In the deliberation process, according to one judge, the panelists "ganged up on one strong, qualified candidate from my home area" in an effort to keep that candidate off the final list of nominees. The committee members had adopted a strategy of defeating attractive applicants in order to create a list of nominees that maximized the possibilities for specific candidates favored by their constituent judges. The incentive for such political maneuvering is increased by the statute which provides that "when there is no [concurrence of the district's judges on an individual for appointment], then [the appointment is made] by the chief judge."[26] Thus, the chief judge or some other judge might try to engineer a deadlock among the judges in order to enable the chief judge to make the ultimate appointment.

Case Study: Inside a Merit Selection Committee

Interviews were conducted with all seven members of the merit selection board in one district. The committee remained essentially intact for two proceedings to evaluate incumbent magistrates for reappointment as well as for one proceeding to fill a newly authorized full-time position. The interview questions focused on the selection process undertaken in 1984 by this Blue Ribbon panel in creating a list of nominees to fill a new full-time magistrate position. In general, the panel followed the designated procedures for advertising the magistrate position in several legal publications, screening written applications, and interviewing finalists before submitting a ranked list of nominees to the judges.

The judges exercised significant control over the composition of the committee. As one panelist stated, "You really can't say no to the chief judge when he asks you to serve on a committee." Lawyers who practice in federal court were especially eager to stay on good terms with the judges, considering it an honor to be chosen. Thus, judges can, without much difficulty, get whomever they desire to serve on the selection committee. In the case of this Blue Ribbon panel, the automatic availability of desired panel members also gave the judges the ability to select a board composed of individuals whom the judges perceived to share their view of the appropriate role for magistrates. The ability to select familiar panelists enhanced the judges' ability to communicate with board members concerning criteria for selection based upon the judges' conceptualizations of the magistrate's role. The communication was strengthened by the committee members' keen desire to please the judges with the list of final nominees. The mutual desire for effective communication allowed the judges to guide the selection committee in the process of evaluating applicants.

Although the judges appointed a Blue Ribbon panel, in part, because they trusted the members' values and judgments, the judges
communicated preferences to the board which directed and defined
the boundaries of the selection process. For example, the chief judge
met individually with the panel chairman and a lay member to explain
the selection process and to convey the judge's perception of the
magistrate's role within the district. The chief judge's expansive view
of the magistrate as an important judicial officer who should broadly
exercise the judicial powers authorized under the statute, including
autonomous work on case settlements and civil trials, was communicated to and absorbed by the panel members. The communication of
this conceptualization of the magistrate's role helped to define the
criteria that the committee applied in screening applications.

The judges communicated to the board members the strength of the
judges' commitment to the recruitment of women and minority candidates. One judge told a panel member to "give extra consideration
to selecting a woman." Communications supportive of locating
qualified women and minority candidates helped to guide the
committee's search process and also established one value to be
weighed when the panel began to evaluate and compare qualified
candidates. Although some communications from the judges supported the goal of increasing diversity and representativeness in the
federal judiciary, this Blue Ribbon panel evinced less sensitivity to the
affirmative action issue than Representative panels, in which women
and minority panelists are present and participating in deliberations.
This Blue Ribbon panel had one female member and no minority
members. Although a female lawyer was ultimately appointed as the
new magistrate, one panelist, lacking the diplomacy usually evident
on Representative panels, complained indignantly that "we bent over
backwards for one of them" when speaking of minority applicants.
The fact that this panelist was insensitive, if not hostile, to the goal of
diversity within the federal judiciary, yet willingly participated in the
affirmative action process by consciously seeking qualified women
and minority candidates, is testimony to the power of the criteria
communicated by the judges to the committee and to the panelists'
desire to please the judges.

Another form of communication took place when the roster of
applicants was communicated to the judges so that individual judges
could veto candidates that they personally found unacceptable before
the committee began its evaluation process. The board members
revealed the applicant list and accepted the veto of candidates because
they wanted to please the judges with their final recommendations.
Some committee members wanted to avoid the discomfort of repeating a well-known incident in the district in which the judges and a

different committee disagreed about the nominees for a bankruptcy judge position.

Additional communication occurred when the panel members interviewed judges whose former law clerks applied for the magistrate position. Although these interviews were ostensibly designed to assess the candidate's work habits and intellectual abilities, committee members also gained a perception of the judge's view of the magistrate role and of the judge's attitude about the possible nomination of the former law clerk. One panelist described such an interview as confirming that "the judge thinks the world of" a particular candidate, the former law clerk who was ultimately nominated and appointed. Another panelist described being very aware that the nomination of the former law clerk would "make the judge very pleased."

The panelists were heavily influenced by their perceptions of the judges' preferences. One panel member declined to describe the general criteria he applied to the selection of the magistrate because he said that his decisions were based entirely upon his perceptions of "what the judges will want." He said he would "select an entirely different nominee if the magistrate would be working for a different set of judges." This board member was explicitly concerned about having his selections fit with the criteria for the magistrate's role that he perceived being communicated by the judges. Another panelist similarly stressed that the committee must be "aware of what the judges want" in order to avoid putting forward nominees "that the judges might reject." Thus, the judges' views on the magistrate's role and appropriate criteria for selection were pivotal influences over the deliberations of the merit panel.

Merit Selection in Other Districts

The survey of chief judges sought to determine whether panels in districts throughout the country shared key characteristics of the merit committee in the foregoing case study district. Several questions tested the degree of contact between the judges and the panelists to detect the opportunities for judges' views on selection criteria and the magistrate role to be adopted and applied by the merit boards.

The case study panel had remained intact for more than one merit proceeding, namely one merit process to fill a vacancy and two proceedings to solicit comments and evaluate incumbent magistrates for reappointment. By keeping the same committee intact, the judges avoided any need for re-educating new committee members about the selection criteria. The statute and the Judicial Conference regulations do not specify whether a new committee should be formed for each proceeding, but most districts in the survey (75.5%) formed new committees for each appointment and reappointment process. The vast majority of the districts which keep their merit panels intact have Representative-type boards (75% of the twelve districts with permanent merit panels). Unlike Blue Ribbon and Proxy panels, which serve to facilitate communication between judges and panelists, Representative committees are premised upon the concern expressed by Congress and the Judicial Conference for increasing diversity in the judiciary. Because members of Representative panels are selected to represent specific legal groups or community interests and are less likely to have prior familiarity with judges, there is a greater incentive for the district judges to maintain committees and avoid repeating the education process with new panelists. Keeping Representative committees intact can facilitate the development of relationships and communication between the judges and panelists. Panelists will be able to perceive reactions to their previous nominee selections and thus be better attuned to the judges' desires in subsequent selection proceedings.

One important way in which judges can influence the magistrate selection process is by actually informing the panelists directly of criteria to be applied in creating the list of nominees. In 60 percent of the districts, the panelists were told by the judges to look for specific qualities in applicants.

Although popular misconceptions of a merit selection process for the judiciary may maintain that panelists should somehow work in isolation away from political influences in making decisions, research on judicial selection has consistently shown that political conflicts are inevitably a part of the merit judicial selection process.[27] Those who would maintain the myth of a pristine magistrate merit selection process bridle at the suggestion that judges influence the panel's deliberations. One court administrator wrote, somewhat defensively, on behalf of a chief judge, that "I can assure you that the process is carefully screened from any judicial involvement until the final list of candidates is prepared." A judge in the case study district, where it was clear there was contact between judges and panelists, appeared or pretended to be naive about the role of judges in the selection process: "The panel goes off and does all the work on its own. We don't have anything to do with them until they present us with the list of finalists." This desire to maintain the myth of "pure" merit selection may have affected the accuracy of responses to questions about contacts between judges and magistrates, yet 37 percent of chief judges acknowledged that the roster of applicants was circulated to the judges before the panel had completed its deliberations. It is not clear if the judges exercised explicit veto power over individual candidates, but the responses certainly indicate a high degree of involvement by judges. By staying informed about developments in the selection process, judges created opportunities for communication, explicit or otherwise, with the panelists in order to guide or influence the proceedings.

In 20 percent of the districts, judges were interviewed by panelists regarding former law clerks who had been the judges' employees. This interview situation provides an excellent opportunity for a judge to reach every committee member with the judge's views on appropriate selection criteria.

The chief judges surveyed presented conflicting views on the value of the merit selection system. Most judges (74.4%) wanted to retain the merit process, but over one-quarter (25.6%) wanted to return to the old method of judges directly appointing magistrates. Some judges recognized, as one judge expressly noted, that "judges continue to determine who is appointed." These judges, therefore, viewed the elaborate merit committee process as unnecessary. According to one blunt chief judge, "I think [the merit process] is a complete waste of time." Another judge expressed dissatisfaction with the work of a Representative-type panel. The Representative panel, lacking contacts and communication with the judges, can tend to look for the "best" person according to generalized criteria and thus nominate a person with the all-around qualifications to be an outstanding judge. This chief judge, however, did not take an expansive view of the magistrate's role ("I don't think the [merit process] is the best way of obtaining a true 'team player'.") and therefore valued different selection criteria than those applied by the Representative panel. Thus, the judge was dissatisfied with the inability to communicate preferences to the committee because the committee did not fit one of the two types, Blue Ribbon and Proxy, that are designed to facilitate communication from the judges.

Although district judges are appointed through a partisan political process of presidential nomination and senatorial approval and most district judges had experience or connections with partisan political activity in order to be appointed to the bench, there was surprisingly little evidence of political party affiliations affecting the selection of magistrates. In two districts, judges were reported to push for magistrate candidates based upon partisan political affiliations, but, in general, the political conflicts over magisterial appointments involved contests between judges within individual districts who had competing values or goals concerning the appointment and utilization of magistrates.

Magistrates are viewed by judges as important resources. They are generally considered to be essential to the management of large and growing caseloads in the federal courts and thus judges emphasize competence rather than patronage in appointing new magistrates. Political conflicts occur over the definitions of selection criteria and competence, but apparently magistrates are too valuable in the resource-scarce judiciary to permit primary emphasis on partisan political considerations. Interviews revealed numerous examples of judges appointing magistrates from the opposite political party or not knowing the partisan inclinations of the selected appointee.

An additional factor that infuses the magistrate selection process, but was not explicitly raised in interviews, concerned the power of attorneys and the organized bar over the selection of magistrates. Studies of judicial selection in other contexts have documented the power of lawyers' groups over the selection of judges.[28] Judicial Conference regulations specifically instruct that "[t]he panel shall consist of lawyers and other members of the community."[29] The implied instruction to have at least two lay members out of the required six or more committee members indicates an expectation that lawyers will dominate the membership of the panels. Moreover, in the numerous Representative panels, the chief judges consistently indicated that they appointed representatives from state bar associations or local federal bar associations. Thus, the magistrate selection process shares with other forms of judicial selection the characteristic of substantial influence wielded by lawyers and bar groups. In the case of magistrates, concerns about groups outside the legal community being shut out of the process may be less compelling since district judges, an especially elite group of lawyers, are clearly designated as the final decision makers on magistrate appointments.

THE RESULTS OF SELECTION

The selection procedures, under substantial influence from the district judges, determine which lawyers will be appointed to magistrate positions and thereby exercise judgment and discretion in influencing the outcomes of litigants' cases. But just who are these individuals? Judges' backgrounds have been an important research focus for social scientists,[30] especially because of the links between background characteristics and judicial decision making.[31] In order to examine the magistrates' backgrounds, biographical data were obtained from information sheets at the Administrative Office. The available data sheets were examined to gain information on magistrates' employment backgrounds, legal education, and age.[32] The tables that follow contain at least some information about 97.4 percent of the full-time magistrates and 84.7 percent of the part-time magistrates serving during October 1986.

Employment Background

One of the purposes of the merit selection process was to eliminate the appearance of patronage that resulted from judges directly appointing former law clerks and other court personnel to magistrate positions. The pattern of appointment for people with close connections to the federal courts continued even after the implementation of the merit committee selection process (see Tables 2 and 3). The category labeled "Federal court personnel" includes former law clerks, assistant U.S. attorneys, U.S. attorneys, federal defenders, clerks of court, bankruptcy judges, and federal probation officers. Ninety-three percent of the magistrates in that category were either former law clerks or former assistant U.S. attorneys.

Virtually the same percentage of former court personnel have been appointed since the start of merit selection as were appointed through the previous direct selection method—at least among individuals who continue to serve as full-time magistrates. The work of the merit panels dilutes the appearance of patronage because the magistrate vacancies are publicly advertised and applications are accepted and screened by panel members. For some reason, the previous appointment pattern persists.

There are several reasons presented by magistrates, judges, and selection board members for the significant numbers of law clerks and other former court personnel appointed. First, law clerks and assistant U.S. attorneys tend to have outstanding academic records, strong intellectual abilities, and impressive writing skills. These are among the qualities that merit committees and judges seek in magistrate appointees. Second, law clerks and other court personnel often possess a commitment to public service careers and an interest in federal law which lead them to apply for magistrate positions. Third, unlike successful lawyers in private practice who might be forced to accept substantial pay cuts in order to become magistrates, law clerks and assistant U.S. attorneys are accustomed to public sector salaries, so the magistrate's salary would not be unattractive. One court official, referring to the first years of the magistrates' existence, attributed the appointments of court personnel to the low salary of $22,000 that the first magistrates received. That explanation, however, was subsequently less forceful because magistrates' salaries increased nearly four-fold over an eighteen-year period to $82,000 in 1989.[33] Moreover, magistrates will continue to enjoy increases whenever federal judges succeed in gaining pay raises.[34] In sum, magistrates and judges argue that law clerks and other court personnel tend to be precisely the kinds of interested, qualified people who are attracted to the magistrate position and whose credentials make them desirable to merit panels and district judges.

All of the preceding arguments are true, but the essential characteristics of the merit selection process make other factors important too. The judges ultimately make appointments. No matter what the merit committee decides about the finalists, the judges are likely to be best acquainted with a nominee who was previously a law clerk, assistant U.S. attorney, or other close member of that federal court's working community. The judges inevitably rely upon their own personal knowledge and assessments of the finalist in making appointments. Thus, former court personnel are in an advantageous position by virtue of the judges' familiarity with them. Moreover, if the former law clerk is a protégé of a sitting district judge, the judges may have even more reason to appoint that person.

Does the continued pattern of appointments for court personnel in the judge-dominated merit selection process mean that the legislative goals of the new procedure have failed to be attained? Not necessarily. The merit process has opened up applications to the entire legal community. Judges have the opportunity to consider candidates who might have remained unknown under the old system of quickly appointing a known individual from the federal courthouse. Although judges continue to appoint many individuals with similar backgrounds, one can never know how many more former law clerks and other court personnel might have been appointed perfunctorily if the merit procedures had not interposed the activities of a selection committee to counteract the previous appearance of possible patronage.

One notable development in appointments after the implementation of the merit process was an increase in the number of former state judges and law professors selected to be magistrates. Several judges stated in interviews that the ideal magistrate would be a former state judge who could step right in and handle civil litigation matters and trials. The increases may indicate that merit selection panels heed or agree with the views of judges who seek appointees with well-developed expertise.

By the very nature of the position, part-time magistrates tend to be individuals who have positions with the flexibility to mix career responsibilities. Busy, successful law practices and salaried corporate positions may not provide the needed flexibility. As one full-time magistrate wrote on a survey form concerning prior experience as a part-time magistrate, "[m]y private practice during those two years declined to virtually none."

Age at Appointment

The average age at time of appointment was nearly identical for full- and part-time magistrates. For full-time magistrates it was approximately forty-two years and for part-time it was forty-one years.

Table 2 Employment Backgrounds of Full-Time Magistrates, by Selection Process

Previous Jobs	Full-Time Magistrates (%)	Selected Pre-Merit (%)	Selected Post-Merit (%)
Federal Court Personnel	59.9 [154]	59.1 [78]	59.8 [76]
Private Practice	69.3 [169]	60.6 [80]	70.1 [89]
Local Prosecution	13.9 [36]	11.4 [15]	16.5 [21]
Federal Government	13.9 [36]	13.6 [18]	14.2 [18]
State Government	12.7 [33]	11.4 [15]	14.2 [18]
Teaching	8.9 [23]	6.1 [8]	11.8 [15]
State Judge	7.7 [20]	4.5 [6]	11.0 [14]
Legal Aid/ Legal Services	4.6 [12]	3.8 [5]	5.5 [7]

Note: Figures in brackets are base $\underline{N}$s for the adjacent percentages. Total $\underline{N}$=259 (132 pre-merit, 127 post-merit). Columns do not total one hundred percent because the table includes more than one employment category per magistrate. In addition, several small employment categories were excluded.

The average age for graduation from law school fell between twenty-six and twenty-seven so that the appointment age indicates that magistrates have an average of approximately fifteen years of legal experience prior to appointment. This average disguises the fact that there are tremendous age and experience ranges for new appointees as part-time and full-time magistrates (see Tables 4 and 5).[35] Age at first appointment ranged from twenty-seven to seventy for current full-time magistrates and from twenty-seven to sixty-six for part-time

Table 3 Employment Backgrounds of Part-Time Magistrates, by Selection Process

Previous Jobs	Part-Time Magistrates (%)	Selected Pre-Merit (%)	Selected Post-Merit (%)
Federal Court Personnel	15.7 [24]	17.2 [16]	13.3 [8]
Private Practice	70.6 [108]	65.6 [61]	78.3 [47]
U.S. Commissioner	16.3 [25]	25.8 [24]	1.7 [1]
Local Prosecution	13.7 [21]	12.9 [12]	15.0 [9]
Federal Government	2.6 [4]	4.3 [4]	0.0 [0]
State Government	5.9 [9]	4.3 [4]	8.3 [5]
Teaching	3.9 [6]	1.1 [1]	8.3 [5]
State Judge	8.5 [13]	8.6 [8]	8.3 [5]
Legal Aid/ Legal Services	2.6 [4]	0.0 [0]	6.7 [4]

Note: Figures in brackets are base Ns for the adjacent percentages. Total N=153 (93 pre-merit, 60 post-merit). Columns do not total one hundred percent because the table includes more than one employment category per magistrate. In addition, several small employment categories were excluded.

magistrates. Consequently, years of legal experience prior to appointment ranged from two to forty-six for full-time magistrates and one to forty for part-time magistrates.

Interviews with judges and magistrates revealed that the diversity of age and experience reflects the different ways in which district court judges conceptualize the magistrate's role. The very youthful appointees under the old direct selection method show the inclination of some judges to view magistrates as permanent law clerks who per-

Table 4 Age at First Appointment for Full-Time Magistrates, by Selection Process

Age	Full-Time Magistrates (%)	Selected Pre-Merit (%)	Selected Post-Merit (%)
27-30	5.8 [15]	10.4 [14]	0.8 [1]
31-35	23.0 [59]	21.5 [29]	24.6 [30]
36-40	22.6 [58]	15.6 [21]	30.3 [37]
41-45	16.3 [42]	20.7 [28]	11.5 [14]
46-50	9.7 [25]	10.4 [14]	9.0 [11]
51-55	11.7 [30]	12.6 [17]	10.7 [13]
56-60	7.0 [18]	6.7 [9]	7.8 [9]
61-65	3.5 [9]	1.5 [2]	5.7 [7]
66-70	0.4 [1]	0.7 [1]	0.0 [0]
Total	100.0 [257]	100.0 [135]	100.0 [122]

form very limited task assignments. The requirement of five years legal experience in the 1979 act eliminated the subsequent appointment of any individuals under thirty years of age.

Prior to merit selection, the age at first appointment was fairly evenly distributed between twenty-seven and fifty-five for full-time magistrates and between twenty-seven and fifty for part-time appointees. Since the implementation of the merit selection process, new appointees have been noticeably bunched into the thirty-one to forty

Table 5 Age at First Appointment for Part-Time Magistrates, by Selection Process

Age	Part-Time Magistrates (%)	Selected Pre-Merit (%)	Selected Post-Merit (%)
27-30	9.0 [14]	14.7 [14]	0.0 [0]
31-35	24.5 [38]	24.2 [23]	25.0 [15]
36-40	23.9 [37]	14.7 [14]	38.3 [23]
41-45	13.5 [21]	11.6 [11]	16.7 [10]
46-50	11.6 [18]	14.7 [14]	6.7 [4]
51-55	6.5 [10]	7.4 [7]	5.0 [3]
56-60	5.8 [9]	7.4 [7]	3.3 [2]
61-65	4.5 [7]	4.2 [4]	5.0 [3]
66-70	0.6 [1]	1.1 [1]	0.0 [0]
Total	100.0 [155]	100.0 [95]	100.0 [60]

age range, with nearly 55 percent of full-time and over 63 percent of part-time appointees falling into that category.

This phenomenon may reflect a prejudice against older applicants that was detected in interviews with some merit selection panel members. Several selection committee members expressed a presumption that older applicants must be either "running away" from career problems or else erroneously viewing the magistrate position as a comfortable job for easing into retirement. This view is certainly at odds with the desire of some judges to recruit experienced former state judges who can immediately handle complex litigation. The increased percentages of full-time appointees in the fifty-six to sixty-five age range may reflect the latter view on the desirability of experience and expertise that is evident in some districts.

Legal Education

The legal education of judges has frequently been studied and the analyses employed have been subject to dispute.[36] Graduation from a law school of only local or regional reputation does not imply the acquisition of an inferior legal education. However, graduation from a state-funded law school may indicate something about one's financial background because these schools are generally less expensive. Attendance at an "Ivy League" private law school can reflect the historical links between those schools and the top socio-economic stratum of society.[37] Arguably, an additional reason to examine law school background is that attendance at an elite law school reflects high academic achievement and consequently, a broad array of lucrative employment opportunities. Thus, for example, the recruitment and selection of magistrates from elite law schools, while not implying that these are the most qualified individuals, has implications for the manner in which the prestige, authority, and salary of the magistrate are viewed relative to the complete range of legal career possibilities.

In Tables 6 and 7, "elite" law schools are defined as Ivy League law schools plus Chicago, Stanford, Michigan, and California/Berkeley as a rough approximation of the top nine schools by reputation.

There are differences in the legal education backgrounds of the full- and part-time magistrates. Greater percentages of full-time magistrates graduated from elite and private law schools, while public school graduates comprise a greater percentage of the part-time magistrates. Assuming the elite and private law school graduates have the widest range of career options due to the prestige of their degrees in the eyes of employers, the data bear out that full-time magistrate positions are more desirable than part-time positions.

Table 6 Legal Education of Full-Time Magistrates, by Selection Process

Law School Type	Full-Time Magistrates (%)	Selected Pre-Merit (%)	Selected Post-Merit (%)
Elite	15.7 [40]	12.5 [16]	19.0 [24]
Public (non-elite)	47.2 [120]	51.6 [66]	42.9 [54]
Private (non-elite)	37.0 [94]	35.9 [46]	38.1 [48]
Total	100.0 [254]	100.0 [128]	100.0 [126]

Table 7 Legal Education of Part-Time Magistrates, by Selection Process

Law School Type	Part-Time Magistrates (%)	Selected Pre-Merit (%)	Selected Post-Merit (%)
Elite	6.5 [10]	5.4 [5]	8.3 [5]
Public (non-elite)	65.4 [100]	66.7 [62]	63.3 [38]
Private (non-elite)	28.1 [43]	28.0 [26]	28.3 [17]
Total	100.0 [153]	100.0 [93]	100.0 [60]

This conclusion comports with the differences in authority, salary, and prestige for the positions. Part-time magistrates are paid, at most, only half of the full-time salary, and many part-timers receive much less, depending upon how many official working hours per week are assigned for their positions. In addition, full-time magistrates in many districts preside over complete civil trials and undertake a wide range of judicial responsibilities, while many part-time magistrates handle primarily petty offenses in national parks. The percentages for part-time magistrates are additionally skewed in favor of public school graduates due to the location of part-time positions. Many national parks and concomitant part-time magistrate positions are located in less populous Western states. The local attorneys who are potential applicants for magistrate positions in sparsely populated Western states, such as Montana and Wyoming, tend to be produced by their own state universities, which provide the only law schools within the state.

When looking solely at full-time positions, it appears that elite and private law school graduates may have a competitive edge in the eyes of judges and merit committees that make selection decisions. This may in part reflect the fact that elite and private educations are strongly represented among the selectors themselves.[38]

Women and Minorities

The merit selection process for magistrates was established in 1979, in part, because the Carter administration was pushing for such procedures to be widely applied in the federal judiciary. The magistrate selection legislation and implementing regulations shared the Carter administration's goal of appointing members of underrepresented groups to judicial office. Under the merit process, as with the Carter-era appointments to the federal bench, an increased number of women and minority magistrates have been appointed (see Tables 8 and 9). The number of magistrates from these groups increased both in absolute numbers and as a percentage of total magistrates.[39]

The specific regulatory instructions to seek a broader applicant pool had the intent of encouraging judges and merit committees to consider candidates from underrepresented groups. Interviews indicated that district judges can guide merit panels toward consideration of members of underrepresented groups by showing the strength of the judges' commitment to broad recruiting during the initial communications between district judges and committees.

The great increase in authorized full-time magistrate positions[40] helped to facilitate the additions of women and minority magistrates,

Table 8 Women and Minority Group Members Among Full-Time Magistrates

Date	Full-Time Magistrates	Women	Minority
1979 [prior to merit selection]	174 (100.0)	15 (8.6)	9 (1.7)
1981 [after merit selection, one year]	200 (100.0)	16 (8.0)	12 (6.0)
1986 [after merit selection, six years]	287* (100.0)	39 (13.6)	24 (8.4)
1986, October	266 (100.0)	42 (15.8)	NA

Sources: Administrative Office of the U.S. Courts, Annual Report on the Judiciary Equal Employment Opportunity Program for 1981 and 1986; October 1986 roster of U.S. magistrates; and Peter G. McCabe, "The Federal Magistrate Act of 1979," Harvard Journal on Legislation 16 (1979): 395.

Note: Figures in parentheses represent percentages.

*Includes all persons who served as full-time magistrates at any time during June 1985 to June 1986

Table 9 Women and Minority Group Members Among Part-Time Magistrates

Date	Part-Time Magistrates	Women	Minority
1981 [after merit selection, one year]	236 (100.0)	4 (1.7)	4 (1.7)
1986 [after merit selection, six years]	183 (100.0)	8 (4.8)	5 (2.7)

Sources: Administrative Office of the U.S. Courts, Annual Report on the Judiciary Equal Employment Opportunity Program for 1981 and 1986.

Note: Figures in parentheses represent percentages.

because incumbents did not have to be replaced in order to increase representativeness within the magistrate system. Women and minority group members could be appointed to newly created positions without waiting for the original magistrates to retire or resign.

SELECTION AND MAGISTRATES' ROLES

The selection process provides the initial influence upon the development of magistrates' precise roles. Because of their control over the appointment process and influence over merit selection panels, district judges can integrate their conception of the magistrates' appropriate roles into their decisions on appointments. The subordinate judicial officers' roles are not finalized, however, by the selection of specific lawyers for the magistrate positions. Magistrates' roles within individual districts develop and evolve because of a variety of factors. Although district judges are the most influential actors in the role definition process due to their statutory authority and practical power within the courthouses, as subsequent chapters will discuss, situational factors and other judicial actors also affect the expectations and task assignments which define the magistrates' roles within the federal courts.

NOTES

1. U.S. Congress, House Report No. 1364, Magistrates Act of 1978, 95th Cong., 2d Sess., 1978, 11.
2. Joseph F. Spaniol, Jr., "The Federal Magistrate Act: History and Development," *Arizona State Law Journal* (1974): 568–569.
3. Peter G. McCabe, "The Federal Magistrate Act of 1979," *Harvard Journal on Legislation* 16 (1979): 395.
4. Elliot Slotnick, "Lowering the Bench or Raising It Higher?: Affirmative Action and Judicial Selection During the Carter Administration," *Yale Law and Policy Review* 1 (1983): 280.
5. U.S. Congress, House Report No. 1364, 17.
6. U.S. Congress, Senate Report No. 74, Federal Magistrate Act of 1979, *U.S. Code Congressional and Administrative News* 1979, 1478.
7. 28 U.S.C. section 631(b)(5).
8. Administrative Office of the U.S. Courts, *The Selection and Appointment of United States Magistrates*, Feb. 1981, 44.
9. Richard Watson and Rondal Downing, *The Politics of the Bench and Bar: Judicial Selection Under the Missouri Nonpartisan Court Plan*, (New York: John Wiley & Sons, 1969).
10. Administrative Office, *The Selection and Appointment*, 44–45.

11. Pacemaker Diagnostic Clinic v. Instromedix Inc., 725 F.2d 537, 545 (9th Cir. 1984) (en banc) *cert. denied* 469 U.S. 824 (1984).

12. For example, Watson and Downing, *The Politics of Bench and Bar.*

13. Larry Berkson, Susan Carbon, and Alan Neff, *A Study of the U.S. Circuit Judge Nominating Commission,* (Chicago: American Judicature Society, 1979).

14. Elliot Slotnick, "What Panelists are Saying About the Circuit Judge Nominating Commission," *Judicature* 62 (1979): 320–324.

15. Elliot Slotnick, "Federal Appellate Judge Selection During the Carter Administration: Recruitment Changes and Unanswered Questions," *The Justice System Journal* 6 (1981): 283–304.

16. E. M. Gunderson, "'Merit Selection': The Report and Appraisal of a Participant Observer," *Pacific Law Journal* 10 (1979): 683–706.

17. Peter Fish, "Merit Selection and Politics: Choosing a Judge of the United States Court of Appeals for the Fourth Circuit," *Wake Forest Law Review* 15 (1979): 635–654; Lynn Haskin, "Serving on the Circuit Judge Nominating Commission's Third Circuit Panel was a satisfying and successful experience," *American Bar Association Journal* 64 (1978): 575–576; Clayton Hoskins, "A Different View of Judicial Nominating Commissions," *American Bar Association Journal* 65 (1979): 723–724.

18. Slotnick, "Federal Appellate," 289.

19. The districts within this sample represent all of the federal circuits and contain a mix of large, urban courts; courts in sparsely populated states; and courts representing a range of in-between settings.

20. Administrative Office, *The Selection and Appointment,* 43–44.

21. Ibid., 5

22. U.S. Congress, House Report No. 1364, 18.

23. Administrative Office, *The Selection and Appointment,* 10–11.

24. John Cooley, "Designing an Efficient Magistrate Referral System: The Key to Coping with Expanding Federal Caseloads in the 1980s," *Civil Justice Quarterly* 1 (1982): 124–150.

25. Carroll Seron, *The Roles of Magistrates in Federal District Courts* (Washington, D.C.: Federal Judicial Center, 1983), 21–29.

26. 28 U.S.C. section 631(a).

27. Watson and Downing, *The Politics of Bench and Bar,* 1969; Gunderson, " 'Merit Selection'," 1979; Fish, "Merit Selection and Politics," 1979.

28. Joel Grossman, *Lawyers and Judges,* (New York: John Wiley & Sons, 1965); Charles Sheldon, "Influencing the Selection of Judges: The Variety and Effectiveness of State Bar Activities," *Western Political Quarterly* 30 (1977): 397–400; Watson and Downing, 1969; Richard Watson, Rondal Downing, and Frederick Spiegel, "Bar Politics, Judicial Selection, and the Representation of Social Interests," *American Political Science Review* 61 (1967): 54–71.

29. Administrative Office, *The Selection and Appointment,* 44.

30. For example, Thomas M. Uhlman, "Race, Recruitment, and Representation: Background Differences Between Black and White Trial Court Judges," *Western Political Quarterly* 30 (1977): 457–470; S. Sidney Ulmer, "Social Backgrounds as an Indicator to the Votes of Supreme Court Justices in Criminal Cases: 1947–1956 Terms," *American Journal of Political Science* 19 (1973): 622–630.

31. For example, C. Neal Tate, "Personal Attribute Models of Voting Behavior of U.S. Supreme Court Justices: Liberalism in Civil Liberties and Economics Decisions, 1946–1978," *American Political Science Review* 75 (1981): 355–367.

32. All 402 available biography sheets on magistrates serving during October 1986 were examined. The information sheets are voluntarily submitted to the Administrative Office by magistrates. Some magistrates did not submit biographical data sheets and others omitted information, particularly concerning employment background. Survey forms were sent by the author to nineteen full-time magistrates who provided no biographical information to the Administrative Office. Twelve forms were returned, although not all of these contained complete information. Thus the tables have slightly different numbers of magistrates for each category.

33. Magistrates are paid 92 percent of district judges' salaries. In 1989, district judges' salaries were $89,500. Committee on the Judicial Branch, *Simple Fairness: The Case for Equitable Compensation of the Nation's Federal Judges* (Washington, D.C.: Judicial Conference of the United States, 1988), 84.

34. Linda Greenhouse, "Rehnquist, in Rare Plea, Asks Raise for Judges," *New York Times*, 16 Mar. 1989.

35. Tables 4 and 5 indicate age at *first* appointment to a magistrate position. For example, several magistrates began as part-time appointees who later had their positions converted to full-time or else obtained a full-time appointment when a vacancy occurred. The table for full-time magistrates includes their ages from the initial appointments as part-time magistrates.

36. Robert T. Grimit, "More important judicial qualities," *Judicature* 70 (1986): 141 (letter to the editor).

37. Sheldon Goldman, "Reagan's judicial appointments at mid-term: shaping the bench in his own image," *Judicature* 66 (1983): 338–340.

38. For example, there is a significant representation of individuals with elite and private law school educations among the district judges appointed during the last four presidential administrations. Ibid., 338.

39. Data on the composition of the magistrate system are drawn from McCabe, "The Federal Magistrate Act of 1979," 395; Administrative Office of the U.S. Courts, *Annual Report on the Judiciary Equal Employment Opportunity Program for the Twelve-Month Period Ended June 30, 1981* (Washington, D.C.: U.S. Government Printing Office, 1981); Administrative Office of the U.S. Courts, *Annual Report on the Judiciary Equal Employment Opportunity Program for the Twelve-Month Period Ended June 30, 1986* (Washington, D.C.: U.S. Government Printing Office, 1986); and the October 1986 roster of magistrates obtained from the Administrative Office.

40. For example, the number of authorized full-time magistrates positions increased from 61 in Spring 1970, to 228 in Fall 1982. Seron, *The Roles of Magistrates*, 11.

Part 3

Magistrates' Roles Within Representative Court Contexts

4

Magistrates' Roles in District Courts

In order to gain an understanding of the roles of magistrates within the federal courts, this study utilized a participant observation methodology that placed the author in constant, personal contact with magistrates during all working hours. By selecting magistrates in both large and small courthouses as observation subjects, this study analyzed the behavior and roles of magistrates within the general institutional contexts in which the subordinate judges work. In the examples presented by the four illustrative districts in the chapters that follow, the court environments under study ranged from a lone magistrate paired with a single judge in medium-sized city (population 100,000) to five magistrates working for eleven judges in a large courthouse building located in a major city (population over 1,000,000). Examining the magistrates within different contexts is important for a number of reasons which will be further illuminated in subsequent chapters. For example, the size of the courthouse and number of judicial actors (i.e., magistrates, judges, lawyers, clerks, etc.) working within the courthouse can inhibit or enhance familiarity and communication between the judicial actors. The level of contact can, in turn, affect the development of role conceptions and expectations concerning the magistrates. In addition, a location in a large city can complicate the magistrates' role development by expanding the size of the relevant legal community and, consequently, detracting from the magistrates' ability to become well-known to the large local bar.

Any analysis of magistrates' roles in the federal courts requires an understanding of the tasks, interactions, expectations, and resources that comprise the working lives of these lower judicial officers. Unlike studies of judges, such as the work of John Paul Ryan and his colleagues on state trial judges, in which scholars describe and analyze the "typical workday" of the judicial officer, this study makes clear that there is no "typical" workday for United States magistrates nationally.[1] The magistrate system was designed for flexible utilization by district judges according to the needs of their respective districts. In addition, control of the magistrates, including task assignments, has been left under district judges in order to preserve the constitutionality of the magistrate system through supervision by constitutionally based, Article III judicial officers. Thus, magistrates' assignments and the organization of their workloads can vary, sometimes dramatically, not only from district to district and courthouse to courthouse, but also among magistrates with offices along the same hallway in a single courthouse.

Although they receive task assignments from district judges, magistrates, as judicial officers with their own legal and support staffs, retain at least some degree of autonomy in designing the organization of their workload. In fact, because they generally are not as involved with the time-consuming business of presiding over trials, events which require definitive scheduling in order to have parties, attorneys, witnesses, jurors, and other actors simultaneously present in one room, the subordinate judges frequently have significant autonomy in deciding when to address particular assigned tasks during their workdays.

Carroll Seron's studies for the Federal Judicial Center provide a starting point for understanding what magistrates do within the federal courts. After a national survey focusing on methods for assigning tasks to magistrates[2] and interviews in nine selected districts,[3] Seron classified magistrates as falling into three different model role categories: (1) Additional Judge, in which "magistrates hear and decide their own civil caseloads, creating an environment whereby magistrates become, in practice, additional judges";[4] (2) Specialist, in which "magistrates hear and recommend action on special areas of the civil docket, most commonly Social Security and prisoner cases"[5;] and (3) Team Player, in which "judges may elect to have a magistrate hear all pretrial matters (on either a regular or selective basis)."[6] As a generalized framework for understanding magistrates' roles in various districts, Seron's typology provides a useful, initial categorization. Detailed observation of magistrates reveals, however, the limitations of the typology, because of the hybrid nature of magistrates' workloads, which mix the categories within Seron's model role types. Although the magistrates examined in this study do not illustrate an exhaustive representation of magistrates' tasks and behavior, the observation methodology builds upon Seron's previous work with surveys and interviews to illuminate more detail and complexity in the magistrates' work and in their consequences for the federal court system.

Table 10 provides an initial "snapshot" comparison of the different tasks performed by magistrates in the districts studied. The follow-

Table 10 Illustrative Monthly Workloads for Full-Time Magistrates Within Districts Studied

District	A	A	B	B	C	C	D	D
Month Task	Apr. '87	Jul. '87	Oct. '86	Jan. '87	Mar. '87	Apr. '87	Mar. '86	Apr. '86
Criminal								
Petty Offense	13	0	6	2	2	8	21	1
Search Warrant	2	4	0	0	6	0	4	3
Arraignment	12	19	0	0	23	37	4	3
Prisoner								
Habeas Corpus	0	1	4	0	1	0	17	11
Civil Rights	0	0	0	9	0	0	7	13
Social Security	9	9	4	5	0	0	12	30
Civil								
Pretrial Conf.	0	0	4	0	27	10	5	6
Settlement Conf.	1	0	8	3	0	1	2	3
Nondispositive Motion	32	35	44	61	87	86	91	99
Dispositive Motion	3	1	0	0	20	19	97	102
Consent Trial	0	0	0	0	0	0	1	1
Consent Case: Dismiss/Settle	0	0	0	0	0	1	7	12

ing chapters will discuss, in detail, the differences between the magistrates' roles in these districts as well as the reasons for and consequences of those differences. Because individual magistrates' tasks may vary from month to month, this "snapshot" is based upon available statistics for randomly selected months and presents merely a rough illustrative comparison to show the variety and quantity of judicial tasks handled by the subordinate judges.

NOTES

1. Ryan *et al.* present descriptions of "Time Management and the Flow of a Typical Day" for both criminal and civil state trial judges. John Paul Ryan, Allan Ashman, Bruce D. Sales, and Sandra Shane DuBow, *American Trial Judges* (New York: The Free Press, 1980), 18–21.

2. Carroll Seron, *The Roles of Magistrates in the Federal District Courts* (Washington, D.C.: Federal Judicial Center, 1983).

3. Carroll Seron, *The Roles of Magistrates: Nine Case Studies* (Washington, D.C.: Federal Judicial Center, 1985).

4. Ibid., 35.

5. Ibid.

6. Ibid., 36.

District A:
Status Conflicts, Unmet Expectations, and Limited Formal Authority

District A has eight full-time magistrates and fourteen active judges serving in four different courthouses. The main courthouse contains five magistrates and eleven judges located downtown in a major city (population over 1,000,000). The three satellite courthouses, located in medium-sized cities (populations 80,000–150,000), each have one active judge paired with one full-time magistrate. A visit to one small courthouse revealed that, like small courthouses in other districts, the judges' and magistrates' chambers were close to each other. In such small court buildings, this proximity facilitates contact and communication between district judges and magistrates and can enhance working relationships, if the judge respects the magistrate's capabilities and is flexible about the exercise of magistrates' judicial authority. In the large court building, the magistrates and the judges are scattered around several floors of a large, urban federal office building. The opportunities for personal contact and concomitant familiarity in relationships are diminished by the physical environment. For example, a judge or magistrate with chambers and a courtroom on the seventh floor, whose normal work routine is thereby limited to taking the elevator every day from the ground floor to and from the seventh floor, would have little reason to pass by the offices of or otherwise encounter other judicial officers. The time-consuming travel process of waiting for an elevator in a large building further discourages the potential for personal contact through specific visits to judges' offices. In addition, the environment and large organization make it difficult for new magistrates to become acquainted with all of the judges. Thus, some magistrates rely upon the district's full-time administrator, the Court Executive, for advice on how best to approach and communicate with particular judges.

In any district, magistrates' task assignments and relationships with judges are influenced by the method of task assignment adopted within a particular district or courthouse. John Cooley, a former magistrate, presented the possible ways to design an effective task referral system[1] and Seron documented the ways in which districts currently assign tasks to magistrates[2]: (1) random assignment; (2)

rotational assignment; (3) judge-magistrate pairings; (4) assignment by a chief administrative magistrate; and (5) assignment at discretion of individual district judges. In district A, a paired assignment system evolved for the three satellite courts because, with a single judge/magistrate pair under one roof and located at a distance from the district's other judges and magistrates, it was inconvenient to consider an alternative, district-wide task referral system. For the large courthouse, the judges made a conscious decision to adopt a system that generally pairs one magistrate with two judges.[3] The pairings are supposed to change annually, but the judges sometimes keep the pairings intact for longer periods. Each judge decides what tasks to send to his or her assigned magistrate. The pairing system is not used for District A's substantial Social Security appeal caseload.

The district is among the country's leaders in number of Social Security case filings.[4] District A and neighboring districts experienced a veritable flood of filings after industrial plants closed and thousands of local workers lost their jobs. Social Security cases are distributed evenly to magistrates throughout the district through centralized assignment from the court clerk's office. As a result, magistrates in District A spend significant proportions of their time on Social Security cases. The careful review of Social Security cases can require close reading of lengthy and detailed medical testimony and therefore reports and recommendations often cannot be produced quickly. Unlike prisoner cases, in which there are often obvious procedural defects or patently insufficient allegations, which can serve as the basis for a quick dismissal, Social Security files can require time-consuming attention and consideration. The magistrates often assign Social Security cases to their law clerks, but because of the caseload, they must inevitably do some of the cases themselves in addition to reviewing the law clerk's work on the other cases.

The magistrates generally are not responsible for prisoner cases. Habeas corpus and civil rights cases by prisoners are reviewed by two staff attorneys assigned to the district court. An experienced senior magistrate supervises these staff attorneys. Although this magistrate was laden with additional responsibilities, unlike in some other districts, he was not rewarded with the title "chief magistrate." After the initial screening by the staff attorneys, prisoner cases meeting procedural and legal requirements may be assigned by judges to their paired magistrates.

A "duty magistrate" system developed for handling preliminary criminal matters. In the large court, magistrates are "on duty" for separate, rotating, one-week periods in which they have exclusive responsibility for processing the criminal cases. Thus, the magistrates normally handle criminal matters only once every five weeks. In the large court, criminal pretrial matters, such as arraignments, bail reviews, detention hearings, initial appearances, search warrants, and arrest warrants, arise virtually every day. In addition, some of the judges have magistrates handle criminal pretrial conferences to coordinate and settle evidentiary and other matters prior to trial.

A MAGISTRATE IN ACTION

The following incident observed at the courthouse provides a picture of the magistrates at work as subordinate yet authoritative judicial officers. In the large courthouse, there is a daily "Duty Call" scheduled at one o'clock each afternoon to handle preliminary criminal matters. On this particular day, the district's magistrates held their regular monthly luncheon meeting, which did not conclude until 1:15. Afterwards, the duty magistrate talked with the author about the magistrates' roles for ten more minutes prior to entering the courtroom. Magistrates, like judges, recognize that lawyers and witnesses are frequently late in getting to court. Therefore, court proceedings generally do not begin and the magistrate or judge will not enter the courtroom until all other relevant actors are present. The magistrate's lack of concern about beginning precisely on time did not indicate callous indifference or an ego-motivated intention to be late. The magistrate acted as any judge does in seeking to have the court's business effectively accomplished, but not feeling rushed by any clock or supervisor. This judge-like behavior, in recognizing that there would be no sanction or rebuke for not starting promptly, was evident in every district. When magistrates preside over a judicial proceeding, they are the judges for those proceedings and are therefore generally free to organize and run the events according to their own wishes.

Prior to entering the courtroom, the subordinate judge encountered two plainclothes federal agents waiting in the reception area of the magistrate's chambers. The agents indicated that they needed to get an arrest warrant. The magistrate told them to wait in the courtroom and they would be handled first in the Duty Call.

The magistrate entered the courtroom wearing a black robe, while a clerk-bailiff instructed everyone present to rise and then announced that court was in session. The magistrate was seated at the bench just like a judge. Although the magistrate system was designed for flexible use according to the needs of various districts, this emphasis on flexibility should not be mistaken for an intent to encourage informality. During formal judicial proceedings in courtrooms, magistrates serve as genuine judges and therefore generally rely on all of the formalism and symbolism applicable to a federal judicial proceeding.

In less structured situations, such as conferences in chambers with attorneys, magistrates, like judges, develop their own styles and levels of formality in attempting to attain such objectives as encouraging settlements or scheduling discovery matters. In the courtroom situation, however, an uninformed passerby would have no way of knowing that the black-robed figure issuing directives from the federal courtroom bench was a United States magistrate rather than a district judge—except in those few remaining districts in which judges refuse to permit magistrates to wear judicial robes.[5]

As the first order of business, the magistrate had the plainclothes officer swear out and sign the arrest warrant by literally reading him an oath in open court ("Do you swear everything contained . . . is true to the best of your knowledge?"). With the careful formality of any judge, the magistrate served as the judiciary's check upon unrestrained police power for arrests.

The second matter was the appearance of a defendant accused of violating the conditions of his probation. The accused allegedly failed to report a drunk driving arrest while on probation. The magistrate carefully read the defendant his rights and asked him if he understood. The magistrate then described the nature of the immediate proceedings for setting bond. As the magistrate proceeded, some confusion arose regarding whether the defendant had filled out the appropriate financial form to accompany his request for appointed counsel. The magistrate sharply chastised the government officials responsible for processing arrestees, speaking to the court generally but looking directly at the Assistant U.S. Attorney: "You were all waiting for me [in the courtroom] yet none of this paperwork seems to be done." The defendant, who had been standing in front of the bench, was taken back to a seat to fill out the necessary forms.

A subsequent matter concerned a defendant in a narcotics case. This defendant was a middle-aged, naturalized citizen from Ecuador. The defendant told the magistrate that although Spanish was his native language, he understood English and did not need an interpreter. Despite his claims, his spoken English was difficult to comprehend. The defense attorney told the magistrate that he had explained to his client that "the Government would not seek detention if the defendant will waive the preliminary exam." Upon hearing the defense attorney's statement about an apparent deal arranged between the prosecution and defense, the magistrate, with eyebrows raised in an exaggeratedly surprised reaction, stared silently at the Assistant U.S. Attorney. The magistrate then questioned the defendant on the knowing and voluntary nature of this waiver. After accepting the defendant's responses, the magistrate set the conditions for release: $50,000 unsecured bond based upon a promise to appear; travel limited to a nearby three-county area; and forfeiture of passport to the Pretrial Services office by the next day.

This brief courtroom scene illustrates several important points concerning these relatively invisible, subordinate judges within the federal district courts. Magistrates are indeed authoritative judicial officers. The interactions between the magistrate and the lawyers clearly demonstrated the assertion and acceptance of judicial power embodied in the magistrate. These subordinate judicial officials act as judges in conducting the activities within a courtroom through the use of discretionary judgments and reliance upon the accoutrements of judicial office. In addition, magistrates' authorized use of discretion in making judicial decisions has significant impact upon the lives of people drawn into the judicial system. In the foregoing example, the magistrate released the defendant under certain conditions for bail, but the magistrate also possessed the power, after holding detention hearings, to send unconvicted criminal defendants to jail while awaiting trial. The deprivation of liberty for unconvicted defendants is one of the most substantial powers granted to the judiciary in a system which formally presumes that defendants are innocent until proven guilty.[6] Despite the exercise of judicial authority and behavior evident in these criminal pretrial proceedings, the magistrates in District A have clear limitations upon their authority and status.

THE MAGISTRATES' AUTHORITY: A PIVOTAL FACTOR

The constraints upon communication created by the physical and organizational environment of the large courthouse, such as those that are experienced within District A, are common to other districts with their primary location in an urban center. Similarly, the choice of a paired assignment system for referring tasks to magistrates is utilized by many districts. District A, however, has one distinguishing characteristic which underlies and affects virtually every other aspect of the magistrate's roles within the district. Unlike all but one other district in the country, the magistrates in District A are *not* designated by the district's judges to exercise the full extent of magistrates' statutory authority by handling full civil cases with the consent of litigants, although they do in fact preside over such cases on rare occasion, as will be discussed later in this chapter. Under 28 U.S.C. section 636(c)(1), which grants to magistrates the authority to handle civil trials and otherwise take responsibility for complete civil cases, the magistrates may act in such a capacity when the parties consent and "when specially designated to exercise such jurisdiction by the district court or courts he serves." The judges in District A have repeatedly discussed, debated, and voted on designating the magistrates under section 636(c)(1). Initially, some opposition among the judges stemmed from concerns about the statute's constitutionality in granting trial authority to magistrates. Other factors continue to perpetuate judges' opposition to designation, because appellate court cases have clearly established that circuit courts and the Supreme Court do not intend to overturn magistrates' authority under the present statutory scheme.[7]

Magistrates and judges within the district assert that there are a variety of factors which underlie this unusual situation in which the district judges refuse to designate their subordinates to hear consent cases. First, the aforementioned concerns about constitutionality have led some judges to conceptualize a limited role as most appropriate for the magistrates. Moreover, there is agreement among a number of judicial officers that because the judges have taken formal votes on the question of designating magistrates, they have, in effect, adopted public positions on a particular policy—public in the sense that their colleagues are aware of how they have voted. Thus, the judges are placed in the position of rationalizing or defending their votes even though the original justifications for their votes have been swept away by appellate case decisions. Although the circuit courts have directly endorsed the designation of magistrates and the Supreme Court has left in place magistrates' consent jurisdiction by denying certiorari in the primary contested case, the district judges are free to manifest their opposition to magistrates' authority by refusing the designate the magistrates. Discussions and votes in district judges' meetings indicate that positions have hardened and that, contrary to the aspirations and expectations of the magistrates, the district has not moved any closer to explicit designation of magistrates for consent trial work.

The judges in District A, prior to the implementation of the magistrate system, had taken great pride in the fact that they handled all matters, including mundane criminal warrants, without the help of a U.S. commissioner. This tradition of *not* relying on other judicial officers carried over in the judges' attitudes about magistrates. Although they were eventually forced by the flood of filings to have magistrates handle Social Security appeals, several judges were reluctant to allow magistrates even to write recommendations in such cases.

In addition, the chief judge for the district at the time when Congress first considered the magistrate legislation strongly opposed creating a new judicial office. The chief judge traveled to Washington to serve as a primary witness opposing the creation of the magistrate system in the Congressional hearings on the matter. This chief judge helped to set the tone for the district on the narrow characterization and utilization of the subordinate judges.

When the magistrate system was first implemented nationwide in 1971, according to one judge, the magistrates were "parceled out in a penurious manner." District A, a relatively large district, was initially given only one full-time magistrate. With only one subordinate to share among several judges, the magistrate was given the limited role of dealing with a specific category of cases, mainly Social Security, and certain other limited tasks. The lack of authorized positions helped to form a limited initial role for the magistrate, because the judges had never utilized the magistrates in broader roles. As one judge said, "I wish we had been given four or five magistrates right at the start so we could have planned and implemented a system."

As one magistrate described the situation, the district's judges have become "victims of their own experience." They are accustomed to the limited magistrate roles in the district and they are not open to suggestions about expanding the magistrates' authority in order to better utilize the lower tier of judicial officers.

The pairing system for referring cases to magistrates helped to perpetuate the view that magistrates should act as subordinates with a very limited role. According to one magistrate, the pairing system in District A has served to "promote a feeling of proprietary interest" among the judges, in which magistrates are perceived as resources possessed by the individual judges rather than judicial officers contributing to the overall work of the federal district court.

In addition, one magistrate expressed the opinion that the judges have strong perceptions, which are essentially erroneous, that some magistrates are incompetent or lazy. Moreover, one magistrate expressed the suspicion that, at least for a few judges, there are elements of sexism and racism in judges' attitudes about the abilities of particular magistrates. Thus, these judges might support designation for particular magistrates, but they will not support the formalized practice within the district because it would apply to all magistrates. The practice of assigning different tasks to magistrates based upon judges' perceptions of their abilities has been documented in other districts. As one chief judge wrote to the General Accounting Office, "some members of the Court believe that there is a substantial difference in the ability of the various Magistrates, which opinion in my judgment has serious impact on the individual Judge's decisions regarding the use of magistrates."[8]

The judges in District A and elsewhere appoint and reappoint the magistrates, so it is difficult to understand why the judges would not be able to get rid of any magistrate who was truly incompetent. Although no one seems to know of any magistrate in the country who was actually rejected upon application for reappointment, several instances are known of magistrates "encouraged" to retire at the end of their terms because the judges were not satisfied with their performance. It is possible that judges feel obligated to keep magistrates with whom they are dissatisfied in order to avoid conflict with other judges or the discomfort of rejecting a magistrate.

A final factor, mentioned by magistrates but not judges, is what one magistrate described as the "Article III syndrome." As one magistrate described it, some judges have "self-esteem concerns" so that they "want to preserve their own status" against the perceived threat posed by the magistrates. Judges and magistrates in other districts within the circuit described the judges in District A as a group containing some "substantial egos" and several magistrates in other districts said that they probably would resign rather than work for those judges.

The Struggle for Status and Authority

The denial of designation and trial authority for the district's magistrates has several effects which shape the magistrates' roles.

Most of the magistrates in District A were selected through the merit selection process. District A employs a Representative-type panel which selects magistrates according to the criteria that panelists perceive as applicable for the best qualified judge. As a result, several magistrates were appointed who have substantial experience and, most importantly, high expectations and ambitions about the role of the magistrate. As the magistrates continued to be assigned limited tasks, disappointment, frustration, and disenchantment were plainly evident in the magistrates' comments. Several magistrates accepted the position because they expected that the judges would eventually designate them to handle trials after the constitutional issues about the magistrates' authority were settled in appellate cases. When the district's judges maintained their firm stand against designation, the magistrates felt extremely disappointed. A high level of dissatisfaction with the magistrate position is discernible in several of the subordinate judges.

District judges commented that some of the district's judges have been disappointed in the quality of applicants for the magistrate position. The judges' comments have, in essence, confirmed the suspicions of the magistrate who said that judges view magistrates as insufficiently competent. When asked about whether higher caliber attorneys may decline to apply for the position precisely because of the limited authority granted to magistrates, one judge admitted that "we [the judges] may have been hoisted by our own petard."

The magistrates, who have regular contacts with their peers across the country through annual meetings sponsored by their circuit, the Federal Judicial Center, and national magistrates' organization, recognize that their lack of designation is nearly unique. Thus, as one magistrate said, the lack of designation is a "slap in the face" by the judges. Several magistrates feel that they have been publicly labeled as not competent to fulfill the complete range of duties authorized under the statute. One interviewee said, in regard to the experience as a magistrate in District A, that "I just didn't feel like a judicial officer, because the judges control everything, tell you how to do things, and tell you what to decide. There is often no room to make a judicial decision, even when the judge's orders will lead to an unjust result." This feeling of being slighted has been exacerbated by the behavior of several judges within the district. For example, at a formal dinner attended by judges, magistrates, lawyers, and influential public officials within the district, one judge gave a speech in which he said that administrative law judges, magistrates, and summary jury trials are the "work of the devil." According to a magistrate, this public condemnation of magistrates as a threat to the Article III federal courts could do nothing but diminish the possibility of magistrates ever attaining the status and respect appropriate for federal judicial officers. Another judge told a magistrate that he would "rather have a third law clerk than have a magistrate" in communicating his preference that the magistrate system not exist at all. Lawyers reported to one magistrate that a judge had "bad-mouthed" the magistrate during a meeting with the lawyers and sharply criticized the magistrate's decisions on nondispositive matters in the civil case at hand.

In addition to the primary manifestation of magistrates' lack of authority, namely the refusal to designate for consent trials, several judges persistently act to ensure that magistrates are not accorded the status of judicial officers. For example, magistrates in District A are addressed with the title "Magistrate." In a number of other districts, magistrates are addressed by the title "Judge." As one magistrate in District A remarked with an expression combining incredulity and awe, "Did you know that magistrates in District [X] are called 'judges'?" When the magistrates from District A were observed at a Federal Judicial Conference meeting for magistrates from three circuits, their conversations focused substantially on the lack of status they were accorded by their district's judges. One magistrate remarked that "I frequently call my colleague 'Judge [X]'." The magistrate continued by saying, "but I always look around to see [if a judge] might be listening." One judge has stated that magistrates should not be permitted to wear robes and insisted that magistrates have "offices" not "chambers" and that they be referred to as "magistrates" and not "judges." The district's court administrator and the magistrates' staffs have been told by judges and the judges' staffs that magistrates are not to use the title "judge," but one magistrate noted that the judges "would never have the guts to tell me that directly." Examples abound of instances in which the district's judges evinced great concern that magistrates not be accorded status and privileges. A judge became very upset once when a secretary made the mistake of creating an alphabetical list of the court's judges which mixed together the magistrates and district judges.

The status differentiation and conflicts between the magistrates and judges within District A have caused the magistrates to have more communication between themselves and a greater sense of group identification and solidarity than was observed in any other district. In spite of the large courthouse setting that inhibited interoffice personal contacts and the dispersed district with three outlying courthouses, the magistrates organized themselves to have monthly meetings.

At an informal level, the shared frustrations about lack of authority and status led the district's magistrates to joke with each other about their status and the judges in the district. For example, one magistrate remarked that magistrates in District A do not step down from the "bench" when they finish a hearing; instead they step down from the "stool." In laughingly criticizing a clearly erroneous decision by a judge, one magistrate said, "Well, [the judges] are not merit selected [as we are], so they're just doing the best that they can."

The solidarity and communication between the magistrates has also led to organized efforts to increase their status and authority within the district. The magistrates have contacted colleagues in other districts throughout the country and read the Federal Judicial Center's studies on the use of magistrates[9] in order to prepare a joint memorandum for the judges. The memorandum, directed to the judges' magistrates committee, outlined the alternative systems for referrals to and utilization of magistrates based on the experiences in other districts. The memorandum clearly was intended to educate the judges on how they could more effectively utilize their subordinates by permitting broader authority and a wider range of tasks. In the memorandum, the magistrates criticized the district's current system for its inefficiency, lack of continuity on cases, and routinization of work. Although the memorandum described but did not endorse magistrate utilization schemes in other districts, the concluding paragraphs argued very directly for the benefits of designating magistrates for trial work within the district. The memorandum did not lead to any change in the magistrates' authority, but it clearly reflected the unity of the magistrates on the subject.

The magistrates have continued to discuss strategies for altering their roles within the district. They pool knowledge concerning which judges can be regarded as supporters or opponents on the designation issue. As the frustration continued and led several magistrates to consider the possibility of resigning, some magistrates toyed with the idea of symbolic actions such as having all or several of the magistrates simultaneously apply for a vacant bankruptcy judge position. The assumption underlying such an action would be that an overt expression of collective dissatisfaction would shake the judges into acting to avoid the possibility of losing several magistrates.

The Anomaly of Formal Status and Informal Practice

The status and formal authority of magistrates in District A consistently reinforced their role as subordinate assistants to the judges. The status accorded to magistrates, which clashes with the incumbents' expectations for their judicial office, created solidarity among the magistrates and a shared sense of dissatisfaction. Surprisingly, this low formal status contrasts with the informal practices in the same district that provided magistrates with opportunities to exercise broad authority and enjoy significant status as judicial officers within specific situations.

All of the magistrates interviewed and observed in District A stated that they occasionally handled complete civil cases with the consent of litigants. One magistrate was able to do consent trials in prisoner cases and cases with "weird plaintiffs" or unusual areas of law, such as admiralty. In other words, as explained by the magistrate, consent cases tend to be the unusual cases that the judges do not want to handle. The opportunities for consent cases were usually few and far between for the magistrates in the large courthouse. One magistrate said he had done fewer than a dozen trials during his six years as a magistrate.

The magistrates paired and located with a single judge in the smaller courthouses generally developed closer working relationships with their respective judges and consequently enjoyed greater opportunities to be assigned consent cases and trials. According to one judge, the use of magistrates for consent trials, which is contrary to the formally expressed wishes of the district's judges and violates section 636(c) of the statute which requires that the magistrates be "specially designated to exercise such jurisdiction by the district court," developed out of necessity because of the significant case backlog in one of the outlying small courthouses. The judge felt compelled to share cases with the magistrate in order to reduce an enormous case backlog that had developed over the years when there previously had not been a judge assigned to that courthouse on a full-time basis. The example of the magistrate in the small court handling consent cases and trials served to encourage other judges to utilize their magistrates occasionally for such tasks. The anomalous nature of this essentially sub rosa practice of referring consent trials to magistrates was most evident in the example of one judge who consistently voted against designating magistrates and denied that he would ever refer significant case responsibilities to magistrates, yet gradually referred precisely such tasks to his assigned magistrate.

This practice of having undesignated magistrates supervise complete civil cases and trials is not without precedent. Prior to 1979, there were at least thirty-six districts nationwide in which magistrates undertook such responsibilities without statutory authorization. The situation in District A is highly unusual, if not unique, because the 1979 statute laid out in detail the prerequisites for magistrates' authority over civil cases, including official designation by the judges for consent trial work. Most other districts automatically followed the statute in designating magistrates, but District A is unusual in using magistrates outside of the requirements of the statute. The practice can continue to exist, contrary to the statute, because it serves the interests of all the actors involved. The magistrates want opportunities to exercise their full authority and supervise trials. One magistrate admitted to feeling very uncomfortable about doing trials, since, without designation, trials are beyond the scope of the magistrates' authority. However, the magistrate ultimately concluded that a magistrate "cannot say no to a judge." The judges want to be able to reduce their caseloads and filter out cases that they regard as less interesting or less important. The litigants who consent to have their cases heard by magistrates probably do not know much about the specifics of magistrates' authority, although many attorneys would know through experiences in other federal courts that magistrates can handle consent cases. Moreover, litigants are probably not aware of the details of the magistrates' authorizing statute or else a losing party would surely challenge the legitimacy of a magistrate's decision in a consent case.

The magistrates in District A have at least occasional opportunities to exercise their full authority and assume their complete judicial role in civil consent cases. Thus, although they want the case referral system changed and they desire immediate designation and more opportunities for consent trials, they are not completely dissatisfied with all aspects of their jobs. One magistrate described enjoying the various task assignments for magistrates, including Social Security cases, but expressed immense dissatisfaction with the magistrate position because of the "low status and irritating treatment by judges."

The frustrations experienced by the magistrates in District A illustrate the difficulties involved in developing a new judicial position. The incumbents' expectations about their status and roles are based upon the broad authority permitted under the magistrate statute, yet their subordinate position and the historical factors supporting a limited role within the district work to constrain further planned development of the magistrate position. Although the official low status of magistrates has a negative effect upon morale, the practical case pressures and informal practices within the district have operated to broaden the magistrates' actual authority and create opportunities for the subordinates to experience, at least on occasion, a full range of judicial tasks. These experiences have served to maintain the magistrates' high expectations despite the continued formal opposition by a majority of judges. The magistrates' roles continue to evolve, albeit slowly, in the direction of broader authority, but without being granted concomitant recognition and status, an undercurrent of dissatisfaction and conflict will remain among the judicial officers within the district.

NOTES

1. John W. Cooley, "Designing an Efficient Magistrate Referral System: The Key to Coping with Expanding Federal Caseloads in the 1980s," *Civil Justice Quarterly* 1 (1982): 124–150.

2. Carroll Seron, *The Roles of Magistrates in the Federal District Courts* (Washington, D.C.: Federal Judicial Center, 1983), 21–29.

3. In order to pair five magistrates with eleven judges, one magistrate is paired with three judges.

4. In fact, during 1986, District A's Social Security caseload exceeded the Social Security caseloads in ten of the twelve *circuits* and accounted for over 14 percent of the Social Security cases nationally. Administrative Office of the U.S. Courts, *Annual Report of the Director of the Administrative Office of the United States Courts* (Washington, D.C.: Government Printing Office, 1986), 373–375.

5. For example, Seron found that judges do not permit magistrates to wear judicial robes in the Eastern District of Kentucky. Carroll Seron, *The Roles of Magistrates: Nine Case Studies* (Washington, D.C.: Federal Judicial Center, 1985), 63n. 67.

6. As many commentators have noted, this formal presumption of innocence is not evident in the practical processing of defendants through a criminal justice system that relies upon plea bargaining and quick disposition of cases. Herbert L. Packer, *The Limits of the Criminal Sanction* (Stanford: Stanford

University Press, 1968); Malcolm M. Feeley, *The Process Is the Punishment* (New York: Russell Sage Foundation, 1979).

7. Pacemaker Diagnostic Clinic v. Instromedix Inc., 725 F.2d 545 (9th Cir. 1984) (en banc) *cert. denied* 469 U.S. 824 (1984).

8. General Accounting Office, *Potential Benefits of Federal Magistrates System Can Be Better Realized* (Washington, D.C.: U.S. Government Printing Office, 1983), 70.

9. Seron, *The Roles of Magistrates in the Federal District Courts*, 1983; Seron, *The Roles of Magistrates: Nine Case Studies*, 1985.

6

District B:
Acknowledged "Judges" and the Incongruity of High Status and Limited Actual Authority

District B has three full-time magistrates and four judges working in two courthouses in medium-sized cities (populations of 100,000 and 180,000). The main courthouse contains the offices of three judges and two magistrates, while the smaller court has one judge and one magistrate. Both of the courthouses are relatively small and facilitate personal contact between the judges and the magistrates. It is not uncommon for a magistrate or judge to walk down the hall to speak with another judicial officer personally about a pending motion or other aspects of cases before the district court. Although such contacts do not necessarily occur daily or even weekly, the magistrates and judges in the district know each other with sufficient familiarity that each claims to feel free to pick up the phone or walk down the hall to contact the others. In the larger courthouse, the judges' and magistrates' chambers and courtrooms are located on three consecutive floors in a federal building. In the smaller courthouse, the judge and magistrate are both on the ground floor of a small building containing only a post office, district court, and a few federal agencies' offices.

Tasks are assigned to magistrates through a paired system in which each magistrate in the larger courthouse is paired with one of the judges in the same courthouse and the magistrate in the smaller court is paired with the judge in the same location. In addition, the magistrate in the small courthouse must spend one to two days each week at the larger court to handle matters for the fourth judge, who assumed senior status but maintained a productive schedule for handling cases.

For a district its size, District B receives a relatively high number of both prisoner and Social Security case filings. There is no separate office to process prisoner cases, as in larger districts that have staff attorneys or pro se law clerks, so magistrates assume responsibility for handling habeas corpus and civil rights cases. Magistrates also review the Social Security cases. The magistrates each have one law clerk to assist in writing reports and recommendations. The caseload, however, is sufficiently high that the magistrates themselves must spend a significant proportion of their time reading and writing about prisoner and Social Security cases.

The criminal pretrial matters are all handled by the two magistrates in the larger courthouse, because the U.S. marshals' office and the holding facilities are located in the larger building.[1]

THE PATH TO HIGH STATUS

When the district was first authorized to select a full-time magistrate, the chief judge selected a very experienced attorney who, twenty-five years earlier, had been a law clerk in the district court. From the very beginning, the chief judge always referred to and addressed the magistrate as "Judge." This manner of reference and form of address were automatically adopted by the other judges in the district, the subsequent judges (including all of the current judges), the district court staff, and practicing attorneys. The use of the title "Judge" is so well accepted in the district that it is the only district encountered in this study in which magistrates' secretaries answered the office telephones by saying "Judge X's office."

The magistrates are accustomed to being addressed as "Judge" by attorneys and court staff members. In fact, the magistrates expressed surprise when they learned that magistrates are not similarly addressed and respected in other districts. District A, as discussed in the previous chapter, represents the extreme but common case of judges resisting any association of magistrates with the title "Judge." In some other districts, magistrates are called "Judge" during court proceedings by attorneys, litigants, and witnesses. However, District B appeared unique in having the district judges initiate, perpetuate, and endorse the use of the title for magistrates. An official who helps to oversee the magistrate system at the Administrative Office expressed surprise when he was told that there was a district in which magistrates' secretaries answer the phone using the title "Judge." The official was very concerned because district judges in many places react vigorously against associating magistrates with that title. When told about this unnamed district (District B), the official cringed and said "they're not supposed to be doing that" and expressed the fear that judges elsewhere might hear about it and become angry.

The magistrates recognize the value of high status. The title "Judge" creates a clear image in the minds of lawyers and parties about expected deference and appropriate formal behavior in the presence of an identifiable judicial officer. Magistrates have, in effect, a more authoritative voice when ruling on motions, guiding settlement negotiations, and undertaking the other judicial tasks within their authority as federal judicial officers. One magistrate described correcting his secretary when she occasionally slipped and referred to him as "the magistrate" instead of "the judge" because he believed that consistent reinforcement of his judicial status, especially to lawyers who are not familiar with magistrates and federal court procedures, helped to enhance his effectiveness.

By endorsing the use of the title "Judge" for magistrates, the judges in the district publicly acknowledged every day the status of magistrates as judicial officers vested with the power of the district court. Rather than discuss or debate the appropriate title, status, and role of magistrates, the judges simply accepted the title utilized in the district when they were elevated to the federal bench. Unlike District A, in which the judges continually considered and debated the appropriate role and status of magistrates, the District B judges easily accepted a form of address endorsing the magistrates' judicial position.

THE REALITY OF LIMITED AUTHORITY

Although the magistrates in District B enjoy acknowledged status as judicial officers, and in fact are the beneficiaries of the clearest, most unequivocal endorsement from district judges in terms of being called "Judge," the magistrates have relatively limited authority over judicial tasks. One might presume that these manifestations of status would have concomitant practical applications for the work of the subordinate judges under the broad authority permitted in the magistrate statute. In other words, judicial officers who are acknowledged by one and all to be "judges" should be working as judges in having responsibility for an array of important judicial tasks. In District B, however, magistrates' work is limited almost exclusively to prisoner and Social Security cases as well as a limited number of nondispositive civil motions. One judge permitted his magistrate to undertake some broader tasks, including settlement negotiations, but for the most part, magistrates spend much of their time on the more limited matters that Seron would characterize as fitting with the "Specialist" role rather than the "Additional Judge" role for magistrates.[2] The activities of the two magistrates in the larger courthouse are limited to such a degree that the judges' staffs even control the scheduling of motions to be heard in front of the magistrates. The judges instructed the magistrates to set aside Mondays for hearing motions, so the magistrates sit the entire day and hear motion after motion while making rulings from the bench at the completion of each oral argument. The magistrate in the smaller court, who works closely with the most innovative judge, possessed the autonomy to handle not only more diverse tasks, but also to schedule his own conferences and hearings. Although the magistrate in the smaller court exercises broader authority, like the other magistrates in the district, he has never had a consent case or a trial. He was appointed as a special master in one employment discrimination case that settled during trial, but there has never been a civil consent case in the district under section 636(c), even though the magistrates are designated to exercise full authority under the magistrate statute. District B is, in effect, a kind of mirror image of District A in regard to magistrates' status and authority. District A magistrates have low status but are sometimes permitted to handle consent cases and trials illicitly. Magistrates in District B are accorded full status, endorsed by the district judges as federal judicial officers, yet they have never had the opportunity to supervise any civil cases by consent of the litigants.

One effect of the magistrates' lack of broad authority is reduced visibility. Although attorneys who litigate regularly in the federal courts know the individual magistrates very well, they evince uncertainty about what the magistrates can do. In addition to mistakes attorneys make about how to address magistrates, such as the attorney in a settlement conference who addressed the magistrate as "Mister," the lawyers are prone to ask magistrates, "Can you decide that issue for us?" or, "Should we file the motion with you?" If the magistrates had broader authority and handled more visible matters such as civil consent trials, their position and powers would become more familiar to the practicing bar.

The Basis for Incongruity

The original full-time magistrate, a former U.S. commissioner appointed to the first authorized full-time magistrate position in 1973, set the tone for the use of magistrates within the district. The original magistrate, who continued to serve until 1987, always had an extraordinary reputation with the judges and attorneys within the district as an extremely knowledgeable, fair, and competent judicial officer. He became a magistrate after spending nearly twenty-five years in private practice where he was a partner in a well-known law firm. As a magistrate, he continued the pretrial criminal work that he had done as a commissioner and handled the rising levels of prisoner and Social Security cases within the district. He developed such a reputation for expertise in these matters that magistrates in other districts mention his name as someone who is able to give advice to new magistrates throughout the circuit. In fact, because of the reputation that he earned, both magistrates and judges within District B sought his advice on how to utilize the subordinate judges and how to handle certain legal matters. This original magistrate was one of the very few magistrates encountered in the study who expressed, as an ideal role conceptualization for magistrates, a very limited role as specialist in pretrial criminal and civil, Social Security, and prisoner cases. Most other magistrates described the ideal magistrate role as encompassing a much broader range of judicial tasks, with many aspiring to have the complete breadth of statutory authority, including consent trials. This original magistrate, while acknowledging that magistrates should assist judges in whatever tasks that judges might assign under the statute, expressed a principled view that magistrates should have a limited role clearly differentiated from that of a district judge.

The second full-time magistrate position was authorized seven years after the first position. The second magistrate was selected by a Representative-type merit panel and assumed his office after Congress had broadened magistrates' authority, including the explicit approval of consent trials. The second magistrate had and continues to have an expectation and keen desire to exercise the full, broad scope of magistrates' authority. Unfortunately for this magistrate's expectations about his role, the judges in the district had adopted the example of the original magistrate, with his limited duties, as the model for how magistrates should be utilized.

The judges never made any conscious, considered decisions about how magistrates should be utilized. Instead, since all of the district's judges were appointed to the bench *after* the original magistrate was appointed, they learned from the respected original magistrate how the subordinate judicial officers were to be utilized. Because the original magistrate had a limited view of his proper role, this view was conveyed to the judges in their socialization and education process as they learned how to be federal judges within District B. Federal judges tend to have many case responsibilities to occupy them, especially in their first years, when they are concerned with learning how to be effective judicial officers. Therefore there is little reason or incentive for judges, on their own, to examine and digest the details of the magistrates' authorizing statute. Judges normally adapt themselves to the preexisting magistrate system operating within their districts. Only after they become more confident and comfortable in their role as federal judges and they begin to have contact with judicial officers from other districts do they begin to initiate innovation and change in the use of magistrates. For the most part, such planned changes come only from a minority of active, interested judges. Most other judges appear content or preoccupied enough to adapt to existing operations, unless there are obvious problems. Thus changes in the utilization of magistrates will often be on an ad hoc basis in response to changes in case filings. For example, the magistrates in District B began to handle some preliminary civil matters only when the judges realized that the court was steadily falling behind in processing the increasing caseload.

In District B the ad hoc nature of policy development and the lack of conscious attention paid by the judges to the magistrate system were evident in an example involving magistrates' orders in prisoner cases. The district, through the clerk's office, had a long-standing policy that whenever a copy of a judge's order, such as an order dismissing a case, was sent to a prisoner-litigant, the judge's signature would be blackened out and only the judge's typed name would appear at the end of the order. This policy was intended to prevent any potential problems from a prisoner utilizing forgery skills to copy a judge's signature and create phony court orders. Magistrates frequently issue reports and recommendations in prisoner cases, usually recommending that the judge dismiss the case for procedural problems or patent lack of substance. These reports are sent to the litigants at the prison. The litigants then have ten days to respond with objections to the magistrate's report and recommendations.[3] At least one magistrate had always sent the prisoner-litigants signed reports and recommendations just as he would send to any other parties in a lawsuit. After more than two years as a magistrate, one of his reports and recommendations was returned to the court because the prisoner in question had been released from jail and the sheriff had no forwarding address for him. The returned envelope happened to arrive in the larger courthouse at the desk of a senior official in the clerk's office who opened it and discovered the magistrate's signature. This official called the magistrate's deputy court clerk to announce that magistrates' signatures should not be sent to prisoners because the same forgery risks existed that prompted the policy regarding judges' signatures. The personnel in the clerk's office who mailed out magistrates' signed orders and reports had never been told that the policy applied to magistrates; the magistrates' staffs and the magistrates themselves had no awareness of the policy at all—so it was clearly a case of magistrates being overlooked when policies and practices were implemented regarding judicial officers within the district.[4]

One important reason why magistrates in District B have never been allowed to exercise full authority is that the judges have never followed through with the district's rules governing consent trials by magistrates. A 1985 addendum to the district's local court rules, entitled "Order Regarding Civil Jurisdiction of United States Magistrates," outlined in detail the steps to be taken by litigants in order to consent to have a magistrate preside over a civil case. The addendum included the statement that the "clerk of court shall notify parties in all civil cases that they may consent to have a magistrate conduct any or all proceedings in the case and order the entry of a final judgment." The author asked the court clerk's office why routine, universal notice had not led any parties to consent. "What notice?" came the reply from the clerk's office. The personnel in the clerk's office had never even heard of the two-year-old addendum to the local court rules—rules which are normally scrupulously followed in regard to other matters. Apparently the judges had adopted standard language regarding consent jurisdiction for magistrates, but no one had ever followed through by notifying the concerned parties. One judge admitted that he had never even thought about the rule and thus assumed that no one had ever pursued implementation. The lack of follow-up on court rules regarding magistrates indicates that judges have not had any reason to pay particular attention to the way magistrates are utilized in the district.

While the judges were comfortable in regarding the magistrates as judicial officers, two judges expressed reluctance about actually having magistrates supervise consent trials, because of unknown potential consequences such as lengthy trials causing backlogs with Social Security cases and civil motions. Thus, one reason for the magistrates' limited authority was the judges' reluctance to enter the unknown realm of magistrate trials; a reluctance not based on philosophical concerns but on a natural hesitance to change a system that seemed to be operating with adequate efficiency.

The second magistrate, who desired broader authority, sought to have the judges consider utilizing the magistrates for a more extensive range of tasks. Because many districts utilize magistrates to the full extent of the statute, including civil consent trials, and magistrates are well-aware of operations in other districts through regular inter-district and inter-circuit contacts in the magistrates' National Council and the Federal Judicial Center's annual seminars, the second magistrate had many examples to draw upon to show the judges how magistrates are given broader authority elsewhere. When the magistrate attempted to raise the issue to the judges, the limited role of the original magistrate was always held up by the judges as the model for magistrates within the district. For example, at one meeting in which the magistrate raised the possibility of magistrates supervising some consent trials, the former chief judge objected that if trials were permitted, then "the magistrates would not have time to do the things that they are *really supposed to do*—Social Security and prisoner cases" (emphasis added). The example and influence of the original magistrate became firmly established in the district to the extent that the judges had difficulty even thinking about alternatives to the current limited roles of magistrates.

The pairing system of task assignments to magistrates also served to perpetuate the limited magistrates' roles within the district. The second magistrate, who sought more responsibilities, including trials, was paired with the most cautious, conservative judge who wanted to keep firm control over cases that were assigned to him. The judge was not philosophically opposed to a broader role for magistrates, but his view of his own role as a judge dictated that he retain control of and closely monitor cases and tasks.

By contrast, within the same building, the original magistrate was paired with a judge who was interested in considering broader utilization of magistrates. However, the example and influence of the original magistrate served to solidify existing limited practices. For example, the paired judge sometimes left lawyers in his chambers during pretrial conferences and walked down the hall to see the original magistrate. On at least one occasion he said to the original magistrate, "I think that these lawyers might be willing to consent to have you hear the case," which would permit the judge to move ahead to his next case. The magistrate responded that it would be improper to have the lawyers consent under these circumstances since an underlying intent of the magistrate's consent authority was to avoid even an appearance of pressure on the lawyers to consent. Thus, according to the magistrate's proper but unusually principled and narrow view of the consent process, it would be improper to have either the judge or magistrate know how or at what point particular parties decided to consent. The magistrate's view accorded with the concerns expressed by Congress in the legislative history that "no pressure, tacit or expressed, should be applied to the litigants to induce them to consent to trial before the magistrates."[5] According to the House Report on the 1979 legislation:

> The consent procedure is to be handled by the clerk of the court. The response of a party is not to be conveyed to the district judge, and the district judge is not to attempt any inducement, subtle or otherwise, to encourage magistrate trials. This language is an important safeguard against what has been characterized as the "velvet blackjack" problem. Some judges may be tempted to force disfavored cases into disposition before magistrates by intimations of lengthy delays manufactured in district court if the parties exercise their right to stay in that court.[6]

In spite of the technical accuracy of the magistrate's interpretation of the statute, it is very common in other districts that judges and magistrates know how consent came about. Seron has documented that districts take different approaches to the issue of making consents completely "blind" and beyond the knowledge of the judicial officers.[7] As one judge in another district said, "if you followed the statute precisely, you'd have a hell of a time getting anyone to consent." The District B judge's interest in considering a broader role for magistrates was thus thwarted because of his pairing with and respect for the original magistrate.

In effect, then, the particular sets of pairings in District B served to perpetuate limited magistrate roles because of a mismatch between views and interests of the judges and their respective magistrates. The magistrate with the limited view and extraordinary reputation thwarted his paired judge's interest in exploring broader tasks for magistrates. Simultaneously, the judge who desired to control and monitor all aspects of cases stopped his paired magistrate's desire to have autonomy and broader responsibilities. The mismatch was apparent to at least one of the judges, who has said, "if I had [the second magistrate], I would have him do some trials and other things." It seems intuitively obvious that a simple reversal of the pairings would have made everyone happy, but the original magistrate was so valuable for his expertise and efficiency in processing the district's steady burden of prisoner and Social Security cases, that his paired judge did not want to lose him.

The paired assignment system was not arbitrarily selected and implemented in the district. In districts such as District B, in which there is not an even ratio of judges to magistrates, pairings require some compromise and coordination. The pairing system emerged in District B, just as it emerges in other districts, because of a concern about accountability. Many judges want to know exactly what the individual magistrates are doing and how productive they are. In District B, before the addition of the third magistrate, the judge in the small courthouse did not have a magistrate in the building. This judge has became a well-known innovator in alternative dispute resolution mechanisms and had adopted, among other things, a policy of assigning some cases to be heard in summary jury trials in order to facilitate settlement. His interest in assigning cases to summary jury trials coincided with the second magistrate's interest in undertaking broader responsibilities, including the supervision of trials, so the second magistrate conducted dozens of summary jury trials for the judge in the small courthouse. This created a problem with at least one judge in the larger courthouse who felt that the summary jury trials were absorbing the magistrate's time and pulling him away from continuing responsibilities for this judge's Social Security and prisoner cases. When the third magistrate was added and a pairing system became possible, pairings were adopted so that all of the judges could have a specific magistrate accountable to them. Therefore the judges would know precisely how their respective magistrates were accomplishing pending tasks.

A Glimmer of Change

The addition of a third full-time magistrate helped to encourage some expansion of the magistrates' roles within District B. The third magistrate was paired with the judge in the small courthouse who was concerned with efficient case processing. This judge allowed the magistrate to control his own schedule for conferences and motion hearings. The judge gave the magistrate substantial independent responsibility for conferences regarding scheduling, settlement, and pretrial matters, in addition to the court's usual complement of Social Security and prisoner cases. The magistrate developed significant expertise and a very positive reputation for facilitating the settlement of cases. The magistrate's effectiveness and value for the district in undertaking a broader range of tasks served as a new example for the district's judges concerning the possibility of expanding the subordinate judges' roles within the district. One judge, who previously expressed the view that magistrates should concentrate on prisoner and Social Security cases, said, after seeing the effectiveness of the third magistrate, that magistrates can appropriately assume a broader range of responsibilities. The example of the third magistrate led the other two judges paired with magistrates to recognize that their subordinate judges can undertake broader tasks than those traditionally assumed by the influential original magistrate. While the other district judges began to recognize new possibilities, they have moved slowly to alter their customary practices with their own magistrates.

It is very likely that the magistrates' responsibilities within District B will grow and change substantially. The original magistrate, whose influence tended to hinder the interest of his paired judge in trying new things, eventually retired. Thus the judges have had an opportunity to rethink the roles of magistrates within the district as they considered the qualities to seek in the new appointee. Simultaneously, a new district judge was added in a third nearby courthouse, which forced the district judges to reconsider how the magistrates will be utilized.

When asked during the course of interviews "Why don't magistrates handle consent cases in this district?" the judges tended to respond that they really had not thought much about the issue. They had simply adapted to the established limited utilization of magistrates and never consciously studied the possibilities for using magistrates. Unlike District A, in which some judges had principled objections to permitting magistrates to handle consent cases, the District B judges evinced no such opposition to the idea.

Because the judges had never previously studied the use of magistrates, they also had never considered how they would develop a new magistrate system. The judges in District B endorsed and perpetuated the status of magistrates as legitimate federal judicial officers. However, like judges in other districts who accord magistrates much lower status, the judges often regarded the magistrates as simply resources to be allocated and utilized by the judges within the district. This compartmentalization of the magistrates into separate, nonintegrated categories—judicial officers deserving of recognition on the one hand, and case-processing resource tools for the judge on the other—was manifested in the fact that the judges had never really considered consulting with the magistrates about how the magistrate system ought to operate within the district. In District A and districts in which magistrates have a very clearly differentiated and subordinate status, it is understandable that judges intentionally decline to seek suggestions from their "employees." In District B, the anomalous position of magistrates, as subordinates who receive orders and yet are judicial officers, served to hinder the judges' immediate recognition of magistrates as colleagues (albeit not exactly equals) who are intimately involved with and, in fact, are experts on many aspects of district court operations.

Effective Performance as a Model for New Possibilities

The exploration of alternative methods for utilizing magistrates within District B derived, in part, from the example of the third magistrate, who received a range of task assignments from the judge in the small courthouse. The effectiveness of this magistrate in accomplishing case settlements and processing civil litigation through the various stages prior to trial served to show the judges in the larger courthouse how magistrates can be more broadly utilized by district judges in order to increase the effectiveness of the entire court.

Judges and magistrates can keep track of the activities of individual magistrates not only through the "grapevine" of conversations with court personnel and lawyers, but also through the monthly case-closing and pending-case statistics submitted to and published internally by the circuit court. Some magistrates expressed surprise at how competitive the judicial officers are within the federal courts and how pressure for productivity is self-generated when magistrates can see their monthly statistics reported in comparison with those of other subordinate judges. The pressure to produce impressive statistics is exacerbated by the need to satisfy the district judges in order to enhance the likelihood of reappointment. While some magistrates and their staffs explicitly expressed the opinion that certain magistrates must be exaggerating their accomplishments every month and therefore the statistics are not to be believed, most magistrates in District B's circuit appeared to maintain an awareness of the general level of productivity reported by others within their districts. In District B, the monthly reports made judges aware of the diversity and extent of tasks accomplished by the third magistrate. For example, a staff member for one judge, upon encountering the third magistrate in an elevator, mentioned some recent case statistics and said, "Wow, fifty nondispositives [rulings on motions] last month. You're always way ahead of us. I always tell Judge [X] that we'd really like to have [you] with us." Although such comparisons and accompanying comments placed the magistrate in the uncomfortable position of making his colleagues look less effective, the comparisons helped to encourage the district judges to consider how they might emulate their more innovative colleague in the small courthouse in assigning tasks to magistrates.

The judges in the larger courthouse control the scheduling of civil pretrial matters before their magistrates. They instructed the magistrates to hold hearings every Monday. This system does not provide the magistrates with the time or opportunity to become more deeply involved in civil cases. The cases come before the magistrates on a particular motion. The magistrates make a ruling and move on to the next scheduled case. The magistrates gain some familiarity with the facts, issues, and litigants and thus may have a feel for settlement possibilities and the likelihood of trial. There is no guarantee that these judges will utilize the magistrates for settlement or other conferences, however, so that the value of the magistrates' knowledge about the case is lost.

By contrast, because the third magistrate controls his own scheduling for motions and conferences, he can allow for sufficient time to pursue the possibility of settlement in virtually every conference, no matter how distant the conference is from the possible trial date. Moreover, if during a conference the magistrate detects progress toward settlement, he can continue to pursue negotiations. When the magistrate, during a motion hearing, gains some sense about settlement possibilities, he can schedule a conference or even order that the parties undertake some form of alternative dispute resolution, such as arbitration, mediation, or summary jury trial.

The effectiveness of the third magistrate was due, in part, to his continual interest in seeking case settlements. For example, unlike several magistrates observed in other districts, this magistrate inquired during virtually every conference, no matter what its scheduled purpose, about the progress of settlement discussions between the parties. Moreover, the magistrate's order instructing litigants to attend a conference often required that either the actual parties or a person with settlement authority be present (often the attorneys themselves). Although attorneys were frequently chastised by the magistrate for failing to follow this provision of the scheduling order, the practice of requiring parties to attend fostered an environment in which a settlement agreement was possible at any given meeting between the two sides. For example, in a Rule 16 conference for scheduling pretrial matters in an age discrimination case, after setting dates for discovery, additional claims, and motions, the magistrate inquired, "have you discussed settlement?" The parties proceeded to discuss their current positions with the defendant offering one thousand dollars but the plaintiff demanding twenty thousand dollars. The parties argued about the facts and the defendant asserted there was no evidence of discrimination. The magistrate pushed the defendant by inquiring, "are you going to be able to get a summary disposition?"—with the clear implication that if they did not believe they were likely to a get a summary judgment, then they should seriously consider settlement for financial reasons. The magistrate then asked if the parties wanted a summary jury trial since that could give them a good idea whether any of their evidence and arguments would be persuasive to a jury. The defense attorney asked the magistrate to explain the concept of a summary jury trial to his client. The magistrate then asked one side to leave the room temporarily so he could discuss settlement possibilities with the other attorney and party. After separately pursuing and questioning both sides' evaluations of the case and settlement possibilities (e.g., pointing out to the defendants that it will cost more than their one thousand dollar settlement offer to proceed with discovery), the conference ended with both sides appearing to have moved a little closer toward a settlement figure between one thousand and twenty thousand. Afterward the magistrate expressed frustration that he could not have found a way to keep the parties in the conference a little longer, since he believed the plaintiff was willing to move down from his original demand. Although the case did not settle, the magistrate was able to gain a very detailed and accurate perception of each side's positions. Thus he remained able to pursue the issue further at a subsequent conference, because the judge had given him significant autonomy and responsibility for handling all pretrial aspects of civil litigation.

In another case, a complex action in which a trucking company filed suit against representatives from various unions and companies who were serving as trustees for a bankrupt company, the magistrate kept two dozen lawyers and clients at the court for nearly seven hours while he walked back and forth between the plaintiffs in the conference room and the defendants in the jury room. The magistrate carried offers and counteroffers between the groups and, at the same time, discussed each proposal with each side and encouraged them to consider alternatives and consequences. Although the case did not settle, the parties, through the magistrate's initiatives, took enormous strides in reducing the distance between their respective settlement offers. It seems clear that the magistrate's ability to make independent decisions about the nature and extent of attention and pressure to apply in various cases paid dividends for the goal of getting cases off the trial docket.

In the larger courthouse, such settlement discussions would have to take place with a district judge rather than a magistrate, since the magistrates' schedules are limited by the judges. However, because of heavier caseload responsibilities, a judge would have less time and interest for pursuing settlement at each available opportunity. Most cases eventually settle before trial regardless of the system utilized, but the granting of authority and autonomy to the magistrate in such instances serves to accelerate the inevitable settlement process and ultimately conserve scarce judicial resources through immediate personal attention by a judicial officer.

In addition to the application of skill and knowledge, the magistrate's reputation was built by appropriate authoritative action and judicial demeanor. The judges, through their social and other contacts with lawyers outside of court, hear about how the magistrates perform. The third magistrate gained a reputation in the eyes of at least one judge as perhaps pushing too hard for settlement. Although other judicial officers might pursue different strategies, the district judges respected the magistrate for being very effective. Numerous instances were observed in which the magistrate asserted himself to control and educate lawyers in judicial proceedings. In the several pretrial conferences observed for this study, the magistrate repeatedly had to scold and educate attorneys about the extensive jointly prepared pretrial order expected by his paired district judge. The magistrate all too frequently began conferences, with lawyers and the magistrate sitting around a small conference table, by saying, "Why didn't you follow the court's order and jointly prepare the required pretrial order?" The stern warnings from the magistrate about disobeying court orders would inevitably elicit a flow of apologies, excuses, or finger-pointing from the embarrassed attorneys. Most often, the magistrate's response, "I won't accept those excuses," insured that the lawyers would immediately act to rectify their errors and, simultaneously, learn about district court rules and the expectations of the judges.

In other instances, the magistrate had to take authoritative stances to curb attorneys' misbehavior. For example, one attorney who had twice previously been late for appearances before the magistrate was over a half hour late this third time. The magistrate, in robe, went on the bench in the courtroom when the attorney arrived and went "on the record" to discuss the attorney's tardiness. The attorney began with an excuse about having to stay in another city to see if a state court trial would begin that day. After quiet but relentless questioning by the magistrate, it soon became apparent that the attorney had known three days earlier that the trial would not be held that day. The attorney then began to claim that his partner's vehicle had broken down, but the magistrate interrupted him by saying, "That's the same excuse that you gave me six months ago when you were late to a hearing. I will not accept that." While the attorney was simultaneously apologizing and fumbling for a new, more original excuse, the magistrate waited patiently until the attorney embarrassedly ran out of things to say. Then the magistrate sternly announced, "if you [arrive late] again, there will be a price to be paid. Do we understand each other?" The warning was effective to the extent that the following week the attorney drove seventy miles to arrive precisely on time for a pretrial conference with the magistrate in the small courthouse. He still exhibited his disorganized habits by not having his pretrial order completed, but he made certain that he was punctual for the first time nonetheless.

Admittedly, a significant proportion of the third magistrate's effectiveness can be attributed to his personal interest and ability in the settlement process. It is clear, however, that his autonomy and broader responsibilities in the small courthouse facilitated the effective application of his interests and skills and therefore the assignment system itself served as an example to the other judges about what broader possibilities exist for utilizing magistrates. This is not to say that the other judges will necessarily provide such authority and autonomy to their own magistrates, since they may view their magistrates as less capable. While not dictating or guaranteeing what course the other judges in the district will follow, the example of the third magistrate at least induced the judges to think about the utilization of magistrates and diminished the usual unconscious adherence to the customary limited role for them.

District B illustrates one manner in which magistrates' roles develop and evolve within a district. The high status and limited authority granted to magistrates developed from continued, unquestioned adherence to the original established pattern of magistrate utilization. Changes in the magistrates' roles resulted not from discussion and planning on the part of the supervising judges, but from ad hoc innovations by one judge who permitted his paired magistrate to demonstrate to the other judicial officers in the district how magistrates can assist the court with a variety of case-processing responsibilities. Further change has developed as personnel changes in the district, namely replacing the original magistrate and integrating a new district judge position into the court's administration, forced the judges to consider how best to utilize the magistrates. Thus, historical and situational factors, rather than just rationally developed role conceptions imposed by the supervising judges, have substantial influence upon the roles performed by magistrates.

NOTES

1. The dearth of criminal pretrial matters for the magistrate from District B represented in Table 10 stems from that magistrate's location in the smaller courthouse where there are no federal jail facilities.

2. Carroll Seron, *The Roles of Magistrates: Nine Case Studies* (Washington, D.C.: Federal Judicial Center, 1985), 35–46.

3. 28 U.S.C. section 636(b)(1).

4. Although at least one magistrate scoffed at the notion that a forged signature could enable a prisoner to gain release from prison or jail, such events have occurred within some prison systems. Lori Mathews, "Convict Set Free on Fake Papers," *Detroit Free Press*, 24 Dec. 1987.

5. U.S. Congress, Senate Report No. 96–74, Federal Magistrate Act of 1979, *U.S. Code Congressional and Administrative News*, 1979, 1473.

6. U.S. Congress, House Report No. 1364, Magistrate Act of 1978, 95th Cong., 2d Sess., 1978, 13–14.

7. For example, according to Seron, "[t]here was a clear consensus among [lawyers] interviewed [in San Francisco] that when a judge raises the question of consent to a magistrate—for whatever reason—lawyers feel that they have little choice but to go along with the suggestion." Seron, *The Roles of Magistrates: Nine Case Studies*, 61.

7

Districts C and D:
Authoritative Independence

DISTRICT C: INDEPENDENCE IN A LARGE COURTHOUSE

District C has five full-time magistrates and eleven active judges in two courthouses. There are four magistrates and ten judges within the large courthouse which was the focus of study, while a judge and magistrate are paired in the smaller courthouse. The large courthouse is located downtown in a large city (population greater than 600,000).

Within the large courthouse there is relatively little contact between the judges and the magistrates. The magistrates are all located on one floor, while the judges are scattered over several floors and can be as far as eight floors away from the magistrates. The magistrates noted that, other than bumping into judges in the elevator in the morning, they have little reason to speak with the judges personally or by telephone.

A primary reason for the dearth of personal contact between judges and magistrates, in addition to the physical setting of the large courthouse, is that the court's system for utilizing magistrates does not foster continued contact between specific judges and magistrates. Rather than assigning cases to the magistrates through any system of pairings, tasks are sent to magistrates by blind rotation. A judge will send the preliminary tasks for a civil case to the clerk's office for assignment to a magistrate and the clerk assigns the matter to the next magistrate in line to receive an assignment. Thus, rather than work for a particular judge, the magistrates must work for all of the judges.

In other districts, such an assignment system would raise accountability concerns, because judges would not know exactly what each magistrate was working on and some judges might come to believe that magistrates were not spending enough time doing tasks for particular judges. Indeed, the assignment system generates risks of diminished coordination within the court and one magistrate has complained that the system can lead either to underutilization of the magistrates or improper use. For example, a judge could misuse the system by sending a long, difficult consent trial to a magistrate and thus make the magistrate unavailable to the other judges. The magistrate asserted that optimal effectiveness in the use of magistrates would require coordination and cooperation among the judges, but such coordination is impossible because of the independence of the judges and their diverse views on precisely how magistrates ought to be used.

INDEPENDENCE AND AUTHORITY: THE AUTONOMOUS JUDICIAL OFFICER

The risk of accountability problems surfacing in District C is significantly less that in Districts A, B, and D, because the nature of the magistrates' workload is different in one very notable respect. Unlike other districts, the magistrates in District C do not have to handle Social Security cases. In other districts across the country, as illustrated by Districts A, B, and D, a substantial proportion of magistrates' time is consumed by the process of reviewing Social Security cases with their attendant detailed medical records and briefs. The magistrates previously handled Social Security appeals, but they persuaded the judges to discontinue the practice of assigning such cases. The magistrates believed, and the judges apparently agreed, that it was a waste of time to have magistrates go through the time-consuming process of preparing a report and recommendation for a Social Security appeal when the judges were subsequently reviewing each case in detail. Thus, the magistrates felt that they had become a wasteful intermediary step which could be omitted by having the judges do one thorough review of each case for themselves. Although the success and possible accuracy of this argument may seem remarkable in light of the fact that magistrates elsewhere are busily processing Social Security cases that must subsequently be reviewed and approved by judges, District C is one district in which the judges could take on the Social Security cases without creating undue burdens upon their existing caseloads. District C is located in a state that has enjoyed relatively prosperous economic conditions in recent years and thus has not experienced the flood of Social Security appeals by newly unemployed people such as those generated by plant closings in Districts A, B, and D. Without any Social Security cases to handle on a time-consuming report and recommendation basis, the magistrates have greater freedom to assist the district court with other matters.

The magistrates informally developed their own system for handling preliminary criminal matters with a rotating monthly "on call" magistrate. Each magistrate is "on call" only once every four months. The district rules require only that the magistrates notify the court clerk concerning which magistrate is "on call" in a given month. The magistrates have been granted the autonomy to develop their own system for administering this aspect of district court operations.

The large courthouse has a pro se clerk to handle preliminary screening of prisoner petitions. Any prisoner cases that are sent by the judges to the magistrates will go to the "on call" magistrate. District C is in a state with both a smaller population and a significantly lower incarceration rate than the states in which Districts A, B, and D are located. Thus, with relatively fewer prisons and prisoners, the prisoner cases filed in District C amount to only 10–25 percent of the cases handled in each of the other illustrative districts. Again, the caseload difference helps to free the magistrates to work on other matters for the court.

The magistrates in District C do not often perform the activities associated with Seron's Specialist-type magistrate, namely prisoner and Social Security cases. The most well-known and respected judge in the district, now deceased, had adamantly insisted that the magistrates *not* become specialists, because of the value in continuously having "a fresh look at the law in a particular area." Instead, the magistrates combine the elements of Seron's Team Player and Additional Judge roles in that, aside from the preliminary criminal matters during their "on call" months, they primarily handle preliminary civil matters as well as their own consent cases. Most judges routinely send their pretrial civil tasks to the magistrates. One judge made a conscious decision to handle every aspect of his own cases because he was new to the bench and wanted to learn the procedures in federal court.

In the large courthouse, daily schedules of hearings and conferences are posted on bulletin boards on every floor. The daily notices are especially useful because the courtrooms are scattered between the third and twelfth floors of a very large, combination federal office and court building. Unlike other courts in which attorneys, litigants, and members of the public aimlessly wander the corridors and ask people in offices about when and where hearings and conferences are to take place, the large courthouse in District C has created a regularized system of accessible public notice concerning the activities of judges *and* magistrates. The listing of judges and magistrates on the same notice and in the same manner serves as both an endorsement and a verification of the magistrates' status as acknowledged judicial officers within the district. The notices are listed according to the last name of the judicial officer (i.e., Doe, D.J., for district judge and Roe, U.S.M., for magistrates) with the district judges' schedules listed first followed by the magistrates' schedules.

The magistrates have the freedom to schedule their own hearings and conferences. Thus they can monitor and control the progress of cases under their supervision according to their assessment of what is needed to process each case effectively.

The magistrates in District C are referred to and addressed with the title "Magistrate." However, in the conferences and hearings in which the magistrates come into contact with attorneys, they are regularly addressed as "Your Honor," just as any judge would be addressed in similar circumstances. The subordinate judges in District C are sometimes hampered in making their role clear to attorneys who are unfamiliar with the federal courts because the state court system in the district contains an officer called a "magistrate" who has extremely limited powers similar to a justice of the peace. This confusion caused by a generic judicial title was evident in other districts, but was particularly noticeable in District C, because of the many state magistrates who are familiar to the local attorneys.[1]

Although the magistrates are not referred to or addressed as "judge," they clearly enjoy the general endorsement of the district judges as full judicial officers. This endorsement is apparent in the tasks that the magistrates undertake, most notably civil trials. The status of the magistrates has been enhanced because of the national visibility of two of the magistrates. One magistrate was actively involved with training other magistrates across the country for the Federal Judicial Center and thus was relatively well-known among magistrates, judges, and other officials within the judiciary. The other magistrate was the president of a small national judges' organization. Although the magistrate admitted that some of the federal judges in the organization secretly objected to the magistrate's office and even membership, the state judges in the organization look up to the magistrate as someone with the status and prestige of a federal judicial officer. This magistrate gave speeches throughout the country and has enhanced the magistrates' reputation through the activities of the national organizational office.

The independence and status enjoyed by magistrates in District C does not mean that the district's judges endorse the magistrates' status as full judicial officers with the same completeness as in District B. For example, in a court proceeding before a district judge, an attorney referred to a magistrate as "Judge [X]." The district judge said, "Who?" The attorney repeated, "Judge [X]" and was informed by the judge, "Don't call him a *judge*, he's only a magistrate." The judge was obviously concerned about public differentiation from magistrates, although differentiating titles does not necessarily imply that the judge would limit the scope of the magistrates' role. In fact, even though some of the judges in District C believe that magistrates should have a narrower role, because the district does not utilize the paired assignment system, the effect would be to limit the kinds of tasks that a particular judge sends into the assignment pool rather than narrowly confining the activities of a specific magistrate.

Civil Litigation Conferences and Motions

Prior to 1983, magistrates did not become involved in civil litigation until after discovery disputes had occurred. The amendment of Rule 16 of the Federal Rules of Civil Procedure in 1983, which required district courts to hold scheduling conferences or otherwise create scheduling orders outlining dates for discovery, motions, and other preliminary matters, gave the magistrates a new, earlier involvement in civil cases. Although some judges prefer to hold their own scheduling conferences so that they can, as one judge said, "keep their finger on the pulse of their caseload," the magistrates in District C have undertaken substantial responsibilities for handling the scheduling of civil litigation.

The magistrates take different approaches to scheduling, settlement, and other conferences. One magistrate holds all conferences in a conference room, while wearing a robe, having the proceedings recorded, and having a court clerk present. The conference has a formal atmosphere because the clerk announces "all rise, the honorable . . . " at the start of each conference and the magistrate, in robe, enters the room. This magistrate is very concerned about the openness of judicial proceedings and the maintenance of an appropriate judicial atmosphere. By having the conferences recorded, the magistrate feels that there can be no risk to the judiciary's prestige and proper role by having "backroom" discussions beyond the gaze of public scrutiny and accountability. The magistrate is willing to go off the record when there is a specific reason, such as during a pretrial conference in which a plaintiff's attorney told the magistrate that the plaintiff had rejected the attorney's recommendation that a settlement offer be accepted. The attorney asked the magistrate to have a subsequent on-the-record conference to discuss the settlement offer and insure that the plaintiff understood the offer. Apparently the attorney was concerned about possible malpractice risks for himself from proceeding to trial and potentially losing on a directed verdict for failure to present the requisite prima facie case.

By contrast, other magistrates in the courthouse utilize the same less formal settings, such as sitting around the table in the magistrate's chambers, that were observed in other districts. The magistrate, without a robe, simply sits down with the attorneys and encourages informal discussions. The informal approach is believed by many magistrates to create the best environment to encourage the open discussions that will lead to settlement.

The magistrates also take different approaches to scheduling and settlement. One magistrate develops a schedule for discovery and motions, tells the attorneys the schedules, asks for any compelling objections to the schedule, and then imposes the schedule upon the parties. At the same time, the magistrate is interested in encouraging settlement discussions and inducing the opposing attorneys to communicate with each other. Another magistrate takes a relatively passive approach to scheduling and settlement. The magistrate asks the attorneys what they think would be an appropriate schedule for motions and discovery and then generally adopts the attorneys' recommendations. This magistrate is also less aggressive about pushing the attorneys on discussing settlement alternatives. As a result, in the conferences observed, the more passive magistrate set much longer time periods for discovery and effectively permitted the cases to progress much more slowly. Judges and magistrates can adopt differing philosophies about the appropriate role of federal judicial officers in aggressively pushing parties toward settlement, rather than passively facilitating the progress of the litigation. Some magistrates and judges clearly believe that their appropriate role is to resolve disputes. Others believe that they provide a forum for dispute resolution, but these judicial officers place a high value on giving litigants the option of having their day in court without undue pressure from the judges.

In conferences, the magistrates act as confident judicial officers guiding the course of litigation according to their assessments of the cases. Magistrates may have to act to protect the interests of litigants. For example, in one conference concerning a personal injury case in which an elderly woman broke her knee when she slipped and fell in a motel room doorway, plaintiff's counsel said that discovery could be done in ten months. "What!" the magistrate retorted. "You've got an eighty-year-old client. You can't let this litigation drag on." The lawyer changed the time to six months, with an apologetic explanation that he was concerned that a busy senior partner would have difficulty scheduling the necessary depositions. Magistrates also assert control over lawyers' behavior during conferences. In one conference involving a suit between two very large corporations, eight attorneys were present. The attorneys included corporate counsel present to observe and support the lead litigators hired from private firms. As the magistrate and the lead litigators discussed the case and disagreed on some of the facts, one of the corporate lawyers, sitting along the wall rather than at the table with the lead counsel and magistrate, loudly interjected with a sarcastic pronouncement that the opposing lead counsel had "misrepresented" the facts in a discovery dispute. The magistrate immediately reprimanded the attorney for interrupting and reiterated his rule that each side have only one spokesperson. The chastisement had a visible effect upon the corporation's attorney and created a tense, but more cooperative atmosphere among the opposing spokespersons.

Criminal Pretrial Proceedings

The magistrate "on call" each month must handle the preliminary criminal matters. The criminal matters give the magistrates their greatest visibility to the public, because newspapers cover the bail hearings and arraignments of persons accused of highly publicized crimes. For example, during the observation period, the magistrates' names were in prominent newspaper articles because of arraignment and bail rulings in a number of highly publicized cases: a prominent restaurateur accused of paying bribes to local police; two Middle Eastern drug couriers arrested with $2 million worth of heroin at an international airport during a sting operation by the U.S. Drug Enforcement Agency; and a reputed organized crime figure accused of intimidating witnesses in federal cases. In addition, a magistrate from District C received national media attention shortly after this study was completed when the magistrate set bail for a nationally known cult figure accused of fraud.

Because the magistrates make the important initial decisions about bail and detention, the district judges avoid the public responsibility for these frequently controversial determinations. Thus the preliminary pretrial proceedings provide an example of the magistrates functioning to spread responsibility for decision making away from the judges. The responsibility for such controversial decisions can also lead magistrates into conflict with other judicial actors with alternative interests, values, and assessments of particular cases. For example, several U.S. marshals and federal probation officials were overheard discussing how they were going to find ways to decline to assist one magistrate because they felt the magistrate was too lenient in setting bail and detaining defendants. One marshal remarked, in regard to the marshals' role providing courtroom security, "[that magistrate] shouldn't get protection [from us]—[that magistrate] doesn't deserve it."

Consent Cases

The magistrates in District C regularly supervise entire civil cases when the parties so consent. A motion filed in a consent case illustrates why litigants accept the magistrates' jurisdiction:

> Due to the problems encounted [sic] in the scheduling of the trial because of witness unavailability (majority of witnesses in this case are fishermen who are frequently out at sea) counsel have agreed among themselves that matter may be tried before a United States Magistrate and jury if this is agreeable to Your Honor. The greater flexibility of the Magistrate's Jury Trial schedule would enable the parties and the magistrate to arrive at a date for trial which would enable all parties and witnesses to be present.

In District C, litigants may have to wait as long as two years to have their cases heard in a trial before a district judge, but if they consent to have the cases heard by a magistrate, they can receive a trial date within six months. Moreover, trial dates for civil cases in front of district judges cannot be definite because if a criminal trial, which can arise at any time, is placed on the judge's docket, the criminal case must take precedence for scheduling because of the requirements of the Speedy Trial Act.[2] As a result, it can be especially difficult for litigants to plan on a definite trial date in front of a district judge. By contrast, magistrates do not handle felony criminal cases. Felony cases constitute the category of cases which magistrates are precluded from supervising under the magistrate statute. Thus, magistrates, unlike district judges, are able to give litigants firm trial dates, especially when the magistrates control their own scheduling, as they do in District C. Definite trial dates alone, however, are not enough to induce most litigants to consent, because in most civil cases one side believes it is in their strategic interest to delay the course of litigation. Often the strategic delays are intended to encourage a settlement favorable to one party, especially when the parties do not have equal resources to continue litigation over a long period of time.

Many magistrates complain that it is difficult for them to develop reputations as effective trial judges in order to encourage more litigants to consent. Because there is a rotation system for assignment of cases and because the magistrates are perceived as having differing strengths and abilities, litigants are often reluctant to consent if they do not know which magistrate will handle the case. In District C, the magistrate who handled the scheduling conference and the settlement conferences will be the magistrate assigned to the case if the parties consent to have the trial in front of a magistrate. Thus a magistrate would already have familiarity with the litigants and issues. Parties can wait to see which magistrate they draw for preliminary matters and then use that information to decide whether or not to consent.

Because magistrates are perceived to have differing levels of skill as trial judges, there is a feeling among some magistrates that judges seek to steer cases to the favored magistrates in order to garner more consents from litigants. When one magistrate received three consent cases in succession in which the scheduling conferences had been handled by judges, it appeared that judges were finding ways to go around the blind rotation system of assigning cases through the clerk of court's office. If, hypothetically, a judge communicated to the clerk that a case should go to specific magistrate, no one in the court would be surprised when the case ended up with that magistrate. Thus, it appears that, contrary to the statute's provisions that litigants not know which magistrate will supervise their consent cases and that judges not become involved in encouraging litigants to consent, judges have some ability to induce parties to consent by giving them their choice of magistrates.

In addition to having the ability to offer litigants their choice of magistrates, the judges are also capable of pressuring parties to consent. In one case during the observation period, a magistrate was assigned a trial two weeks prior to the trial date in a case in which the magistrate had not done any of the pretrial proceedings. The case involved a very modest amount of money claimed by an individual against an employer under a federal labor statute and thus was not the kind of complex, interesting, or important case that the judge would want to retain. The parties had consented to trial before a magistrate but one of the parties subsequently chose to have the trial before the judge. The judge met with the parties in a pretrial conference and asked them again if they would prefer to have the case heard by a magistrate. At least one party expressed a preference to have the case heard by the judge, so the judge said, "Well, since this case has been pending for months, we'll begin the trial at nine o'clock tomorrow morning." One party, shocked by the judge's pronouncement, protested that they were not prepared to begin the trial on the following morning. The judge replied that he would begin the trial the following morning, but that if the trial were heard by a magistrate, then they would have time to see about a later trial date. The parties quickly consented to the referral and the magistrate handled the trial a few weeks later. While this is an example of coercion by the judge, one magistrate argued that such actions by the judge are simply a way of "calling lawyers on the game playing and delaying that goes on in civil litigation." In other words, the judge can use the magistrates as an additional tool to control civil litigation. Although magistrates often argue that having consent cases simply gives the litigants an additional choice that they otherwise would not have and that the litigants can always decline to consent, the aforementioned example crosses the line of supplying the litigants with a choice and constitutes improper pressure by the judge.

ISOLATION THROUGH AUTONOMY AND ORGANIZATIONAL SETTING

The magistrates in District C are isolated from each other and from judges as they perform their tasks each day. This is not an isolation in the pejorative sense of being removed from reality with attendant negative consequences for status, visibility, or decision making values. Instead, it is a relative isolation in that the magistrates operate independently without the same supervision, constraints, and burdens as magistrates in many other districts. They have little reason to remain in close contact with other judicial officers within the court.

As previously described, the large courthouse with judges scattered over many floors creates a physical setting in which magistrates do not have personal contact with the judges. Moreover, the lack of a paired assignment system means that the magistrates have no reason to be in contact with any particular judge and no judge has reason to monitor the workload and performance of an individual magistrate. As a result, the magistrates work independently, without communication and contact with the judges. The communication between judges and magistrates within the court is further inhibited by memories of a minor scandal in which a judge was embarrassed by revelations that he had discussed a pending case with an assistant U.S. attorney. The episode made the judges and magistrates especially careful about not having inappropriate discussions concerning pending matters.

The magistrates' chambers are all located on the same floor. Although they are well-acquainted and friendly with each other, they have little reason to talk to each other. There is an evident willingness to advise each other on matters which may be new to a particular magistrate, so that the magistrate handling a jury trial for the first time felt free to consult with a more experienced magistrate about a new evidentiary issue. However, because of their autonomy, they do not have the concerns about a lack of status and authority which draw together magistrates in other districts for communication and coordinated action. In fact, given that the District C magistrates are located on the same hallway, it is remarkable how little they know about what their colleagues are doing. For example, the magistrate who wears a robe and conducts all conferences in a formal, on-the-record atmosphere apparently assumed, until learning otherwise from the author, that all the other magistrates had the same view and practices regarding the desirability of formal, open judicial proceedings. In fact, other magistrates usually hold informal conferences in chambers. Moreover, the magistrates have no reason to be aware of the kinds of tasks that their colleagues are undertaking. Each magistrate is busily involved in completing an independent set of civil pretrial tasks.

The level of autonomy in District C also appeared to affect the feelings of job satisfaction among the magistrates. Unlike virtually all other districts in which magistrates expressed serious concerns about numerous matters (e.g., the treatment of magistrates by judges, the repetitive workload on Social Security and prisoner cases, the need to reform the manner of assigning cases to magistrates, and the inability to communicate new ideas to district judges), the magistrates in District C appeared to be quite satisfied with their roles and task assignments. In fact, they did not seem to have much awareness about the concerns and problems of magistrates in other districts, because, unlike other magistrates, they felt no incentive to become involved in efforts to seek reform by learning about alternative operations existing in other districts. During an interview with a District C magistrate, the magistrate received a telephone call from an officer in the national magistrates' organization asking the magistrate to become involved in the political work of the organization to increase magistrates' status, salary, and benefits. Although the magistrate was very polite, the evident lack of interest the magistrate showed in issues which magistrates in other districts regard as vital underscored the relatively high degree of job satisfaction that exists among the independent magistrates of District C.

DISTRICT D: COOPERATION AND INDEPENDENCE

District D contains five full-time magistrates and eleven active judges divided between three courthouses. The large urban court building houses three magistrates and seven judges and the two outlying courthouses each have two active judges and one magistrate. Although all but one of the magistrates and a number of the judges in the district were interviewed, the focal point of the study in the district was one magistrate in one of the smaller courts. This magistrate works for two active judges and one senior judge in the small courthouse located in a moderately large city (population over 300,000).

The magistrates in District D have all been designated by the court to exercise the complete range of magistrates' authority, including consent cases. The actual tasks assigned to the magistrates vary, depending on the courthouse situation and the particular judges with whom the magistrate is associated. Unlike the magistrates in District C, the District D magistrates have a significant caseload of Social Security and prisoner cases, much like the magistrates in Districts A and B. In fact, District D, like District A, has been among the nation's leaders in Social Security case filings and has experienced surges in such filings due to a difficult economic situation and concomitant plant closings within the district. Although they handle a relatively burdensome load of Social Security and prisoner cases, like the District A and B magistrates, the District D magistrates also handle a wide range of preliminary civil proceedings. Moreover, unlike Districts A and B, District D is one of the leading districts in the country for civil consent cases referred to magistrates.

The actual extent to which magistrates perform each kind of task associated with the Seron typology, namely Social Security and prisoner (Specialist), preliminary civil (Team Player), and consent cases (Additional Judge), varies in each courthouse. In one small courthouse, the magistrate receives very few consent cases because the judges in the courthouse have been less inclined to send cases to him and because of his own emphasis on getting cases to settle. The magistrate was originally appointed prior to the implementation of merit selection and his personal and political connections to the federal court were with judges from one political party. Subsequently, the judges from the other political party were appointed to sit at that small courthouse where they found this magistrate already securely in place. Two of the judges who have served in the courthouse during the magistrate's tenure, both from the other political party, regard the magistrate with a certain amount of hostility and contempt. Obviously, in a courthouse in which there is a lack of both personal relationships and professional respect between magistrates and judges, the judges will limit their subordinate's actual authority and influence. The magistrate gets all of the Social Security and prisoner cases assigned to the courthouse, but only one of the judges who has served in the courthouse in the past few years appears to rely consistently upon the magistrate for conferences and all other aspects of civil litigation.

In the large courthouse, magistrates previously received the complete range of tasks and consents through a random draw system. When several new judges were appointed to the bench in the large courthouse, judges involved in personal and political disputes with more senior incumbent judges changed the way cases were assigned to magistrates. Some of the newer judges claimed that the magistrates were not accountable to the new judges. They viewed the magistrates as working for the incumbent judges with whom the subordinate judicial officers had already developed relationships. One judge said that he initially assigned a task to a magistrate and he did not get anything back from the magistrate for eighteen months, so he decided not to send things to the magistrates anymore. The new judges were not told how to use magistrates, so they tended not to use the magistrates much at all. The newer judges, in the course of pursuing other administrative changes within the court and seeking to reduce the power of the incumbent chief judge, changed the system of task assignment to magistrates by creating a pairing system in which each magistrate works for two judges.

Throughout the period of changes and conflicts occurring in the large court, the magistrates claim that no judges told them of any dissatisfaction with the previous assignment system. The magistrates had become pawns in the larger struggles between the district judges over resources and power. The new assignment system placed the magistrates in the large courthouse in close contact with some judges who are not supporters of the magistrate system. These judges said such things as: "I cannot believe that they pay them [the magistrates] almost as much as I [a district judge] am paid"; "I'd rather have a third law clerk than a magistrate. A law clerk is much more useful to me"; and "Magistrates ought to fill out time sheets so we know exactly what they are doing—just like employees at a law firm." During interviews, the magistrates emphasized the positive aspects of the new system. They said, for example, that under the new assignment system they need only please two judges, not seven. They claimed that pairing allows the judges to get to know the magistrates and eventually will allow the magistrates to receive the broadest possible range of assignments after proving themselves to their paired judges. Although the magistrates seemed earnest in expressing these positive opinions about the increased supervision of their work, they were noticeably diplomatic and careful in making comments about the district judges.

Although some of the district's judges have criticisms of the magistrate system, the status and authority of the magistrates has been firmly established within the district's courthouses. Unlike in District A, the magistrates' critics among the judges still accepted the magistrates' authority to handle consent cases. The chief judge helped establish the tone in the district through complete support for magistrates' authority to exercise the full range of duties under the statute. The chief judge actively sought to make the magistrates' position as a judicial officer well-known. He organized open meetings with bar leaders and local attorneys so that the magistrates could introduce themselves and explain their authority, roles, and availability for consent cases.

THE MAGISTRATE AS ALL-AROUND PERFORMER
FOR THE COURT

The magistrate in one small court performs the broadest possible range of tasks for the district court—everything from Social Security and prisoner cases to consent trials. Like the comparable magistrates in other districts, this magistrate was the first full-time magistrate in the courthouse. Thus the magistrate had the opportunity to shape the magistrate role directly, in the courthouse, without fighting against the natural obstacle of previously established practices and traditions. Working with a judge who was very supportive of utilizing the magistrate position as broadly and effectively as possible, the magistrate was able to make suggestions about how best to use the new judicial office.

Because the courthouse is small, there are ample opportunities for the magistrate to have contact with the judges in the building. It is a very easy matter to walk down one flight of stairs in order to see any judge personally. The limited number of judicial officers in the building, as well as their cooperative attitudes and mutual respect, enabled the courthouse to experiment with different uses of the magistrate and led to the evolution of an effective system. For example, the magistrate perceived particular difficulties with civil rights cases that might hinder settlement. Plaintiffs often want more than money; they want psychic satisfaction from presenting grievances during their day in court. At the same time, defendants have an incentive for early resolution, because the longer a trial is delayed, the greater their potential liability for backpay. Thus the magistrate drafted an order which the judges signed that mandated that all Title VII (employment discrimination) case pretrial work go directly to the magistrate. The immediate and effective attention given by the magistrate to parties in employment discrimination cases had a ripple effect in making the magistrate known and in encouraging parties to consent in other kinds of cases. The magistrate drafted a similar order which led the judges to send all antitrust and securities cases to the magistrate, but eventually the burden of other cases on the magistrate led the judges and magistrate to rescind the order. Thus, the close contact, cooperative atmosphere, and lack of a rigidly defined conception of the magistrate role allowed the judges and magistrate to develop a system for utilizing the magistrate which fit the needs of the court for effective case processing.

The magistrate's ability to define his own role was also due to the fact that the two active judges in the district were appointed to the bench after the magistrate assumed office. Thus the magistrate himself taught the judges how the magistrate could be used and what duties the magistrate had been performing. The judges adapted themselves to the existing patterns, with the effect of solidifying the magistrate's influence and reaffirming the established pattern of utilizing the subordinate judge broadly.

Although the magistrate in this small court serves as a jack-of-all-trades, this does not imply that he is the master of none. After the magistrate established himself as an effective judicial officer with a positive reputation as a trial judge among the local bar, the magistrate and the judges had created the broadest possible basis for deciding how best to utilize the magistrates' skills and abilities. For example, one judge uses the magistrate to impanel juries, so that the judge's time is not taken by time-consuming voir dire procedures when another capable, experienced judicial officer is available for the task.[3] The magistrate does settlement negotiations for one judge because the judge feels his own objectivity in a trial may be affected by knowledge of prior settlement discussions.

Because there is only one magistrate in the small courthouse, lawyers know who will get their cases if they consent to have civil cases heard by the magistrate. Due to the small number of local lawyers who practice in the federal court, it was relatively easy for the magistrate to prove himself and become known.

District D publicizes the consent option and makes it available to litigants by giving each party in every civil case a form which describes the magistrate's authority and requests that the litigants make a decision about consenting to have the case heard by a magistrate. The standard practice of notifying each party with a detailed explanation surpasses the haphazard practice of notification in some other districts. Some other districts, such as District B, have failed to follow through on notification and in others, based upon the oral explanations of magistrates' authority observed at conferences and hearings, it appears that the notice provision may be buried in the details of the local court rules. The notice in the small courthouse specifically names the magistrate to whom all consent cases will go, thus maintaining the magistrate's visibility and making the litigants' choices more certain.

The magistrate has the freedom to schedule his own tasks, except for a standing practice of spending Monday mornings impaneling juries for one judge. Because the magistrate has autonomy, it is relatively easy for the magistrate to establish his own style for handling scheduling, discovery disputes, and settlement negotiations. Unlike some of the judges in the district who utilize detailed and strict standard pretrial orders, the magistrate is able to use a more flexible approach to preliminary matters that relies upon his evaluation of the parties, issues, and attorneys in each case. The magistrate requires attorneys to cooperate with each other in discovery with what he calls the court's "cards up and on the table approach to discovery." If a dispute arises, he tells attorneys "don't file a motion—make a phone call or write a letter. The court expects the attorneys to cooperate and work things out." If, however, as in one conference with an out-of-town lawyer, an attorney insists upon being combative and seeking judicial intervention for every trivial pretrial dispute, the magistrate is quick to lecture the attorneys and issue orders to prevent such disputes. By developing his own style and reputation as a judicial officer, the magistrate has created a role in which consent to the known magistrate becomes a clear, calculable alternative for lawyers who assess how their particular cases would fare in front of the court's judges. In fact, the magistrate has performed so well and developed such a positive reputation that one judge on the district's circuit court of appeals, which sees matters on appeal that have been decided by the magistrates within the circuit, says that "consent to Magistrate [X] leads to better results than going with the judges."

Although the magistrate is an alternative judge for lawyers who wish to consider consenting to have civil cases referred, the magistrate can also differentiate himself from judges in order to attempt to resolve cases. For example, at a pretrial conference concerning a civil rights suit over conditions at a county jail, the magistrate dissuaded the six attorneys from consenting to his jurisdiction. The magistrate recognized that the nature of the institutional litigation and risk of a controversial, expensive remedial order meant that the case "needs to have a district judge's name at the bottom of the page." The magistrate, without risk that the parties would consent, could take a more active role in advising the parties on negotiation without fear that he would eventually have to decide the case. The magistrate proceeded to educate the attorneys about the limits of federal courts' ability to order remedies and the relatively limited extent of constitutional violations recognizable by the federal courts. The magistrate also offered to help in any way to actualize the parties' mutual desire to solve the jail's problems without the expense and publicity attendant to a trial. The magistrate participated in a discussion about how to proceed with the case and successfully renovate the jail without permitting the press or the county commissioners to become interested in the case. All of the participants recognized that media attention and involvement by elected officials would make the case more adversarial and difficult. Ultimately, with the magistrate's assistance as a facilitator of discussion, the jail's deficiencies began to be redressed without a trial or politically inflammatory publicity. In addition, the magistrate gave the parties informal advisory opinions on legal issues to help them past sticking points when they disagreed about specific issues during the course of settlement discussions.

The availability of a magistrate possessing the skills and reputation of an additional judge, as well as the flexibility to accomplish other kinds of tasks, creates risks that the district judges will seek to over-utilize the magistrate beyond the permissible boundaries of the statute. In the small courthouse, there are some indications that at least one judge has stepped beyond statutory limitations in attempting to utilize the magistrate as a valuable resource for case processing. The judge admits that in cases which he feels are being unnecessarily delayed by the attorneys, he has given the lawyers the choice of having the case dismissed or consenting to the magistrate's jurisdiction in order to seek a continuance from the magistrate. Such actions can place the magistrate in an awkward position, since there is an apparent expectation on the judge's part that the magistrate will grant a con-tinuance. Most obviously, however, this method of encouraging con-sents violates the letter and spirit of the statute's prohibition against pressure applied by judges upon litigants.

The magistrate in the small courthouse undertakes all of the tasks assigned to magistrates in other districts, enjoys support from the judges and recognition from the bar, and works with the judges to effectively utilize the magistrate position in assisting with the court's responsibilities. In carrying out this broad role, the magistrate fulfills the elements of all three roles in the Seron typology without exclusive-ly or primarily fitting a single role. Thus, this small courthouse in District D provides an example of the most flexible and diversified magistrate role, which, because of the level of communication with and support from the judges, provides the opportunity to adjust the magistrate's responsibilities to fit the needs of the district.

NOTES

1. This confusion over the appropriate title for the subordinate judicial officers has been noted by the Judicial Conference. A number of magistrates have advocated changing the title to "Associate Judge" in order to avoid association with lowly state officials. *The Federal Magistrates System: A Report to Congress by the Judicial Conference of the United States*, (Washington, D.C.: U.S. Government Printing Office, 1981), 61–62.

2. 18 U.S.C. section 3161.

3. The Supreme Court eventually declared this practice to be impermissible in felony cases. *Gomez v. United States*, 57 U.S.L.W. 4643 (1989).

Part 4

Developmental Factors and Consequences of Magistrates' Roles

8

Factors That Determine Magistrates' Roles

The previous chapters' descriptions of illustrative magistrates in representative court contexts provide the basis for analyzing the roles of magistrates within the federal judiciary. Although magistrates are affected by some common role expectations, the factors which guide and constrain magistrates' behaviors can vary widely from district to district. Thus, the magistrates' roles, the behaviors that are characteristic of magistrates within the federal courts,[1] will differ depending upon the operation of defining factors at a given historical moment. As the four sample districts demonstrate, a magistrate's role cannot be regarded as static, because identifiable factors can foster change within specific court contexts.

JUDGES' CONCEPTUALIZATIONS OF MAGISTRATES' ROLES

The study of the four illustrative districts as well as the interviews and observations conducted in the other districts consistently confirmed that the judges, and their expectations concerning the magistrates' appropriate roles, served as the predominant influence over the behaviors and expectations of magistrates. The judges' influence stems not simply from the inherent power of their expectations as superiors and supervisors over the magistrates, but also from the statutory, constitutional, and case law underpinnings of the magistrate system, which give legal authority and actual power to the judges' conceptualizations. Legal considerations are not an exclusive influence over judges' expectations by any means. Given the political and constitutional framework of the judiciary, however, legal factors, such as the magistrates statute, have a degree of primacy in setting the boundaries and guiding the development and actualization of the judicial officers' roles.

The district judges' formal authority does not inherently guarantee that they will have the primary actual influence over role definition for the subordinate magistrates. It is possible in the context of some political institutions, for example, that the actor vested with formal legal authority for decision making may not in fact serve the role of primary decision maker for that institution. Illustrations of this political reality include the predominant role of prosecutors and plea bargaining over the determination of criminal sentences that are under the formal authority of a trial judge,[2] and the traditional role of senators in determining federal judicial appointments that are under the formal authority of the president.[3] Thus, in the case of magistrates' roles, it was possible that judges would not actually determine what roles magistrates would perform. In reality, however, the judges possess the legal and actual power to determine the magistrates' tasks and status, and thus have a predominant influence over role definition. The magistrate legislation places control over magistrates' tasks clearly in the hands of the district judges. The control and supervision of magistrates by district judges serves as the primary basis for the constitutionality of the magistrate system in both the legislative history[4] and relevant judicial opinions.[5]

In several districts, interviews with judges and magistrates made clear that the judges had difficulty precisely envisioning the appropriate judicial role for magistrates. Thus, many judges equated magistrates with their perceived closest approximation among existing judicial actors, namely law clerks, and limited the magistrates' work to law clerk-type legal tasks. The high number of former law clerks and other court personnel appointed as magistrates under the old direct appointment system served to reinforce the limited role conceptualizations that many judges possessed for the new magistrate position. Some judges simply appointed their law clerks to the magistrate positions, continued the clerks' duties and in effect created permanent law clerks with the title "Magistrate." In one district, the chief judge outmaneuvered another judge to ensure that his former law clerk, rather than the other judge's clerk, would be appointed to the first full-time magistrate position. The new magistrate was assigned the same Social Security and prisoner reviews that had absorbed his life as a law clerk. Although he had a new title, he was viewed by lawyers and other judges as the chief judge's law clerk, specializing in particular categories of cases, especially Social Security appeals.

The limited role of the magistrates' predecessors, the U.S. commissioners, also served to give the judges a limited view of the magistrate role. In 1967, just prior to the passage of the initial magistrate legislation, nearly one-third of the commissioners were non-lawyers.[6] In addition, commissioners had very limited duties for warrants and petty offenses.[7] Moreover, many of the first magistrates, especially part-timers, were simply the same lawyer-commissioners continuing their limited duties and roles under the new title of "Magistrate." Thus, the judges' first impression of the magistrate role often developed from a close association with the well-established, but very limited, role of commissioners. The association of the new magistrate position with the old commissioners' limited duties was enhanced because of the manner in which the magistrate system was implemented. When the magistrate system was established nationwide in 1971, after the two-year, five-district pilot program, there were about eighty full-time and 442 part-time magistrate positions replacing the 600 commissioners.[8] Because of the overwhelming number of part-time positions, which were viewed as especially similar to the old commissioners' role (and often were held by the incumbent lawyer-commissioners), most district judges' first exposure to the new magistrate role was in the form of a veritable continuation of the old commissioner role.

The legislative history and magistrates statute also limited the judges' conceptualization of the magistrates' role. The magistrate system was intended to upgrade and professionalize the lower tier of the federal judiciary by replacing the less qualified, inconsistent commissioners with licensed attorney-magistrates. Congress also intended that the new position be utilized in a flexible manner according to the wishes and needs of the district judges. Thus, the judges did not receive specific guidance on how to utilize magistrates and the guidance that they did receive, in the form of the statute's language, specifically listed very limited duties for the magistrates, namely the powers of the old commissioners, preliminary criminal matters, and "additional duties" to assist the judges.[9] The "additional duties" section, while granting flexibility and implicitly encouraging broad, innovative uses, gave limited guidance to the judges by listing only three examples of magistrates' duties: service as special masters, civil and criminal pretrial proceedings, and prisoners' petitions.[10] Under Rule 53 of the Federal Rules of Civil Procedure, the use of special masters, whether magistrates or attorneys, is limited to "exception[al]" cases. Therefore the first listed item did not provide a basis for broad conceptualization of the magistrate role. The second listed sphere of duties, preliminary civil and criminal matters, while potentially broad, did not encourage wide utilization or give examples concerning how a magistrate ought to be utilized. In not presenting examples or alternatives, there was no basis for combating the narrow conceptualizations of magistrates' roles possessed by judges. The third listed example, prisoners' cases, provided a concrete example that might affect judges' conceptualizations of the magistrate role, but because it involved a limited sphere of activity equivalent to the work already performed by many law clerks, it also helped to reinforce the view of the subordinate judges as judicial actors with a limited role.

The specific example of prisoner cases also fit with judges' interests and growing needs in many districts. Several judges testified at legislative hearings that they desired to utilize magistrates to address their growing prisoner caseload burdens.[11] Thus the district judges' needs for law clerk-like review of prisoner cases coincided with their limited vision and nonexistent experience regarding the possibilities for the magistrate position.

The findings from this study corroborate Seron's assertions regarding the effect of various models of judges' organizational orientations upon their conceptions of magistrates' roles.[12] For example, according to Seron, judges who view the magistrates in the professional model of additional judges or as participants in the courts' dispute processing function will define the magistrates' tasks very differently than those judges who utilize a bureaucratic model of magistrates as merely assistants to the judges. In particular, the judges observed and interviewed for this study often could be readily divided into two categories that roughly match Seron's conclusions. Judges who evinced a willingness to use magistrates broadly tended to view themselves and the magistrates working for a common enterprise—the federal courts. By contrast, judges who limited magistrates' activities frequently spoke as if they embodied the federal court and therefore the magistrates' purpose was to assist them personally. Despite this congruence with Seron's well-developed conclusions based upon organizational theory, one must be cautious about the application of her models to the behavior of judicial actors. To the extent to which Seron's conclusions imply that judges make rational, calculated decisions on the use of magistrates based upon their views of the courts' proper organizational characteristics, one must bear in mind that many judges do not possess firm conceptions of the magistrates' proper roles; therefore, the roles can be established and evolve for a variety of other reasons.

For example, the previously discussed factors, which encouraged an initial conceptualization of magistrates in limited roles, served as the basis for implementing task assignments and status that bore a great similarity to the role of law clerks. Once the magistrates' roles develop within a given district, they tend to establish a pattern which will change only under certain circumstances. Thus the initial views of judges serve to influence the continuing definition of magistrates' roles. The narrow views initially employed in many districts often continued to linger more than twenty years after the magistrates statute was first passed into law, essentially because many judges did not rationally reassess the appropriate roles for magistrates. Instead, the judges simply adopted the existing role definitions and patterns of utilization for the subordinate judicial officers.

FAMILIARITY AND COMMUNICATION BETWEEN JUDGES AND MAGISTRATES

Contact, or the lack thereof, between magistrates and judges can affect the expectations of both actors and thereby influence the definition of the magistrate role within a courthouse or district. For example, one judge claimed that no one told him anything about magistrates when he became a judge in a large courthouse. His lack of contact with magistrates, which made him angry when he later learned that he could have used the subordinate judges for Social Security cases and other matters, helped to shape his views that magistrates should have a limited role.

The district judges' familiarity with the personal qualities and skills of the magistrates, a familiarity most often gained through direct contact and communication, rather than by reputation and hearsay alone, can enable the subordinate judges to obtain greater opportunities to exercise authority. A common characteristic of smaller courthouses is that judges and magistrates have frequent contact. As a result, magistrates are able to make themselves known to the judges. Consequently, in the districts examined for this study, the subordinate judges in smaller courthouses generally undertook the broadest range of judicial tasks. If a district judge possesses a settled conceptualization of a limited role for magistrates, then personal contact may be insufficient to gain broader authority for the subordinate. If the judge is uncertain or ambivalent about the appropriate roles for magistrates, however, then communication and contact create opportunities for magistrates to demonstrate their judicial qualities and skills.

It is communication and familiarity, rather than organizational setting itself, that contribute to the development of the magistrates' roles. Although smaller courthouses generally facilitate contact between judges and magistrates through their natural proximity within the court environment, communication and familiarity are possible and can have expansive effects upon the magistrates' roles in large courthouses as well. In the large court settings, the level of personal contact depends upon the initiative of individual judges and magistrates. Several magistrates in large courts described calculated strategies for regularly visiting the judges for whom they work. A few judges make efforts to keep in regular contact with magistrates in order to monitor the rate of progress on certain tasks and to show their personal concern for the magistrates. These judges also expressed an intention to assign a variety of tasks to magistrates so that the subordinate judges would not become bored or disenchanted with an unending flow of Social Security or prisoner cases.

The contact and communication between magistrates and judges are affected by the different levels of status and authority possessed by the two judicial officers. The status of magistrates was clearly differentiated from that of the judges in every instance in which face-to-face interactions between judges and magistrates were observed. Even those judges who claimed to regard the magistrates as colleagues were beneficiaries of deference and clear status differentiation in contacts with the magistrates. The shared expectation among both judges and magistrates that the magistrates are indeed subordinate to the judges was apparent in each setting. In the several situations in which magistrates introduced the author to district judges, the magistrates universally stepped back to allow the judges to take over and determine the flow of the conversation. Many of the magistrates were obviously friendly and familiar with the judges. Although some magistrates claimed to be on a first-name basis with particular judges, in no instance observed did the magistrates call the judges by their first names. By contrast, judges would sometimes refer to magistrates by first name. The deference accorded to judges serves to color the contacts within courthouses and limit the possibilities for genuine equal partnership in developing administration and case-processing systems within a district. These status differences pervading the atmosphere of contacts between judges and magistrates, which are to be expected because of the judges' legal powers and actual influence over the selection, retention, and task assignments for magistrates, were observed in courts with both limited and broad roles for the subordinate judges.

It can be very difficult for magistrates to forthrightly express opinions and concerns to judges because of the magistrates' subordinate position and because the magistrates do not wish to tarnish their images and relationships with them. For example, if a magistrate were assigned such a tremendous load of Social Security cases that it was impossible to complete the cases at an acceptable pace, the magistrate may fear that any communication to the judge about the problem will be perceived by the judge as an admission that the subordinate judicial officer is incapable of handling necessary job responsibilities. Even though relatively few magistrates have been pressured to retire or resign, magistrates continually discussed their clear recognition that reappointment for additional terms was determined at the judges' discretion. Magistrates' concerns about maintaining positive images in the eyes of judges can seriously hinder honest communication about the level and organization of workloads within a courthouse. Thus, magistrates may have legitimate and valuable suggestions about how to improve the administration of justice within a particular courthouse, yet fear that any suggestion will be misperceived and tarnish the subordinate judges' reputations for diligence and productivity.

In several districts, magistrates and judges take steps to formalize communications between judges and their subordinates in order to reduce the inhibitions that exist regarding communications from magistrates to judges. In one courthouse, the most experienced magistrate expresses concerns and suggestions in the form of joint communications from all of the subordinate judges in the courthouse. In another district, the magistrates meet regularly and submit formal written memoranda to the judges to express their concerns, again with the messages coming from all of the magistrates at once, rather than risking the perception that an individual magistrate is complaining about the judges' administration of the district. A respected senior judge in one district initiated a role for himself as a "liaison judge" between the judges and magistrates. He noticed that the magistrates' cars were in the courthouse parking lot every Sunday afternoon and he accurately perceived their presence at the court as an indication that the judges were assigning too many tasks. Because the district had a random task assignment system, none of the judges knew how overburdened the magistrates were by the constant flow of assignments from various judges. In order to protect any individual magistrate from appearing inadequate by lodging a complaint about the workload, the judge initiated private monthly meetings with the magistrates. This senior judge then took the magistrates' individual and joint concerns to the other district judges without identifying which individual expressed the complaint or suggestion. The judges and magistrates in the district were satisfied with their system of regular communication that is sensitive to the personal and professional concerns of each magistrate. In other districts, a single judge is designated as "liaison judge" or "magistrates' judge," but the creation of this formal communication mechanism will not necessarily facilitate openness unless the judges take an active interest in the magistrates and their concerns.

The monthly judges' meetings held in most districts would provide an excellent opportunity for magistrates and judges to discuss the district court's needs and accomplishments.[13] The inclusion of magistrates at such meetings requires, however, that the subordinates be recognized by the district judges as judicial officers. In most districts within this study, the judges do not include the magistrates in their monthly meetings or in other regular meetings. Often this exclusion of magistrates reflects the view that as subordinates, magistrates need not be consulted about the administration of district court. In other instances, the judges ignore the magistrates simply because they have never thought about including their subordinates. Thus, situations arise in which judges contemplate administrative changes within a district, including changes affecting the tasks and roles of magistrates, yet never consult their subordinates about the effects the changes will have upon the magistrates' work. Some chief judges initiated meetings with magistrates on a regular basis in order to draw these lower judicial officers, who have the most experience with many aspects of court administration (such as preliminary criminal matters and the processing of prisoners' cases), into the planning and administration process. Obviously, the inclusion of magistrates into regular, formal communication processes requires a recognition by district judges that magistrates' roles and functions can have unique and profound effects upon the administration of the district courts.

Contact and communication between magistrates and judges can enhance the judges' view of magistrates and broaden the subordinate judges' roles within a district if the magistrates can overcome the potential constraints upon communications imposed by their organizational settings and subordinate positions. Interpersonal familiarity derived from personal contact between magistrates and judges can alter judges' conceptualizations of the magistrates' roles, but there is a risk of a narrowing effect if the magistrates' qualities and actions do not meet the judges' expectations. In at least two districts within this study, judges referred to individual magistrates as "dumb" or "incompetent" and thereby revealed the double-edged nature of communication and familiarity.

EXPECTATIONS OF MAGISTRATES

The expectations that magistrates have about their own roles stem from perceptions about the limits imposed upon their activities and authority by judges; knowledge of what magistrates are doing in other districts; recognition of the status, prerogatives, and benefits enjoyed by other judicial actors; and conceptions of the ideal role for the subordinate judicial office.

Magistrates can quickly gain a relatively accurate perception of the views held by their district's judges. The kinds of tasks that are referred to the magistrates; the communication and formal orientation, if any, provided by the judges and the other magistrates; and the behavior toward magistrates exhibited by the various judicial actors within the courthouse all contribute to the magistrate's perceptions of the judges' views. The magistrate who primarily receives Social Security appeals and prisoner petitions will not only recognize the limited nature of tasks assigned by the judges, but will also likely receive less deference and recognition in the courthouse. Thus the magistrate will usually have less status, because of few opportunities for visibility in courtrooms presiding over judicial proceedings involving a wide range of attorneys. Although most full-time magistrates wear robes while handling preliminary criminal matters, only a small portion of the bar is normally involved in criminal cases. Such magistrates will have a difficult time becoming known to the other attorneys within the district based upon preliminary aspects of criminal cases alone. Magistrates who are given a wide range of tasks will, by contrast, legitimately possess broader expectations about the potential breadth of magistrates' authority, while simultaneously enjoying recognition and status as federal judicial officers through involvement with a more diverse cross-section of the local bar.

Magistrates gain their clearest understanding of the judges' utilization of magistrates and expectations for magistrates through direct discussions with district judges. Normally, supervising judges will be interested in using the selection process and interviews to orient the finalist applicants to the magistrate position within the courthouse. Surprisingly, however, several magistrates said that they were given only the most general understanding of the magistrates' duties. Thus, although applicants for the position may be told by the judges that they will be responsible for all Social Security cases as well as preliminary civil matters, the new subordinate judge may be surprised to learn that the actual composition of work assignments entails significantly more of one described task than the other. One magistrate described coming into the court on the first day to find several years' worth of backlogged Social Security cases waiting on the desk. Because no other magistrates or judges in this large courthouse visited the office, neither to advise nor welcome the newcomer, the magistrate had to experiment and invent a system for organizing and reviewing the cases.

In many courts, the judges and newly appointed magistrates are well acquainted. In some instances, the collegial relationship between the judge and magistrate may create opportunities for the magistrate to ask questions and make suggestions. In other cases, the judge, although well acquainted with a former law clerk or assistant U.S. attorney, has already established a hierarchical relationship and possesses a settled conceptualization of both the individual person and the magistrate role. In these cases, the new magistrate simply steps into the existing system of case processing within the judge's chambers. The new magistrate in such situations is likely to be perpetually responsible for entire, predictable categories of limited tasks.

Usually the judges will not tell magistrates directly how cases are to be decided or processed. The magistrate will simply begin submitting reports and recommendations to the judges on civil motions or Social Security and then the judges will review the magistrates' work according to judicially and statutorily mandated standards. The feedback from the judges' reviews will help the subordinate judges gain an understanding of the district judges' expectations for the magistrates and thus inform the subordinates' own expectations about their roles within the court. The feedback from the judges can take the form of direct communications about decisions or how to make decisions. For example, magistrates in two districts were called into judges' chambers and told very directly that they were to review Social Security cases according to the specific standards which the judges themselves would apply. Some judges, in an indication that they not only view the magistrates as legitimate federal judicial officers but also as colleague-judges, said that they would accept a magistrate's reasonable determination even if the judge would have made a different decision. In these cases, the district judges have modeled themselves as appellate judges reviewing the magistrates as lower judges, rather than regarding the subordinate as merely preliminary decision makers on matters which must ultimately reflect the district judges' own views.

In many respects, magistrates are like any other judge having an opinion reviewed by a higher court in that they feel disappointed if a district judge reverses one of their decisions or disagrees with a report and recommendation. Most magistrates, viewing themselves as judges, take such reversals in stride as a natural and inevitable phenomenon within the federal courts. Some magistrates have reason to be annoyed when the rejected report and recommendation returns to the magistrate with all of the earmarks of review and reversal by the judge's junior law clerk rather than by the judge. In addition, many magistrates resent any indication that the judges are going over their work with a fine-toothed comb. In the area of Social Security, for example, in which the magistrate's determination is based on a limited standard of review looking for evidentiary support in the administrative law judge's decision below, magistrates often expect the district judges to respect reasonable determinations made by a legitimate federal judicial officer. Thus, a reversal may be perceived as implying personal criticism of the magistrate's decision making.

In some courthouses, the magistrates receive very little feedback at all. In District C, the illustrative district in which magistrates are relatively independent and autonomous, the magistrates rarely hear what happens after they submit a report and recommendation to a judge. The magistrates simply move on to the next case and the next set of tasks. In most instances, the magistrates never see their decisions again, regardless of whether their determinations were reversed or approved.

Magistrates' expectations are shaped by what they observe in other districts. There are numerous opportunities for magistrates to learn about how their colleagues are utilized in other districts. Many magistrates attend regional training conferences taught by experienced magistrates during their first year. The Federal Judicial Center sponsors annual conferences for magistrates by region (e.g., the Sixth, Seventh, and Eighth Circuits comprise one region) and each circuit generally has at least one conference each year for judges, magistrates, and clerks of the court. These gatherings create opportunities for magistrates from different districts and courts to become acquainted and compare notes about how the magistrate system is operating within their respective courthouses. The publications from the Federal Judicial Center and the General Accounting Office, including the two primary studies of magistrates by Seron, are distributed to judges and magistrates. Although few judicial officers actually seem to read the publications, the reports are available for perusal and are cited by judges and magistrates as a source of ideas for innovations. Magistrates can also follow the case statistics reported by their colleagues within circuits that publish such statistics internally. Thus it is quite clear who is getting consent trials and who is forced to spend all of their time on prisoner and Social Security cases. The magistrates' national organization, the National Council of Magistrates, holds an annual meeting and serves to connect magistrates on issues of common interest, including tangible items like pension benefits and more intangible matters like status and prestige. It is through the contacts that develop during these forums that magistrates learn about the broad use of their colleagues elsewhere. Communications from officially neutral entities such as the Magistrates Division of the Administrative Office and the Federal Judicial Center can feed magistrates' expectations by continually supporting a broadening of magistrates' authority in every district. The representatives from the Administrative Office and Federal Judicial Center who conducted the annual conference observed for this study were clearly supportive of magistrates' aspirations and endorsed magistrate-speakers' digressions from topics on developments in constitutional law to subjects concerning magistrates' salaries, pensions, and status. Magistrates also learn about practices elsewhere through attorneys who return to the district after handling cases in federal courts in other districts. Awareness of the broad roles of magistrates in many districts can increase the expectations of magistrates and exacerbate conflicting role expectations between judges and magistrates.

Magistrates' expectations about their roles are influenced by their awareness of the authority and prestige enjoyed by other actors within the judiciary, especially their primary reference group of non-Article III judicial officers, bankruptcy judges. The advantages enjoyed by bankruptcy judges in title, autonomy, and support services are noted by magistrates and serve as a focal point for magistrates' expectations about what a federal judicial officer is entitled to possess and enjoy.

Magistrates' views on their ideal roles are premised on their universally adopted assertion that they are legitimate federal judicial officers. The magistrates' shared view that they deserve the authority and status of federal judicial officers can clash sharply with the notions of judges who conceptualize magistrates as personal assistants. Because the judges are more influential within the district courts for both legal and practical reasons, the role conflict regarding magistrates' roles will be forcibly resolved in favor of the judges' view unless conditions develop to permit change within the district court. The use of the term "forcibly" should not imply an open conflict, but instead recognizes that the judges' superior power, especially over the assignment of tasks, inevitably limits the magistrates' ability to effectuate a particular role conception if it is opposed by the more powerful judges.

The magistrates' shared consensus on their legitimate status and roles as federal judicial officers was evident in the speeches and discussions at the annual magistrates' conference observed for the study. For example, one speaker complained that too much language in various federal statutes and rules permits specified decisions and actions by a "U.S. district court or magistrate." A reference book commonly used by lawyers and law students is entitled *Federal Rules of Evidence for United States Courts and Magistrates*, and thus implies that the magistrates are somehow not a component of the federal courts.[14] The magistrate-speaker found this repeated differentiation of magistrates from the district court to be highly objectionable because, as he said, *"we are* the district court." Another magistrate was insulted that a member of Congress in 1979 had insisted that magistrates handle criminal misdemeanors only with consent because, according to the member of Congress, *"real* judges" should really handle such matters. The magistrates view themselves as legitimate judicial officers and therefore as "real" judges, albeit with more limited authority than district judges. The magistrates take umbrage at anything which implies that they are not judicial officers within the federal judiciary. As another speaker said, "If you and I are not 'judicial officers' of the district court, then I don't know who is."

A Typology of Magistrates' Ideal Role Expectations

Beyond the common shared expectation of status as judicial officers, magistrates' expectations about the ideal roles for magistrates diverge according to individuals' personal goals, experience, skills, and understanding of Congressional intent. Unlike Seron's model role typology for magistrates (i.e., Specialist, Team Player, and Additional Judge), which was based upon an analysis of tasks actually performed in nine districts and the organizational relationships between judges and their subordinates,[15] the typology of ideal roles that follows emphasizes magistrates' normative expectations expressed in interviews and conversations. The typology has been developed from both a standard interview question (i.e., "What role should magistrates play in the district courts?") and more extensive discussions with magistrates during the course of observations in various district courts and at the magistrates' annual conference. In characterizing this typology as concerning "ideal" types, the emphasis is on the magistrates' inclusion of their personal goals within the normative expectations that comprise the typological categories. However, the label "ideal" should not be misperceived as representing purely what the magistrates would like to see develop, but rather a combination of what role they would like to perform, what tasks they believe magistrates are effective in accomplishing for judges and the district courts, and what they believe to be the magistrates' proper relationship to judges and the judiciary under the statute. These factors will obviously be shaped by what tasks each magistrate actually performs and other aspects of professional and personal experience.

The normatively based typology illustrates the diversity in magistrates' expectations and simultaneously points to the possibilities for conflicting expectations between magistrates and judges (see Table 11). Although magistrates' normative expectations are illustrated, individuals differ in the extent that they attempt to shape their roles to meet their ideal expectations. Role conflict, manifested in career dissatisfaction, can usually be detected to some degree in every case in which the magistrates' expectations clash with the judges' conceptualizations and practices. Some magistrates may resign, others may use whatever limited means are at their disposal to push for reform, and others may simply endure the disappointments and bide their time until retirement. In any case, conflicting expectations can result in expressions of dissatisfaction, often diplomatically muted, concerning the magistrate position in its current roles within a district.

Magistrates' ideal role expectations can be characterized as fitting within one of eight model role categories: (1) Autonomous Federal

Table 11 Typology of Magistrates' Ideal Roles

Role	Description
Autonomous Federal Judge	Broad authority. Own docket of civil cases. Status as colleague to district judges.
Lower-Tier Trial Judge	Receive simple or small cases. Significant autonomy. Free district judge to handle complex cases or new legal issues.
Trial Preparer	All preliminary aspects of civil and criminal cases. Permit judge to concentrate on trials.
Filtering Facilitator	Filter out cases through the innovative and aggressive pursuit of settlements.
District Judge's Surrogate	Replicate judge's decisions on motions and petitions. Limit discretionary judgments. Reduce need for supervision by judge.
Categorical Specialist	Single category or limited kinds of cases. Develop expertise to increase efficiency in processing cases.
Jack-of-All-Trades	Complete range of tasks, from simple motions to trials. Variety enhances incumbent's enthusiasm and maximizes flexibility.
Judge's Assistant	Deference to judge's wishes. Limit authority and innovation unless initiated by judge.

Judge; (2) Lower-Tier Trial Judge; (3) Trial Preparer; (4) Filtering Facilitator; (5) District Judge's Surrogate; (6) Categorical Specialist; (7) Jack-of-All-Trades; and (8) Judge's Assistant.

Autonomous Federal Judge. Some magistrates view themselves and their role in the judiciary as mirroring the role of Additional Judge reportedly performed by their colleagues in the District of Oregon.[16] These magistrates believe that magistrates should have their own separate docket of civil cases for trial and that the 1979 Act clearly demonstrated the Congressional intent to endorse magistrates not only as federal judicial officers but as full-fledged trial judges. The magistrates who see their role as that of Autonomous Federal Judge perceive the 1979 Act as effectively enabling them to fulfill the need for additional judgeships in regard to every area except felony trials and sentencing. Four magistrates stated very explicitly that they want to be district judges and at least two of them have actually applied for judgeships in districts that use merit application processes for appointing Article III judges. Many district judges would argue, in agreement with the words of the district judge who said, "the magistrates all want to be judges," that this ideal role is based solely upon the personal aspirations of individual magistrates. While this ideal role probably stems from an emphasis on these magistrates' personal goals, several magistrates persuasively argued that magistrates could make their best contribution to the district's case processing by taking the most expansive possible role.

Lower-Tier Trial Judge. Some magistrates conceive of their ideal role as trial judges for simple and small cases, so that district judges will be freed to concentrate on large, complex cases and cases that may involve the development of new law. Civil suits may be filed in federal court under diversity jurisdiction if the cases are between parties from different states and involve an amount over $50,000. The federal courts do not develop their own common law for such cases, but instead apply appropriate state law.[17] Because of diversity jurisdiction within the federal courts, there are many lawsuits that do not involve new developments in federal law, but are instead decided upon applicable state law. At the time of the study, the amount in controversy had not yet been raised from $10,000 to $50,000, so that a relatively simple automobile accident could arrive in the federal courts through diversity jurisdiction because of the price of automobiles. In addition, some cases brought under federal statutes may be for relatively small amounts of money. In cases in which the law is clear, but the judge or jury needs to resolve a factual dispute to determine the existence of liability, or in cases in which the amount at issue is relatively small, magistrates in the role as Lower-Tier Trial Judges could spare the district judges from expending their limited time and resources for minor cases. This conceptualization of the magistrates' role risks fulfilling one critic's prophecy that the magistrate system would "create a dual system of justice" by preventing the poorer litigant from having a case heard by a real Article III judge.[18] Magistrates argue, however, that, because all magistrates are either merit-selected or merit-reviewed for reappointment, there is no reason to believe that the magistrates are any less qualified and capable than the district judges who reach the bench through the partisan political process of senatorial courtesy, presidential appointment, and senate approval. Therefore, the creation of a de facto lower trial court system within the federal courts would not necessarily result in unjust outcomes.

Trial Preparer. This role most closely approximates Seron's Team Player model role, because the magistrate would handle all preliminary aspects of civil and criminal cases so that the judges could devote their time to trying cases. The magistrate would decide motions, meet with attorneys in pre-trial and settlement conferences, and eventually pass the case to the judge when completely prepared for trial. The judges would not be distracted by preparatory or administrative tasks, because the magistrate would handle virtually everything up to the point of trial. On the other hand, there is a risk that judges would lose their ability to, in the words of one district judge, "keep their fingers on the pulse of the case," by meeting with attorneys and gaining preliminary understanding of issues and settlement possibilities through involvement in preliminary phases of the cases. In addition, there is a concern that such hierarchical specialization will increasingly contribute to the "transformation of the courts—this time into a 'bureaucratic' judiciary."[19]

Filtering Facilitator. Some magistrates see their ideal role as filtering out cases through the innovative and aggressive pursuit of settlements. Magistrates can be interposed into cases and, because they need not be the ultimate neutral trial judges for the cases, they can seek innovative means for encouraging settlement. This might involve becoming intimately involved in settlement negotiations; presiding over various types of alternative dispute resolution processes, such as mediation, arbitration, or summary jury trials; giving advisory opinions on legal issues during settlement negotiations; or generally facilitating settlement opportunities through a willingness to actively participate in any appropriate process that might help to move the parties closer together. The magistrate thus becomes the key figure responsible for keeping cases from going to trial and thereby reduces the caseload burden upon the judges who can devote their courtroom time to difficult cases not amenable to settlement. This role for magistrates creates risks of coercion and pressure upon litigants that are inappropriate for a judicial branch which is supposed to provide a neutral, available forum for resolving disputes according to formal legal procedures.

District Judge's Surrogate. Magistrates also see themselves as surrogates for particular judges, especially under paired assignment systems. As a District Judge's Surrogate, the magistrate would concentrate on replicating the judge's methods and values in behavior and decision making for hearings, review of written documents, and conferences. Because decisions other than consent trial dispositions will ultimately be made final under the signature of a district judge, the magistrate would feel obligated to try to act as the district judge would act in working for settlements and making recommendations on motions. This ideal role emphasizes the constitutional and statutory framework for the magistrate system which place a premium upon supervision and accountability under the control of district judges. This role would defeat whatever benefits could be derived from having the magistrate, as independent decision maker, make considered judgments about issues, motions, and cases. Judges would lose the fresh perspective that magistrates can provide by independently approaching each decision. If judges approve reports and recommendations that both they and the magistrates perceive to follow the path that the judge probably would have followed, the motion or issue in question may, in fact, never receive any complete, open-minded judicial review. The judge may simply approve what is assumed to be the decision that the judge would have made anyway. As the Supreme Court's decision in *Raddatz v. United States* made clear, the district judge is not necessarily required to review completely the determination made by the magistrate even in a procedure in which the district judge is technically undertaking a complete or de novo review.[20] At least one court has raised the possibility that undue influence by a judge over a magistrate's decision making may implicate due process issues.[21]

Categorical Specialist. This role is very similar to Seron's model role of Specialist. The magistrate would become an expert in particular categories of activities and would work exclusively on those tasks. Unlike the Seron model role, in which the Specialist worked primarily on either Social Security or prisoner cases, this Categorical Specialist role might include a broader range of activities. For example, a magistrate might specialize in Title VII employment discrimination cases, evidentiary motions, or other particular categories of cases and tasks. This role carries with it the risks of specialization in which the decision maker's supposed expertise comes to rigidify decision making according to specific values. Thus there is never a fresh look at cases within the category. There is a serious risk that cases will be unfairly predetermined according to past experience without a reasonable opportunity to distinguish from previous cases or recognize the desirability of new trends in the law which would be sensitive to changing conditions and values within society.

Jack-of-All-Trades. It is possible to characterize the foregoing role categories not as ideal roles, but as the multiple purposive roles that an individual magistrate would undertake according to the parties' circumstances and the needs of the district. In this way, the magistrates' roles become more like Clinton Rossiter's famous cataloging of presidential roles,[22] in which there is a clear recognition that no single role necessarily dominates the professional performance of the position incumbent. A more closely analogous example would be the ten purposive roles fulfilled by state judges, as complied by Charles Sheldon from three studies of judicial roles.[23] A magistrate whose ideal role is Jack-of-All-Trades believes that the magistrate should be performing all of the aforementioned roles without concentrating on or being limited to any particular ideal role. Arguably, this conceptualization provides the most flexible use of magistrates, but as a practical matter such a magistrate could easily be locked into Social Security or prisoner cases if the district has a particularly heavy workload in those areas. It is clear from talking to the magistrates that this ideal role presumes that the magistrate would in fact be used in all roles, rather than evolving into any one or limited combination of listed ideal roles.

Judge's Assistant. A few magistrates, often evincing a very cautious diplomacy in their interview responses, characterized their ideal role as simply doing whatever tasks the judges might decide to send to the magistrate. This ideal role not only accepts the legal and practical subordinateness of the magistrate position, but actually endorses the judges' complete power and discretion to determine what role the magistrate should play. While the Autonomous Federal Judge ideal role reflected some emphasis on the magistrates' personal aspirations, the Judge's Assistant ideal role seems to embody a suppression of personal goals in favor of deference to constitutional and statutory control by the district judges. If a magistrate adopted this role, which implies a degree of passivity on the part of the magistrate in regard to the district court's administration, the judges and the district would lose the value of innovation that can develop when magistrates actively seek to shape their own roles within a court.

Ideal Roles, Magistrates' Expectations, and Role Development

The magistrates' ideal roles can provide them with a standard of behavior and performance that influences their activities within the court. If the judges limit the magistrates' authority to a level below that of the magistrates' ideal role, then the magistrates can use the standard of the ideal role to push the judges, through suggestion or example, to broaden task assignments. When the possibilities for reform seem slim, then the ideal role can be a primary source of frustration, because the magistrate recognizes or believes that the judges could and should permit the exercise of broader authority. If the magistrates' ideal roles imply a limited range of tasks or passive participation in court administration, such as in the Categorical Specialist or Judge's Assistant roles, then the extant practices and expectations within a courthouse can continue to define the magistrate's role to the exclusion of reforms and innovations which might have contributed to effective case processing. Sometimes judges limit magistrates' authority simply because, as in the case of District B, district judges are not aware of and have not thought about other possible utilization schemes even though the judges have no personal or principled objections to giving the magistrates broader authority. Although it may reduce job dissatisfaction because the incumbent's expectations are lower, a limited ideal role may hinder experimentation and innovation, because no actor's interests and expectations motivate behavior aimed at encouraging reform. In addition, the magistrates' ideal roles, even in courthouses which strictly constrain magistrates' activities, may guide the incumbents' attitudes and behaviors in hearings or conferences. A magistrate with a broader ideal role may assert a judicial demeanor that commands respect and deference in a way different from the magistrate who concentrates on replicating a judge's decision making or otherwise directing public behaviors toward such very specific goals as assisting a judge with a narrow task.

LAWYERS' EXPECTATIONS

Lawyers' expectations about and understanding of the magistrates' roles influence both the way magistrates are treated within the courthouse and their overall effectiveness in contributing to the work of the district court. If magistrates are not regarded as judicial officers, then there will not be consents to the magistrates' authority for trials even if the district's judges are willing to delegate complete civil cases.

Lawyers' expectations concerning magistrates are influenced by the district's judges. If the judges consistently and publicly endorse the magistrates' legitimacy as federal judicial officers, as in District B in which district judges address the magistrates with the title "Judge," then the practicing attorneys will adopt the prevailing practices.

Litigators are normally very concerned about maintaining good relationships with judges, as illustrated by Chapter 3's descriptions of the behavior of attorney-selection committee members who attempt to please the judges with their list of magistrate nominees. Thus lawyers will emulate the judges' attitudes and follow prevailing practices within the district without being overly concerned or even knowledgeable about the statutory and constitutional limitations on magistrates' authority. As previously mentioned, at least thirty-six districts permitted magistrates to preside over civil trials prior to actual statutory authorization in 1979.[24] Although magistrates' authority to supervise trials was challenged on appeal in some districts, the widespread utilization of the not-officially-authorized practice is indicative of lawyers' propensity to go along with judicially-initiated practices that are not patently unlawful.

Judges can also have adverse effects upon lawyers' perceptions of magistrates by treating the magistrates as limited subordinates or by criticizing specific magistrates and the magistrate system generally. In addition, judges have adverse effects upon lawyers' perceptions of the magistrates' roles by pressuring lawyers to consent to the subordinate judges' authority. Examples of questionable tactics employed by judges to coerce attorneys to consent arose, during the study period, in at least two districts. Although attorneys can be pressured to go to trial with the magistrate presiding, the resentment at the forced procedure can detract from the magistrate's ability to prove to the attorneys that consent trials represent a desirable option.

Judges can influence lawyers' views, but they cannot necessarily dictate views to the lawyers. In one district in which the chief judge organized informational meetings to encourage attorneys to consent to magistrate-supervised trials, the meetings had little effect upon attorneys and litigants. The willingness of parties to consent depends on several factors, including trial strategy, settlement positions, and familiarity with the magistrate's abilities.

Lawyers are influenced by magistrates' behavior or role performance that they observe within the courthouse. In regard to one respected magistrate, several lawyers noted that the magistrate's performances as a trial judge and settlement facilitator had earned the respect and cooperation of attorneys throughout the district. When the magistrate came up for reappointment at the end of his term, unlike the situation in other districts in which comment letters from attorneys trickle in unless specifically requested by the committee, the public announcement of this magistrate's reappointment drew dozens of letters. The letters were universally positive, even from attorneys who had received adverse rulings and judgments from the magistrate. In this district, the magistrate had earned virtually the same respect and treatment that the bar accorded to district judges. By the same token, attorneys who perceive that a magistrate performs poorly will treat that magistrate differently, be less willing to consent to magistrate trials, and develop a narrower view of the magistrate's appropriate roles.

In many districts, because of the title, role, and prestige differentiation between magistrates and judges, attorneys have less regard for the magistrates. This diminished respect for the magistrates may be manifested in ways that are not obvious to the magistrate. For example, one attorney confided that "when a judge tells you to do something, you jump. But when a magistrate tells you to do something, well, you do it, but it's not the same." In some instances, it is very obvious to the magistrate that the attorney regards the magistrate as being of lesser importance. The magistrate may be forced to marshal resources in order to maintain his or her desired judicial role. For example, in a District B case in which an attorney attempted to go over the magistrate's head to the judge in order to get a conference rescheduled, it was clear that the attorney never would have attempted such a maneuver if the district judge were presiding over the conference. After an attorney approached a judge about rescheduling, there would be nothing that the attorney could do but comply with the judge's orders. In the District B example, the magistrate hurried to contact the judge to ensure that the judge upheld the magistrate's decision. Thus the magistrate, because of the relatively new judicial office and uncertainty about appropriate status and role for the magistrate position, must often actively seek to maintain proper behavior and respect on the part of attorneys.

Seron's interviews with lawyers in selected districts indicated that lawyers respected magistrates and were satisfied with their performance in broad judicial roles.[25] During the observation periods for this study, however, several instances arose in which it appeared that attorneys were treating the magistrates very differently than district judges. Some of these examples were obviously due to attorneys' ignorance about the magistrate position, such as when attorneys called a particular magistrate "Mister," rather than using an appropriate judicial title. In other cases, however, it appeared that the attorneys did not view the magistrates as complete judicial officers, despite the magistrates' obvious efforts to perform a broad judicial role requiring discretion and judgment during both hearings and conferences. In one instance, an attorney arrived at a hearing without having filed the required motions and briefs, and without any papers, notes, or even a calendar to schedule the next hearing or conference. The attorney strolled in smiling and empty-handed as if attending a casual meeting, even though the magistrate was robed and sitting on the bench in the courtroom with a court reporter present. The attorney seemed startled but unfazed when chastised by the magistrate. The magistrate later said, just as several of his peers responded when asked about the subject, that he did not detect any lower level of respect or appropriate behavior from attorneys. He claimed that this attorney was probably always unprepared, but it was a little difficult to imagine that the attorney would still be employed by a law firm if he treated district judges with the same disrespect and nonchalance he evinced before the magistrate. In several instances in different districts, lawyers indicated that they would not attend conferences scheduled by magistrates despite a court order requiring them to appear. Usually the magistrate's staff would attempt to impress upon the lawyer that there could be serious consequences if the magistrate's order were ignored. In regard to certain kinds of hearings, such as hearings for prisoners' civil rights cases, some magistrates just shrugged their shoulders when a state assistant attorney general would fail to appear. It seems less likely that a district judge's schedule would be so disrespected. In one case, a magistrate had ordered a lawyer to remain at an all-day settlement conference as negotiations continued even when it was obvious that the lawyer had expected to leave after a brief meeting. By the middle of the afternoon, the aggravated lawyer became incensed at the settlement offer that the magistrate had carried back from a meeting with the opposing party in a separate room. The lawyer walked right up to the magistrate and practically yelled, "I am appalled that a federal judge would carry this illegal offer to us. This is unethical." Again, it was difficult to imagine that the attorney's anger would be expressed so openly and undiplomatically to a district judge. These episodes were noticeable exceptions to the norm of professional courtesy that lawyers exhibit when dealing with magistrates as well as other attorneys, but they gave indications of how lawyers may differentiate magistrates from judges.

Unlike judges' expectations, lawyers' expectations do not significantly define the magistrates' roles. The lawyers are influential, however, because the broad ideal roles desired by most magistrates are dependent upon cooperation and respect from the local bar. A magistrate cannot preside over trials unless the lawyers are willing to regard the magistrate as a trial judge. Likewise, a magistrate cannot be effective at facilitating settlements unless the lawyers trust the magistrate. If lawyers do not consent to have cases heard by magistrates, then, even if the judges would like to encourage trials, judges will be forced to give their subordinates more limited tasks and the lawyers' expectations about magistrates will have served to influence the development of the magistrates' actual roles.

ESTABLISHED PATTERNS FOR MAGISTRATE UTILIZATION

The development of the magistrates' roles within district courts can be heavily influenced by established patterns, or the lack thereof, for utilization of magistrates. The extent of existing practices can limit the expectations of judges, magistrates, and lawyers, because they lack familiarity with alternative utilization schemes. The strong identification and association of specific individuals with the magistrate position can create a model and standard for subsequent magistrates. The qualities of the individuals who become model magistrates within districts can influence the selection of new magistrates by the judges, the assignment of tasks to magistrates, and the behavior of judges, magistrates, and lawyers in relation to the magistrates' roles.

Interviews revealed that many judges have never given much thought to the ideal roles of magistrates or to alternative methods for utilizing magistrates. Frequently, as in Districts A, B, and D, the first magistrate appointed within a particular courthouse will, with the judges, set a pattern for magistrate utilization that will automatically be followed by new judges and magistrates subsequently appointed to office in the courthouse or district. In District A and other interview districts, the first magistrate was utilized in law clerk-like tasks because of the district's caseload characteristics and the judges' expectations concerning the magistrate position. The introduction of new magistrates or changes in the caseload will not necessarily result in changed tasks and a broader role, because the judges, magistrates, and lawyers are accustomed to having the subordinate judges perform in the established roles. One disgruntled magistrate, referring to the well-established limited role for magistrates in his district, characterized the judges as "victims of their own experience." In District B, the first magistrate developed a tremendous reputation for skill and competence in Social Security and prisoner cases and, in addition, held a principled view that magistrates should perform limited roles. As a result, when new judges and magistrates were assigned to the court, even though they did not share the magistrate's view that a limited role was required or even desirable, the established practices and respect for the original magistrate's knowledge hindered consideration of any broader, alternative systems for utilizing magistrates.

In District D, the original magistrate in the illustrative courthouse established a pattern for broad utilization of magistrates, including consent trials and acceptance of magistrate-initiated innovations. The judges within the courthouse simply adapted to the prevailing, successful practices without questioning the broad authority exercised by the magistrate. The same phenomenon was observed in a similar courthouse in which the magistrate, in effect, taught the judges how magistrates should be utilized. Thus judges' expectations and conceptualizations were, at least partially, derived from and limited by their experiences with magistrates. For these District D judges it would be difficult to imagine limiting the utilization of magistrates to the narrow tasks assigned in Districts A and B. In District D, the lack of existing practices when the first magistrate was appointed facilitated the implementation of broad authority for magistrates, because the innovative appointees and open-minded judges did not have to combat any preestablished normative standards for the magistrates' roles.

The performance of original magistrates also influenced the selection of subsequent magistrates. Magistrates fulfilling law clerk-like functions often set standards for subsequent appointment decisions in the same ways that subordinate judges exercising broad authority led district judges to seek appointees with the qualities of trial judges. In both instances, it is not only the task assignments which comprise the influential existing patterns, but also the skills and traits of incumbents which are replicated by the judges in subsequent appointment decisions.

Established patterns can remain a powerful influence over magistrates' roles unless judges within the district become dissatisfied with magistrates' contributions to the court or become amenable to alternatives suggested by the magistrates or sources outside of the district.

METHOD OF TASK ASSIGNMENT

The method of task assignment can influence magistrates' roles by affecting judges' attitudes and expectations toward their subordinates or by limiting magistrates' opportunities to prove their abilities to the judges.

In the districts examined for this study, the paired assignment system seemed to have the strongest effect upon magistrates' roles. In District A, one magistrate commented that the paired assignment system "promotes a feeling of proprietary interest" for the judges. The judges begin to feel that they own the services of specific magistrates and therefore are unwilling and unable to consider alternative utilizations that would give the magistrates broader authority. The possibility for granting broader authority to magistrates in District B was clearly hindered by a mismatched pairing that placed an ambitious magistrate with a cautious judge and a conservative magistrate with an open-minded judge. If the pairing had been reversed, one pair would certainly have undertaken innovative experiments that might have led the other district judges to broaden the range of tasks assigned to magistrates. The paired system reinforces notions that the magistrates work for individual judges, rather than the district court, and therefore leads judges to limit magistrates' authority in order to maintain control over personal judicial resources.

The paired assignment system may also prevent opportunities for magistrates to prove their abilities. In one district, the judges sent consent trials and settlement conferences to the experienced, original magistrate who possessed an established reputation. When new magistrates were added to the district, a pairing system was undertaken that fit with the physical arrangements of the district's three courthouses. Judges gave their paired subordinates more limited tasks and sought ways to send complex tasks to the original magistrate, thus preventing the newcomers from ever learning about and proving their ability to do more complicated assignments. An innovative new chief judge led a change to a district-wide random assignment system which, although geographically inconvenient, because lawyers had to travel to different courthouses for hearings and conferences, eventually led to broader authority and a wider range of tasks for all magistrates.

Magistrates' roles, job satisfaction, and expectations may also be affected by the nature of the assignment system, rather than its form. The assignment of certain kinds of tasks to magistrates at the time of filing can help standardize and perpetuate magistrates' roles without continual evaluation and reexamination by the judges. By contrast, an ad hoc system of assigning tasks, while maximizing the judges' control and discretion, forces the judges to make individual decisions about tasks. These decisions will reflect the judges' expectations about the magistrates' roles and, moreover, indicate the judges' assessments of the capabilities of individual magistrates. One magistrate in a small courthouse, who receives all civil motions automatically, strongly asserted that he would be personally insulted if judges used an ad hoc basis for choosing matters to assign to him. He would feel as if decisions about assignments, especially decisions in which a matter was not assigned, would convey a message to the magistrate as well as to local attorneys that the judge does not trust the magistrate's abilities. Although practices in other districts demonstrate that there can be myriad benign reasons for a judge to retain specific tasks, it is possible that the process of making choices about the delegation of tasks could affect the perceptions of other judicial actors about the magistrates' roles and abilities.

In two courthouses, the judges have adopted or maintained paired assignment systems specifically to create narrower limits on the magistrates' authority. These practices were fueled by the judges' concerns that they could not keep close track of magistrates' activities if the subordinate judges were not personal assistants. While random assignment systems can create opportunities for magistrates to prove their abilities to judges all over the district, there are attendant risks that judges may perceive magistrates to be no longer accountable. Thus, assignment systems have sometimes been adjusted both to expand and contract the magistrates' roles.

NATURE OF THE DISTRICT'S CASELOAD

The emphasis of this study has been upon the expectations of various actors, especially district judges, and attendant effects upon the development, continuation, and change of magistrates' roles within the courts. The expectations, attitudes, and behaviors of the various judicial actors do not, however, operate in isolation. Specific environmental circumstances, such as the physical courthouse facilities, some of which inhibit contact and communication, constrain and shape magistrates' roles. One important uncontrollable factor, namely the quantity and composition of case filings within a district, can significantly affect the magistrates' roles. The nature of the caseload can limit task assignments in particular ways regardless of the judges' expectations and magistrates' aspirations for a broad role.

The quantity of case filings can determine what tasks judges are able to do and, therefore, what tasks are available to be referred to magistrates. In the case of *DeCosta v. Columbia Broadcasting System, Inc.*,[26] the busy, lone district judge in Rhode Island assigned a trial to the lone magistrate by consent of the parties prior to statutory authorization for consent trials in the 1979 Act. The magistrate involved in the case, an experienced former military court judge, had received the case assignment because the court's high caseload was occupying the time of the district judge. Although the magistrate became well-known to other magistrates because of his work in this seminal case, an interview conducted with the magistrate for this study revealed that he is no longer assigned any trials. Magistrates in neighboring districts who know the magistrate personally and are also familiar with his recognition for the *DeCosta* case have expressed surprise that the role of this "trailblazer" has actually become more limited during the past thirteen years. There seems to be a common assumption among many magistrates that once judges in a district "open their eyes" and recognize the value of a broad role for magistrates, then the subordinate judges' authority will become established and the broad role will continue. Thus magistrates who object to being placed into a limited role assume that their roles will permanently change if they are given the opportunity to conduct consent trials regularly. In fact, the Rhode Island example illustrates the influence of external, environmental factors upon the magistrates' roles. Unlike the lone judge during the early 1970s, Rhode Island now has several judges, due to new appointments and the continued contributions of judges on senior status. In addition, the district has also experienced a relative decline in case filings. Thus, the current trial caseload can be handled by the district judges without any need to refer complete civil cases to the magistrate.

The composition of a district's cases will also affect task assignments to magistrates. A key feature that distinguishes the independent magistrates of District C from the magistrates in the other three districts studied is that District C magistrates do not handle Social Security cases. The District C magistrates asserted that having judges handle Social Security cases avoids a potentially unnecessary layer of review on such cases and frees the subordinate judges for other tasks. The other three districts, however, have been among the nation's leaders in Social Security case filings, particularly during years in which their districts were hit hard by economic difficulties that did not beset District C. As the magistrates in the other three districts often point out, the District C judges might have a very different view of their own abilities to handle Social Security cases if they were swamped with hundreds of such cases. Under those circumstances, they might behave more like judges in other districts who send the Social Security cases to magistrates in order to free themselves to conduct trials and other matters. Likewise, substantial caseloads in other categories of cases can determine the magistrates' roles. For example, magistrates in districts near federal land may find their time inevitably consumed by a steady stream of petty offense and misdemeanor cases. Depending upon the assignment system used within a district, a magistrate in a courthouse near several prisons may be similarly occupied by habeas corpus and civil rights cases.

Judges' decisions about task assignments and their conceptualizations of magistrates' roles have predominant influence upon the definition of magistrates' roles. Judges' views and actions will, however, be influenced by the needs and case pressures within the district court. Magistrates are a resource for the courts, so judges' utilization of them will be determined, at least in part, by the courts' specific perceived needs that require application of additional judicial resources.

MAGISTRATES' ROLES AND THE PROCESS OF CHANGE

The literature on utilization of magistrates produced by the Federal Judicial Center, the General Accounting Office, and the Administrative Office supports broad utilization of magistrates.[27] These exhortations, despite their prevalence and unanimity, do not seem to have significantly altered the magistrates' roles. Other specific factors are more important determinants of change. Not surprisingly, because the factors discussed throughout this chapter affected the development of magistrates' roles, these factors were also observed influencing role changes.

Most obviously, as the Rhode Island example illustrates, changes in the composition and quantity of case filings within a district can cause changes in the magistrates' roles. Even if all other factors have created an environment conducive to a broad role, a sudden change in case pressures can narrow or expand the breadth of tasks assigned to magistrates. For example, case pressures within particular courthouses in District A resulted in assignment of broader tasks to the magistrates paired with judges in the smaller, satellite courthouses.

In District A, the assignment of broader tasks in the smaller courthouses eventually led some judges in the large courthouse to broaden task assignments for magistrates in the urban center. This phenomenon, namely change through example, was common to many districts that experienced expansion in the magistrates' roles. Sometimes change can be encouraged by the example of a single, explicit demonstration of magistrates' potential, such as a single magistrate successfully handling a complex consent trial. The other judges in the district can observe the results of the trial and listen to attorneys' views about the process before considering whether they should assign more of such tasks to the subordinate judges.

Examples which encourage change normally arise with some identifiable catalyst. As mentioned previously, the catalyst might be a reduction or increase in certain kinds of case filings, with the result that the range of magistrates' tasks either expands or contracts to fit the district's needs. An individual can often serve as a catalyst. In several small courthouses, creative individuals appointed to magistrate positions made suggestions to judges, took on additional responsibilities, and demonstrated through effective performance that magistrates could assist the court by assuming a broader range of responsibilities. The effectiveness of such individuals' initiatives was dependent upon the judges' being amenable to experimentation and to reconceptualization of their subordinates' roles.

Judges can also serve as catalysts by experimenting with new ideas learned from other judges or described at judicial meetings. A new judge appointed to a district will normally adapt to existing practices while learning to be a federal judge, but in a few districts new judges have had definite ideas about alternative dispute resolution mechanisms and other reforms which, when implemented, effectively broadened the magistrates' roles. For example, judges in several districts have initiated the use of summary jury trials by having magistrates preside over the non-binding courtroom proceedings. Although the other judges in these districts have not always adopted the use of summary trials, the mechanism has enabled some judges to see how their subordinates can be utilized more broadly.

Situational catalysts can also provide examples for new roles. In two small courthouses within this study, judges were temporarily disabled by medical problems, so magistrates had to carry the major burden in the courts by assuming substantial responsibility for everything except felony trials and sentencing. Interviews with judges in other courthouses indicate that these situations attracted notice and earned new respect for the individual magistrates while demonstrating the breadth of possible uses for the subordinate judges. The retirement of a magistrate can also create an opportunity for change, as illustrated by District B and the reevaluation of the magistrate system in conjunction with the retirement of an experienced magistrate who had initiated a limited role.

District A illustrates the difficulties facing magistrates who attempt to suggest planned changes in the face of opposition from the district judges. The magistrates have united and acted in concert to develop reforms that will increase their status and sphere of authority. The judges, however, ultimately make the decisions so that, even though District A magistrates have seen their roles expand through evolution and the example of their own satellite courthouses, any new policies or comprehensive changes depend upon formal endorsement from the recalcitrant judges. Magistrates in other districts were observed meeting together and discussing strategies for approaching district judges. In nearly every instance, the magistrates' recognition that the judges possess power over both task assignments and reappointments dictated that the subordinate judges move forward in a cautious and diplomatic fashion.

CONCLUSION

As the discussions in this chapter have indicated, the recognition that the judges are the central figures does not imply that judges are making informed, calculated decisions about the utilization of magistrates or that judges solely determine the magistrates' roles. Judges in various districts define the magistrates' roles in terms of their own customary experience with law clerks, who serve as personal assistants. Some judges conceptualize their own work as part of a larger enterprise, the federal judiciary, rather than seeing themselves strictly as individually and personally embodying the judicial branch. Thus, judges who manifest this discernible attitude appear to be more willing to view the magistrates as actors fitting within the broader needs of the courts, rather than as personal resources for the judges.

Magistrates themselves can influence the development of their roles, depending upon the circumstances within individual court-houses. The availability of communication with the judges, opportunities to demonstrate magistrates' abilities, district caseload characteristics, and judges' amenability to innovation significantly affect the magistrates' influence.

Established patterns for magistrates' utilization and status within courthouses serve as powerful determinants of subsequent role continuation or change. The examples of roles performed by previous subordinate judges provide the socializing environment and education for subsequent district judges, magistrates, and attorneys. As examples such as District B have shown, judges may be amenable to broadening the magistrates' roles, yet the lack of overt dissatisfaction with the existing patterns can serve as a disincentive to evaluating and reassessing the effectiveness of the magistrate system.

The statutory design of the magistrate system evinced a clear intention to permit the district judges to define the magistrates' roles according to the needs of particular courts. Although this study has determined that the judges do indeed have significant power over the definition of magistrates' roles, the expectations of other actors, primarily magistrates and attorneys, as well as situational, environmental, attitudinal, and experiential factors serve to make the development of magistrates' roles a complex and changing process. The pressures and resource demands upon the federal courts have dictated that magistrates' roles generally evolve or change in the direction of expanded tasks. One magistrate characterized the development of the magistrate system as a process of "expansion, recognition, and acceptance; expansion, recognition, and acceptance." As the Rhode Island example shows, however, the flexibility in the magistrate system and the interaction of influential factors can, contrary to magistrates' aspirations and expectations, lead to a contraction of magistrates' authority as well.

NOTES

1. Bruce J. Biddle, *Role Theory* (New York: Academic Press, 1979), 58.

2. Charles E. Silberman, *Criminal Violence, Criminal Justice* (New York: Vintage Books, 1978), 383.

3. Walter F. Murphy and C. Herman Pritchett, *Courts, Judges, and Politics* (New York: Random House, 1986), 134–136.

4. U.S. Congress, House Report No. 1364, Magistrate Act of 1978, 95th Cong., 2d Sess., 1978, 10–11.

5. Wharton-Thomas v. United States, 721 F.2d 922, 927 (3rd Cir. 1983); Pacemaker Diagnostic Clinic v. Instromedix Inc., 725 F.2d 537, 544 (9th Cir. 1984) (en banc).

6. U.S. Congress, House Report No. 1629, Federal Magistrates Act, *U.S. Code Congressional and Administrative News*, 1968, 4256.

7. Joseph Spaniol, Jr., "The Federal Magistrates Act: History and Development," *Arizona State Law Journal* (1974): 566.

8. General Accounting Office, *The U.S. Magistrates: How Their Services Have Assisted Administration of Several District Courts; More Improvements Needed* (Washington, D.C.: Government Printing Office, 1974), 1.

9. Peter C. McCabe, "The Federal Magistrate Act of 1979," *Harvard Journal on Legislation* 16 (1979): 349.

10. U.S. Congress, House Report No. 1629, 4262.

11. Testimony of the Hon. Edward S. Northrop, U.S. District Court for the District of Maryland, U.S. Congress, Senate Committee on the Judiciary, *Federal Magistrates Act: Hearings Before the Subcommittee on Improvements in Judicial Machinery on S.3475 and S.945*, 89th Cong., 2d Sess., 1966, 52.

12. Carroll Seron, "The Professional Project of Parajudges: The Case of U.S. Magistrates," *Law and Society Review* 22 (1988): 559–563.

13. Seron has noted that innovative districts find ways to foster communication between judges and magistrates, including the inclusion of magistrates in regularly scheduled meetings of the court. Carroll Seron, "Magistrates and the work of federal courts: a new division of labor," *Judicature* 69 (1986): 359.

14. *Federal Rules of Evidence for United States Courts and Magistrates* (St. Paul, MN: West Publishing Co., 1975).

15. Carroll Seron, *The Roles of Magistrates: Nine Case Studies*, (Washington, D.C.: Federal Judicial Center, 1985), 35–37.

16. The District of Oregon enjoys legendary status among magistrates because of the broad authority and high status granted to its subordinate judges. Ibid. 38–39; General Accounting Office, *Potential Benefits of Federal Magistrates System Can Be Better Realized* (Washington, D.C.: U.S. Government Printing Office, 1983), 18.

17. Erie Railroad Co. v. Tompkins, 304 U.S. 64 (1938).

18. Dissenting Views of the Hon. Elizabeth Holtzman, U.S. Congress, House Report No. 1364, 42.

19. Judith Resnik, "Managerial Judges," *Harvard Law Review* 96 (1982): 437.

20. In *Raddatz v. United States*, 447 U.S. 667 (1980), a district judge was permitted to uphold a magistrate's determination about the credibility of wit-

nesses by simply reviewing a transcript of testimony rather than listening to the actual testimony.

21. The Third Circuit in *Wharton-Thomas v. United States* noted that "[e]ven if it be assumed that the district judge influences the magistrate, this would not amount to non-Article III interference. There is no reason to even speculate that district judges would improperly attempt to influence a magistrate's decision, but any such conduct would implicate due process, rather than Article III." 721 F.2d 922, 927 n. 8 (1983).

22. Clinton Rossiter, *The American Presidency*, (New York: New American Library, 1960).

23. Sheldon characterized judges as fulfilling the following purposive roles: (1) Law Interpreter; (2) Law Maker; (3) Adjudicator; (4) Administrator; (5) Peacekeeper; (6) Task Performer; (7) Policy Maker; (8) Ritualist; (9) Pragmatist; and (10) Constitutional Defender. Charles H. Sheldon, *The American Judicial Process: Models & Approaches* (New York: Dodd, Mead & Co., 1974), 90.

24. U.S. Congress, House Report No. 1364, 4.

25. Seron, *The Roles of Magistrates: Nine Case Studies*, 59–68.

26. 520 F.2d 499 (1st Cir. 1975) rev'g in part 383 F.Supp 326 (D.R.I.1974).

27. For example, the General Accounting Office studied the magistrate system and recommended that: "The Judicial Conference should take a more active role . . . . [to] [e]ncourage district courts and judges who are restricting the use of magistrates to explore methods to increase the use of their magistrates." General Accounting Office, *Potential Benefits*, 34.

9

The Consequences of a Subordinate Judicial Officer

This study of magistrates' tasks and status in various districts revealed that the roles of magistrates, namely their characteristic behaviors and the sum of relevant actors' expectations, can differ dramatically from courthouse to courthouse. Despite these divergent roles, by viewing the U.S. magistrates from a more macroscopic perspective, the magistrates' common functional consequences for the judiciary and the political system can be identified. These consequences are discernible across diverse districts and throughout the federal judiciary.

The consequences of magistrates' roles can be best understood through a general adaptation of Robert King Merton's structural functional analysis, most famously applied by Merton to illustrate the functional consequences of the urban political machine.[1] Structural functionalism posits that organizational structure has functional consequences that determine its contribution to the political system. In this instance, the organizational structure includes the overriding statutory design of a flexibly utilized tier of subordinate federal judicial officers and the characteristics of particular districts and courthouse environments that define the magistrates' roles and tasks. The functional consequences can be examined according to Merton's scheme which distinguishes manifest from latent functions in order to "preclude the inadvertent confusion ... between conscious *motivations* for social behavior and its *objective consequences*."[2]

Manifest functions are "those objective consequences for a specified unit," in this case the political system of the federal judiciary, "which contribute to its adjustment or adaptation and were so intended."[3] Thus, one can examine systemic results from the intentions of legislative and judicial actors in creating and implementing the office of U.S. Magistrate and in shaping particular roles for magistrates within the district courts. By contrast, the latent functions are the unintended and unrecognized consequences for the political system. Although consequences are frequently and matter-of-factly referred to as functional in contributing to or maintaining a system, consequences—both manifest and latent—may also be dysfunctional when they do not lead to positive or maintaining effects.[4] Thus, a net balance of functional consequences must be considered in assessing the magistrates' functions within the federal judiciary.

THE FEDERAL COURTS AS A POLITICAL SYSTEM

Functional analysis and the concept of function are drawn from the biological sciences where, in an analogous context, function is understood to mean the "vital or organic processes considered in the respects in which they contribute to the maintenance of the organism."[5] In political science, the "organisms" that are affected or maintained by political actors or phenomena are usually conceptualized as systems. For the purpose of examining the functional consequences of magistrates' roles, the system under examination is the federal judiciary conceptualized as a political system.

Sheldon Goldman and Thomas Jahnige have developed a complete, elaborate model of the federal courts as a political system which can usefully serve as the basis for examining the U.S. magistrates.[6] The federal judiciary can be conceptualized as a political system because, like other systems that political scientists study, it exhibits boundary-maintaining characteristics and is involved in the authoritative allocation of values or valued things for society. As Goldman and Jahnige point out, "[c]ourts primarily allocate values by deciding cases and issuing rules of procedure and other court orders."[7] The judiciary's influence over the allocation of values may be most obvious in judicial determinations of broad-reaching policy, such as affirmative action, school desegregation, and abortion, but the conflict-resolving decisions affecting individuals, the formal and informal mechanisms for dispute resolution, and the procedures for accepting, filtering, and deciding cases all affect power relationships and have effects on the allocation of valued items within society as well. Interactions occur among politically relevant members of the system, both from inside (e.g., judges) and outside (e.g., interest groups, members of Congress, etc.) of the judiciary itself, and magistrates are "authorities" within the universe of relevant members because they are "occupants of systemic roles who exercise discretion and influence in making decisions for allocating such valued things as wealth, power, prestige, and ideals."[8] The federal judiciary's "regime rules" determine the way authorities such as judges and magistrates may make decisions and allocate values.[9]

Like other political systems, the federal judiciary is an open system which is "constantly subject to stresses or disturbances that emanate from the environment."[10] This environment includes the social, economic, and political forces and institutions which affect general society and the courts. The demands upon the federal judicial system emanating from relevant political actors and the environment are most often transmitted through litigation, but other methods, such as a presidential appointment of a new Supreme Court justice with an alternative judicial philosophy, and Congressional attempts to limit federal court jurisdiction, can be construed as demands upon the system. These demands, both litigation and the other forms, along with supports for the federal judiciary, constitute the inputs for this political system. The federal judiciary processes these inputs by filtering them out of the system (e.g., dismissal for lack of standing or procedural flaw) or by converting the demands into outputs in the form of judicial opinions, rules of procedure, or less formal communications from the courts. The courts' outputs stimulate responses and additional activity in the environment and return to the court as feedback, such as new litigation, new judicial appointments, or other forms of demands and influences upon the federal judicial political system.[11]

A key presupposition involved in any analysis using systems concepts is that systems, including political systems, seek to adapt and survive. For example, Donald Matthews' study of the U.S. Senate suggested that "folkways . . . are highly functional to the Senate social system. . . . Without these folkways, the Senate could hardly operate with its present organization and rules."[12] The prevalent presupposition that the federal courts constitute a political system and manifest this predominant system characteristic of adaptation and survival finds support in numerous studies, particularly those focusing on the Supreme Court. For example, Goldman and Jahnige point to the famous "Switch in Time that Saved Nine" by the Supreme Court during the 1930s in which the Court,[13] while under pressure from other political actors, most notably President Franklin Roosevelt with his "court-packing plan,"[14] responded to political pressures by joining mainstream political forces in upholding social welfare legislation and economic regulation.[15] Robert Dahl's famous article on the Supreme Court's place in the mainstream of national politics[16] and Chief Justice Warren's great efforts to generate a unanimous opinion in the controversial *Brown v. Board of Education* racial segregation case[17] both can be interpreted to support the notion that the federal judiciary manifests system-maintaining behavior. In all three examples, the judiciary adapted and responded to the environment in order to maintain its power, legitimacy, and political effectiveness.

David Easton has described relevant actors within political systems as obtaining information about the consequences of their behavior from the flow of feedback demands. In their effort to maintain the system, "[t]his puts the authorities in a position to take advantage of the information that has been fed back and to correct or adjust their behavior for the achievement of their goals."[18] Easton continues that "[w]ithout feedback and the capacity to respond to it, no system could survive for long, except by accident."[19] In the context of the judiciary, courts must be responsive to the composition and volume of cases filed in order to filter out or process these demands effectively within the constraints of their political authority and resource limitations. Easton's emphasis is related to manifest functions or intended consequences by relevant actors, but as mentioned previously, the analysis that follows will also incorporate Merton's ideas on latent functions and dysfunctional consequences.

MANIFEST FUNCTIONS

Resources for Efficiency

The most obvious manifest function of the magistrates in all of their roles is to assist the judiciary with its work. The federal courts as a political system must seek to prevent "demand input overload,"[20] namely more demands (i.e., cases, claims and influences) than the courts can effectively filter and process. The regime rules of the judiciary, most notably rules concerning jurisdiction, mootness, standing, and justiciability serve to limit the quantity and form of demands. Another way to process demands is to increase the resources of the system. As Chapter 2 described, because of the inadequacies of the U.S. commissioners and the partisan political difficulties attendant to the creation of new judgeships, the office of U.S. Magistrate was created with the explicit intention of providing more resources for district courts. The magistrates' contribution to the system's efficient processing of cases and hence survival as a system can be seen clearly in the 466,078 matters handled by U.S. magistrates in 1987.[21] If the courts became unable to process cases according to expectations, people who have looked to the courts to resolve disputes or advance policy positions might seek to advance their interests outside of the legal and governmental processes. As a result, societal conflicts might find their expression in activities that disrupt and destabilize society and political minorities might lose effective protection of their constitutional rights. By providing resources to the federal courts in the form of the myriad tasks that magistrates are authorized to perform, this lower tier of judicial officers contributes to the continued operation and survival of the federal judicial political system. In examining the development of the magistrate system, Steven Puro and Roger

Goldman found that magistrates make a "significant contribution to federal judicial operations."[22]

Gatekeeping and Filtering

Lawrence Baum has found that "[c]ourts possess and utilize a variety of what may be called gatekeeping powers, powers with which they help to determine which demands they will address and how fully they will consider the demands they do address."[23] Gatekeepers are "the major structural inhibitors of demand input."[24] According to Goldman and Jahnige, gatekeepers "are systemic authorities who, by enforcing regime rules and through discretionary action, control demand input."[25] Magistrates serve as gatekeepers for the federal judicial political system, especially in regard to particular categories of cases like prisoners' habeas corpus and civil rights filings. Magistrates in many districts, for example Districts B and D, have the primary responsibility for prisoners' cases. During 1987, magistrates handled 27,002 prisoner cases, including 2,589 federal habeas corpus, 7,184 state habeas corpus, and 17,229 civil rights petitions.[26] William Bennett Turner's study of prisoners' civil rights cases indicates that gatekeepers' enforcement of regime rules successfully minimizes the number of prisoners' cases that advance through the federal judiciary. As a result, only 4 percent of prisoners' cases ever go to trial and 68 percent are terminated even before the defendants file a responsive pleading.[27] This does not imply that magistrates are maliciously recommending dismissal of prisoners' cases—these claimants have not complied with procedural and jurisdictional requirements (regime rules), such as exhausting state remedies or asserting a proper federal constitutional issue—but it does indicate that, in functional terms, the subordinate judges are serving the important purpose of preventing prisoners' cases from absorbing system resources.

Magistrates serve this gatekeeping function for other kinds of cases as well by considering and presenting recommendations on dispositive motions for dismissal in civil cases. For example, motions for dismissal under Rule 12(b) of the Federal Rules of Civil Procedure[28] frequently go to the magistrates for substantive evaluation. A district judge often will then simply review the magistrate's work to determine if the case should be dismissed and therefore be precluded from advancing beyond the entry "gate" of the judicial system. The judge may officially be the final decision maker, but magistrates usually undertake the close review of the briefs and arguments and then make the important determinations. Magistrates' reports and recommendations may simply be a third brief considered by judges, along with the briefs from plaintiffs and defendants, in cases where the judges actually apply de novo review to issues. Very often, however, by being a neutral judicial officer and subordinate colleague to the judges, a magistrate can have more influence on the judge's ultimate determination than any litigant's brief and therefore influence the judge's final decision by framing and analyzing issues in a particular way. In addition, some judges say that they will defer to reasonable determinations by a magistrate even if the judge might have reached a contrary conclusion.

Magistrates' functions for reducing the demands upon the judicial system can be extended beyond gatekeeping and include the various activities by magistrates that filter cases out of the system and limit the courts' formal outputs. For example, one ideal role identified by this study for magistrates was that of Filtering Facilitator, because many magistrates are involved in settlement conferences and other activities that help to resolve cases prior to the final formal processes of trial and judgment. In addition, the nondispositive decisions by magistrates concerning civil discovery and reports and recommendations on dispositive pretrial matters can have filtering effects. These preliminary decisions in litigation can often, in effect, shape and determine eventual case outcomes. When a magistrate is asked to decide a nondispositive evidentiary motion, although the case will still be alive after the magistrate decides the motion issue, the net effect may be to preclude the admissibility of evidence considered essential for one side's case and therefore effectively force that side to agree to a settlement. In 1987, magistrates handled over 150,000 motions and conferences.[29] Although one would have to examine each matter individually to determine if and how the magistrates' actions contributed to filtering cases out of the judicial system, it was obvious in the observation studies that the magistrates' decisions and interactions with parties contributed substantially to many litigants' decisions to offer or agree to settlement terms. In his review of Seron's studies, Puro agreed that magistrates and their decisions appear to have definite effects upon case development and outcomes:

In the 1985 study, Seron finds that "attorneys do not challenge magistrates' work on dispositive or nondispositive motions as a matter of course" (p. 108). This finding suggests that magistrates' decisions are affirmative steps in defining the litigation process, and not, as some suggest, another layer for a hearing or a delaying tactic.[30]

It is clear that legislative and judicial actors intended for the magistrates to undertake gatekeeping and filtering activities, especially in regard to prisoners' cases. The three specified examples of appropriate duties for magistrates that were contained in the legislative history of the original 1968 act included assignment as special master in civil actions, conducting pretrial and discovery proceedings in civil and criminal cases, and reviewing prisoners' applications for post-conviction relief.[31] All of these examples involve the magistrates in gatekeeping, filtering, or contributing to those two activities on behalf of the judicial system. Furthermore, the testimony before Congress when the first magistrates legislation was under consideration made it clear that many judges wanted the magistrates to handle particular categories of tasks, especially the review of prisoners' cases. When the Supreme Court interpreted the statute to limit the magistrates' authority to conduct hearings in prisoners' cases in *Wingo v. Wedding*,[32] Congress revised the Magistrates Act in 1976 to ensure that magistrates could be completely involved in filtering and processing prisoners' cases. In an earlier era, when observers and participants were more naïve or less forthright about the political nature of courts and judicial processes, judicial actors might have claimed that they were enforcing intrinsically important procedural rules rather than filtering cases out of the judicial system. For example, in an analogous context, George Cole has pointed out that prior to the expansion of social science research on the courts in the 1960s, plea bargaining was "one of the best-kept secrets of criminal justice practitioners."[33] According to Cole, "[i]t was little discussed earlier because there were doubts about its constitutionality and because it did not seem appropriate to a system committed to the adversary process."[34] Although the clearly discernible legislative intention to have magistrates engage in gatekeeping and filtering may have been previously characterized as enforcement of jurisdictional and procedural rules, many magistrates and judges now forthrightly declare that the magistrates are intended to filter cases away from the courts and reduce the burden of litigation.

Magistrates as a Source of Already Socialized District Judges

One method for preserving and sustaining a system is to ensure that the components of the system are adequately maintained and replaced. In the federal judiciary, the judges are the central element responsible for processing inputs and producing outputs, as well as their own gatekeeping, filtering, and other system-maintaining activities. When new judges are appointed to the federal bench, their contributions to the functioning judicial system depend upon their ability to quickly understand and apply prevailing norms and procedures. Robert Carp and Russell Wheeler have documented how new district judges receive limited instruction and assistance in this socialization process.[35] Therefore, judges may take a significant period of time to become fully-operational, contributing components of the judicial system. During the observation study, new judges in two districts were observed undergoing the often slow process of learning how to be an effective district judge. One new judge had retained all case tasks so that he could learn everything possible about litigation in the federal courts. Although this knowledge and understanding will eventually be useful to him and the courts, he was foregoing all opportunities to utilize the magistrates for gatekeeping, filtering, and other case processing activities. The other new judge was observed consulting frequently with a senior judge about how to handle a variety of aspects of federal law because his previous professional experience had been devoted to work in the state courts. According to one experienced judge who was interviewed during this study, it takes five years for new district judges to completely learn their jobs and become effective. The federal judicial system could better utilize its resources for system maintenance, input processing, and output production if new judges were already socialized and knowledgeable about the workings of the federal courts.

Several observers have noted that the U.S. magistrates provide a ready-made pool of experienced judicial talent who possess knowledge and expertise concerning a wide range of federal court activities. Legal commentators have promoted the magistrate experience as providing a training ground for federal district judges.[36] By appointing district judges from the ranks of magistrates, the office of U.S. Magistrate could serve the function of maintaining the personnel resources of the judicial system. Furthermore, the judicial system would benefit by attracting better candidates for the magistrate position, because outstanding lawyers could realistically view the office as a steppingstone to a federal judgeship.[37] In this way, the American judicial system could enjoy some of the benefits presumably derived in other judicial systems, such as Germany, in which law students select a career path for becoming a judge and then undergo special training and professional experiences on a specific judicial career ladder.[38]

The passage and implementation of the 1979 legislation which explicitly authorized magistrates to preside over civil trials increased the potential value of magistrates as experienced federal trial judges. One commentator subsequently put forth a detailed proposal for reforming aspects of the magistrate statute in order to better utilize these experienced lower-tier federal judicial officers as district court judges.[39]

It is clear that judicial actors recognize the beneficial potential of drawing district judges from the ranks of the magistrates. Testimony by a magistrate, during Congressional hearings on the magistrates legislation, referred to ambitious magistrates "who view[] [their] role and function as perhaps a training ground for making [them] eligible for consideration for appointment to the U.S. district court or the U.S. court of appeals bench."[40] At least four magistrates in this study indicated that they would like to become district judges. Two of the four have actually applied for district judgeships in states which utilize open application procedures. In another district, a chief judge said during an interview that for several years he had been urging the state's U.S. senators to put forward the district's most experienced magistrate for the next district judge vacancy. Moreover, a number of magistrates have actually become Article III judges. Nineteen former full-time magistrates served as district judges in 1988. In addition, four former part-time magistrates were district judges and one former full-time magistrate was on a circuit court of appeals.[41]

The fact that a number of magistrates have been appointed to district judgeships and that the issue has been mentioned and discussed in law reviews and legislative hearings indicates that magistrates can serve a cognizable function as ready-made judges for the judicial system. The actual effect of this function is minimal, because of the small number of magistrates who have received appointments. The selection process for district judges, with all of its overtly partisan maneuvering, acts to limit the possible expansion of this manifest function of the magistrates. Normally, a lawyer must be politically active or at least politically well connected in order to receive senatorial or presidential support in the appointment process. Magistrates, during their terms as magistrates, are precluded from developing such political connections, because as judicial officers they cannot become involved in partisan political activity. At least one judge left the magistrate position specifically to become involved in partisan politics and thus facilitate appointment possibilities for a district judgeship. Without the opportunity to participate in partisan politics, magistrates must rely on their previously developed political reputations and social relationships with politicians, or else hope that they will be selected through an open application process. During the Carter administration, merit selection processes were implemented and utilized to select circuit judges and many senators adopted merit committee procedures for the nomination of district judges. However, not only have these merit selection opportunities been reduced or eliminated during the Reagan administration,[42] but the operation of the supposedly merit-based procedures often ultimately involved the same sorts of partisan political considerations that characterize the usual nomination process for federal judges.[43]

Although the effects of this manifest function can be expected to remain quite limited, it is worth noting that one state has four district judges who were formerly full-time magistrates. The Eastern District of Louisiana has three judges who were magistrates and the Middle District of Louisiana has one such judge. Because that state was not included in the study, it is unclear whether these judges had the necessary political connections prior to appointment as magistrates or if their service as magistrates impressed the relevant political actors involved in federal judicial appointments. Although the Louisiana case may simply reflect the application of political patronage, it illustrates the concept of appointing magistrates to judgeships. Other states might benefit by utilizing magisterial positions as a training ground for judgeships if they could develop and implement merit-based appointment procedures.

Magistrates as a Source of Innovation

The flexibility that Congress imbedded in the design of the magistrates legislation was intended to permit districts to develop their own creative plans for effectively utilizing the magistrates. According to the Administrative Office, the legislative history of the first statute made clear that "[t]he courts were expected to be innovative and experiment with the types of functions assigned to magistrates."[44] In the House report on the 1979 act, the legislative history of the subsequent statutory revisions "manifested Congressional intent to allow continued experimentation toward achieving the most effective use of magistrates in the Federal system."[45] The magistrates, as ambiguously defined statutory creations, were expected to provide the judicial system with a flexible resource that could lead to innovations in processing demand inputs.

The use of the term "innovations" need not imply that the magistrates are involved in the introduction of completely new procedures and approaches to case processing, although in some instances that is true. Magistrates can contribute to innovations in the form of more modest reforms and incremental changes in procedures that serve to enhance the judicial system's filtering and processing capabilities.

Although many districts utilized the magistrates in a manner similar to that of the familiar judges' law clerks, several districts within the study evidenced the magistrates' function for introducing innovations. Because of magistrates' significant responsibility for prisoners' cases, magistrates have developed experience and expertise which has enabled them to contribute to changes regarding this specific category of cases. One district within the study, along with other districts nationwide, was involved in instituting a new procedure regarding the payment of costs for prisoners' case filings. In the usual federal case, the claimant must pay a filing fee of $120. Prisoners, who must usually represent themselves, because they have no right to appointed counsel for a discretionary appeal or a civil case, normally file a petition to proceed in forma pauperis so that court fees will be waived. The new procedures in which the magistrates have been involved require the prisoners to make partial payments of court fees. The fees are calculated from the amount of money that the prisoners have in their personal accounts at the correctional institutions.[46] The procedure serves as an additional gatekeeping device to keep prisoners filings, many of which are frivolous, out of the federal courts unless the prisoners are actually willing to invest a portion of their personal funds into the pursuit of the case.

On a more national scale in the prison law area, a magistrate served on the national committee that recommended standardized procedures, involving heavy reliance upon magistrates, for processing prisoners' civil rights cases.[47]

In two districts within this study, magistrates have undertaken their own innovations to address prisoners' cases. In one district, a magistrate goes to the state's largest prison every Thursday afternoon to conduct hearings or meet in conferences with the prisoners and the state's attorneys. The magistrate's willingness and ability to go to the prison saves the state and federal governments the expense of transporting and guarding prisoners at the federal courthouse for proceedings on habeas corpus and civil rights cases. In addition, by actually going to the prison, the magistrate can often help resolve disputes simply by being present and seeing the prisoner-claimant face-to-face. Prisoners from the state's other institutions can be brought to the large prison for their cases and it is easier and less costly to move them within the state correctional system than to take them to the downtown federal courthouse. The magistrate gained the cooperation of the state Attorney General and prison officials, who remodeled a large room into a courtroom for the magistrate. The officials recognize that they benefit from the magistrate's presence not only because of the number of cases that are resolved more quickly, but also because their staff members, who are usually defendants and witnesses in each case, do not have to leave work each time they are involved in a court proceeding. They can simply be called to the prison courtroom when they are needed, rather than spending an entire day waiting at the federal courthouse for the case to proceed.

According to eight prisoners from two of the state's correctional institutions who spoke with the author about the magistrate, the magistrate has gained a reputation among the prison population for his fairness and neutrality. The magistrate's reputation contrasts sharply with the prisoners' view of the state ombudsman, state judges, and prison officials in charge of grievance procedures, all of whom are viewed as merely employees of the state who take orders from the prison administrators. Thus, when the magistrate decides or otherwise guides resolution of a dispute, the prisoners are less dissatisfied and therefore less likely to file additional actions over the same issue or reject the legitimacy of the judicial proceedings. Both of these results help to avoid demand inputs and preserve the judicial system.

In order to gain perspective on this magistrate's innovation, his effectiveness should be contrasted with prisoners' cases observed in other states and districts. In other districts, prison administrators were observed taking two days off work in order to drive up to 400 miles to be present at conferences and hearings held by magistrates—proceedings which often yielded no progress toward resolution of the cases. In other instances, either the prison officials or the states' attorneys would fail to appear or else someone would forget to bring the prisoner to the proceedings and therefore the parties who did appear wasted their time and taxpayers' money. In all instances in which prisoners were present in court, expenses were involved for transporting and guarding these litigants. The size of some judicial districts and the location of correctional institutions within states may make it difficult if not impossible for magistrates to hold hearings at all prisons, but for the district in this study, the magistrate's innovation accomplished very positive effects for the judicial system's ability to process prisoner cases.

The visits to the prison also allowed the magistrate to perform roles other than that of a judge. The magistrate was observed listening patiently to complaints by prisoners that did not raise constitutional issues. For example, one prisoner came to the hearing room to complain that he wanted to get married and because he had AIDS-related complex, which might some day become AIDS, he hoped to get his sentences made concurrent instead of consecutive. The magistrate listened to his concerns, explained that there were apparently no constitutional issues for the federal courts, and advised him to contact the governor's public service office. The magistrate's visits to the prison enabled him to listen to concerns and advise prisoners about which agencies outside of the judiciary could be approached to resolve the problem. Some might argue that the magistrate should not be performing the role of a prison ombudsman, but the magistrate clearly had more credibility than the correctional officials responsible for non-legal complaints. Furthermore, the magistrate was effectively screening complaints away from the federal judicial system.

Magistrates in other districts have contributed to innovations in various other areas of law and aspects of case processing. One magistrate worked with a judge to consolidate several hundred asbestos-related personal injury claims and then settled or heard the cases in groups to spare the judicial system the expense of hearing each case individually. Because the magistrate had developed a very positive reputation with the local bar, it was possible for him to initiate innovations that required litigants to consent to his authority for civil cases.

In another instance, a magistrate was distressed at the lack of quality in the opposing briefs for Social Security cases within the district. He learned that the briefs for the claimants often were written in a standard format by paralegals and the briefs for the U.S. Department of Health and Human Services were written in a standard format by law students working as legal interns. Unfortunately, the use of standard formats by inexperienced underlings frequently meant that the two briefs did not agree in identifying and addressing the relevant issues. The magistrate ordered counsel for both parties to appear for a short hearing in every case. By embarrassing the attorneys who were attempting to argue from the standardized briefs in the first few cases, the magistrate forced the regional Health and Human Services office to select more carefully which cases it genuinely wanted to pursue and forced attorneys for both sides to take care in evaluating and presenting cases.

Other magistrates have assisted their districts by voluntarily assuming responsibility for patent, antitrust, discrimination, and other kinds of cases in which they felt they would be more interested, available, and hence effective than the district judges.

Congress intended that the statutory language permit flexible utilization of magistrates and create opportunities for districts to experiment with new processes. Although the magistrates were, in a sense, the primary object of innovation when the legislation was passed and implemented, they have subsequently expanded their role and function for innovations by initiating procedures which have contributed to more effective gatekeeping, filtering, and processing within the judicial system.

LATENT FUNCTIONS

Merton described latent functions as those consequences for a specific unit, here the federal judicial system, which contribute to its adjustment and adaptation, but are unintended and unrecognized.[48] The following descriptions and analyses of the magistrates' latent functions emphasize the unintended consequences for the judicial system. Although some of these consequences are undoubtedly unrecognized, the concept of latent functions is used more broadly here to include unintended consequences which also might be recognized by some of the actors within the judicial system.

Magistrates and the Development of Case Law

As a country with its legal system based upon the English common law system, the United States depends upon the concept of *stare decisis*[49] and the development of case law to provide both growth and stability in law and legal practices. Judges must build upon the decisions of other judges in order to develop the putative legal rules and concomitant rationalizations that will ultimately serve to allocate values and preserve the judicial system. Because the magistrates effectively serve as judges, especially in civil cases for which they are wholly responsible when the litigants consent, the subordinate judges must see that new developments are adequately explained and disseminated in judicial opinions. Moreover, in other areas of the law, such as civil motions, prisoner cases, and Social Security law, because the magistrates have significant and, in some districts, sole responsibility for these tasks, if the magistrates do not develop the law, then the expansion and refinement of case law in the common law process has been altered from its usual path of development.

When magistrates gained specific authority to preside over complete civil cases, it was feared that the development of case law would suffer. Moreover, there was a concern that the development of case law in specific categories, such as prisoner and Social Security cases, would suffer because the subordinate judges did not have the ability to publish opinions. In the words of one commentator, "[o]ne danger is inhibiting collective judicial exploration of affected areas of law. Magistrate opinions possess very low visibility. Not only are they presently unpublished, but even if publicly available they would lack the precedential weight of decisions by district judges."[50]

During hearings concerning the 1979 revision of the magistrates statute, several witnesses urged that the subordinate judges' opinions be published in order to prevent the hindrance of legal development in areas in which magistrates hear a high proportion of cases.[51] According to magistrates, when they inquired about having their opinions in civil cases published in *Federal Supplement,* the standard reporter for federal cases at the trial level, district judges manifested their concerns about differentiating their status from that of magistrates by vigorously opposing and effectively blocking any effort to publish magistrates' opinions. A representative of West Publishing informed one magistrate that the actual reason was a lack of space in *Federal Supplement.* A number of magistrates expressed the view, however, that the status concerns and power of the district judges lie at the heart of West's decision not to publish magistrates' opinions.

Although magistrates do not have their opinions directly published in *Federal Supplement,* their opinions are reported as those of the district judge when, for example, a district judge adopts and endorses reports and recommendations by magistrates.[52] Magistrates' opinions on procedural matters are published directly in *Federal Rules Decisions* when the magistrates submit their rulings on procedural motions and West Publishing decides that the opinions merit publication.[53]

Although the absence of planned, comprehensive mechanisms for publication indicates that the case law development consequences of magistrates' opinions can be classified as latent, because the potential problems do not seem to be widely recognized by district judges, it is not clear whether these results are functional or dysfunctional. The determination of whether the magistrates have functional or dysfunctional consequences depends on whether the publication of opinions is viewed as enhancing or detracting from the judicial system's filtering, gatekeeping, and case-processing goals. Although case precedents are presumed to be functional in developing principles of law that can be applied to subsequent cases, publication of magistrates' decisions may alternatively be considered dysfunctional in contributing to the deluge of published opinions which confuse and obscure rather than contribute to the development of law. One magistrate expressed the view that the entire *Federal Supplement* could be burned or cease to exist, since only an occasional case truly involves a new issue. For the most part, this magistrate asserted, lawyers will rely upon the more authoritative appellate opinions in the *Federal Reporter* and only utilize *Federal Supplement* when no other authority is available.

In any case, regardless of how one perceives the value of published opinions, magistrates are influential judicial decision makers who are, for the most part, excluded from participation in the dissemination of judicial opinions and the formal development of case law.

Magistrates as Agent-Mediators of the
Judicial System

One judge characterized magistrates as the "front line judicial officers [who are] really dealing with the public." Magistrates handle the preliminary criminal proceedings including warrants, preliminary hearings, and arraignments, so that magistrates are the first judicial officers whom many people see when they come into contact with the federal judicial system. In many districts, the magistrates handle the preliminary civil proceedings and, in the course of preparing cases for trial, they have the most frequent and close contact with parties and their attorneys. Magistrates also handle the categories of cases in which claimants approach the federal courts without the benefit of professional representation. Prisoner, Social Security, and civil rights cases tend to be the instances most likely to involve a pro se litigant and magistrates have significant responsibilities for all of these categories of cases. Thus, in many districts, magistrates may indeed be characterized as the "front line" judicial officers who have personal contact with the public in the course of undertaking gatekeeping, filtering, and case-processing activities that determine which cases will eventually reach a district judge.

It would be reasonable to presume that because magistrates are federal judicial officers, they act as the impartial, authoritative umpires and facilitators who help to resolve and filter cases. In the course of undertaking judicial tasks, magistrates are also, however, accomplishing other system-maintaining functions by serving as agent-mediators between the judicial system and the citizenry making demands from the political environment. The closest analogy for analytical purposes would be from Abraham Blumberg's observation study of defense attorneys.[54] Blumberg concluded that defense attorneys, rather than fulfilling their ideal role of zealously representing the interests of the criminal defendant, actually serve as a mediating buffer between the defendant and the criminal justice system. The defense attorney educates the defendant about processes, tries to prepare the defendant for the eventual outcome—usually a guilty plea, and works with the prosecutor to orchestrate a smooth proceeding. The magistrates have analogous functions for the judicial system's operations, because they frequently educate, "cool out," or attempt to control litigants and attorneys.

Magistrates were observed in several districts educating attorneys and litigants about the practices in the federal court system. As educators, the magistrates are often placed in the position of justifying judicial procedures and facing whatever personal discomfort might follow from direct contact with confused, angry, and disappointed members of the public. For example, magistrates are placed in the position of educating attorneys about and enforcing judges' pretrial orders. Often judges may issue standard pretrial orders which contain page after page of detailed requirements about deadlines for discovery and the timing and format of motions. Because such orders do not take into consideration the individual circumstances of each case, the pretrial orders can create onerous burdens on litigants, especially a pro se litigant or an inexperienced attorney. Whether the pretrial orders are reasonable or not, the magistrates frequently must meet with attorneys at the preliminary conferences and hear complaints and questions about the complex requirements. The magistrates must educate, persuade, and threaten the attorneys into compliance with the court's orders. In observing pretrial conferences in one district for an extended period of time, it was quite apparent that none of the attorneys who met with the magistrate really understood and followed the judge's pretrial order. In conference after conference the magistrate had to explain the judge's orders and often pressure the attorneys into meeting together immediately to draft the required papers. In this district, the judge required the opposing attorneys to meet with each other to draft a document listing witnesses, exhibits, and objections prior to trial. This order clearly clashed with the procrastination ethic that apparently exists among lawyers and also collided with the adversarial attitudes of litigating attorneys by forcing them to work together. When this order created difficulties and petty spats between attorneys, it was the magistrate who had to sit through the heated and often childish arguments about whose fault it was that the judge's orders were not followed.

In two districts, magistrates presiding over a conference and a hearing involving pro se litigants in civil rights cases had to sit for long periods of time listening to plaintiffs shout their way through cathartic tirades about the injustices they had suffered and the difficulties for lay people trying to understand legal procedures. In one case, the magistrate allowed the plaintiff to continue an angry monologue for a solid hour and did not interject until the plaintiff began to repeat himself. Then the magistrate patiently explained how the federal judicial system works and how legal procedures may preclude recovery for a clear injustice if the case does not fit within specific jurisdictional requirements. In the other episode, the magistrate listened to the plaintiff for about thirty minutes before trying unsuccessfully to explain legal procedures to the plaintiff. In the second example, the magistrate attempted to persuade the plaintiff to find a lawyer to present the case. In trying to dissuade the pro se litigant, the magistrate tried to spare the judicial system any disruptive difficulties inherent in having demand inputs presented by individuals who lack knowledge about law and have not been socialized into the professional norms of the legal community that permeate the activities within the system. The magistrate also attempted to help the plaintiff by providing a realistic assessment that the case would fare poorly without an attorney. Thus the magistrates in both instances mediated between the judicial system and citizens attempting to press demands upon the system. In doing so, the magistrates helped to shape demands into an acceptable form for filtering or processing by the federal courts. They also provided the litigants with education and justifications on behalf of the judicial system.

Magistrates commonly face these situations in prisoners' cases as well. In cases involving prisoners, magistrates are especially likely to face openly hostile, vocal, and bitter pro se litigants. In many of these cases, magistrates are placed in the potentially uncomfortable position of defending and explaining regime rules which serve gatekeeping functions against individuals who perceive that they are intentionally excluded from the benefits of the judicial system.

As the first judicial officers to see criminal defendants, magistrates also receive the public criticism from and deliver socializing information to those individuals facing severe sanctions from the state. In a preliminary appearance of a defendant arrested for parole violations, the defendant loudly asserted that he should be sent to a particular jail because the federal holding facility was plagued with unconstitutional conditions. The magistrate listened to the defendant's strident criticisms of the federal criminal justice system, educated the defendant about rights and procedures, and then sent the defendant off to the usual federal jail. Afterwards, the magistrate admitted that he believed that the jail contained patently unconstitutional conditions of overcrowding and sanitation problems, but he was forced into a position of participating in and defending the system because of the practical and political difficulties involved in trying to find space for defendants in other jails.

Magistrates also serve an agent-mediator function when they are involved in settlement negotiations. While magistrates may conscientiously seek to encourage fair settlements, they also have an interest in the judicial system's goals of minimizing the number of cases that go to trial in order to save the system's resources. The fact that many magistrates view a successful case settlement as a "victory" indicates that they are not strictly impartial facilitators who are ambivalent about whether a litigant insists upon taking a case to trial.

In describing the magistrates as agent-mediators who shape the demand inputs for the system and justify the system's legitimacy to doubting members of the public, it should not be implied that magistrates are the only judicial actors serving these functions. Attorneys, court clerks, law clerks, and even judges serve these functions when they have contact with attorneys and members of the public. Magistrates have assumed significant responsibility for these system maintaining functions because judges have referred so many of the preliminary, public contact tasks to these subordinate judicial officers. As a result of the magistrates' direct contact with the public, the judicial system defends its legitimacy and limits the nature and quantity of demand inputs.

Magistrates as a Coercive Tool for the Judicial System

One might view the magistrates' activities as agent-mediators as constituting a kind of coercion or untoward pressure, especially in encouraging settlements. The observation study revealed, however, additional ways in which the magistrates function to give the judicial system an extra tool to pressure claimants into compliance with the system's interests. The great flexibility that was designed into the magistrate scheme has created opportunities for judges to utilize magistrates in a variety of ways—including methods that pressure attorneys. For example, Seron documented that lawyers feel pressured to consent to magistrate trials whenever judges raise the issue of consent.[55] Even if judges do not intend to pressure litigants in every case, the opportunity exists and is utilized to force litigants to shape their cases (i.e., consent to a magistrate trial) according to the interests of judicial system rather than the interests of the client. In one district, a judge told lawyers in a number of cases that they could either consent to the magistrate or else face trials with unknown visiting judges. The judge was making a factual observation rather than an overt threat. The effect of the magistrate's availability, however, was to lead the attorneys to opt for the judge's preferred course of action, which was to consent to the magistrate. In another district, a judge told lawyers in one case that they would be required to begin a trial the following morning if they did not consent to the magistrate's authority. The availability of the magistrate gave the judge extra leverage for removing an unwanted case from his docket.

One can argue that lawyers can always reject judges' suggestions about consent and that the consent option simply offers litigants an additional option that they otherwise would not have had. In reality, however, as continual actors in the judicial system, many lawyers will feel required to act upon their perceptions of the judge's desires rather than their strategic preferences for the client's best interests. The lawyers will be appearing before the judges in future cases and many attorneys will go to great lengths to avoid displeasing the judges.

Congress recognized this risk and attempted to design the statute to discourage any involvement by judges and magistrates in the consent decision. Contact between judicial officers and litigants has been inevitable in many districts because of the education function of the judicial officers and the often well-intentioned interests of judges in providing lawyers with alternatives. While there may be no adverse net effect to the interests of justice from appearing in front of a competent magistrate, the creation of magistrates with broad authority has undoubtedly given the judiciary an additional tool for shaping the demand inputs entering and moving through the system.

Dispersed Responsibility for Decision Making

Magistrates' authority to use discretion and engage in substantive decision making that significantly affects judicial outcomes serves to disperse decision making responsibility within the judicial system. When outcomes from the judicial system meet the outside political environment, the resulting feedback, in the form of demands or supports, will be shaped and focused according to perceptions about the system's processing characteristics. For example, when judges are accused of "letting criminals off lightly" in sentencing decisions, the feedback is often directed at the judges in the form of legislation requiring mandatory stiff sentences or otherwise limiting judges' discretion in sentencing. Criminal justice scholars have discussed how specific judicial outcomes (i.e., sentences for offenders) cause negative public reactions and subsequently rebound to affect the judicial system in the form of legislation.[56] The magistrates provide the judicial system with another actor to "take the heat" and become the focus for feedback from judicial outcomes. Thus, feedback demands which might threaten the maintenance of the judicial system are dispersed and directed at a number of actors, rather than developing a concentrated focus upon a single actor or the system itself.

Although magistrates' decisions in conferences, hearings, and trials generate or contribute to outcomes that affect the interests of parties and attorneys, the best example of magistrates' decisions which generate publicity and reactions are in bail and detention decisions. Magistrates bear the primary responsibility for determining the conditions of release for criminal defendants and, under the Bail Reform Act of 1984, magistrates possess the authority to hold people in jail pending trial. These decisions, more than any other, place the magistrates in the glare of the public spotlight, as evidenced by the many detention hearings in District C that attracted newspaper reporters and observers from the general public. Bail and detention decisions also place the magistrates in the most difficult position vis-à-vis the public, because of their respective differences in understanding the purposes of bail and detention. As judicial officers, magistrates are expected to consider relevant factors to determine what conditions of release will ensure that the defendant will appear in court and that the community will not be exposed to undue dangers posed by the presence of the accused. Public opinion, on the other hand, is not guided by the legal presumption of innocence and there is often a popular expectation that individuals accused of serious crimes should automatically be kept in jail. Fear of crime among the citizenry gives the public different interests and a different perspective than judicial officers.[57]

There have been a number of examples of adverse press attention and public reactions focused upon magistrates because of bail and detention decisions. For example, in one district the magistrate became the object of an extremely critical newspaper editorial and a lampooning editorial page political cartoon after an individual accused of federal gambling law violations disappeared after being released on bail. The U.S. Attorney had advocated detaining the defendant until trial, but the magistrate determined that $600,000 was a sufficient sum to insure that the defendant would appear in court. The magistrate was proven wrong. The magistrates, as a little understood and relatively invisible tier of judicial officers, provide a good dispersal mechanism for the judicial system. In this case, the newspaper appeared to lack an understanding of the magistrate's status as a judicial officer because the editorial continually referred to him as "*Mr.* [X]." The adverse public reaction and negative feedback is not directed at particular structures and processes of the judicial system, but rather at an individual judicial actor, the magistrate, who is not well-known or understood. Thus, the presence of the extra tier of judicial officers making controversial decisions may serve to preserve the legitimacy of the district judges while diluting and dispersing attacks upon the judicial system.

A similar example occurred at a national level, but in this instance, illustrating either the fickle winds of press attention or a lack of understanding of the difficulties underlying bail and detention decisions, the national press castigated a magistrate for detaining an individual and not setting bail. This example arose when the Supreme Court issued a decision recognizing the constitutionality of the Bail Reform Act of 1984.[58]

> [The magistrate] sent . . . a janitor with eight kids, to jail until the case could go to trial. But those that the gods would humble, they first make magistrates. A federal jury took just 25 minutes to find

that [the defendant], who had exculpatory alibis, was not guilty. By then this innocent man had spent 71 days in jail.[59]

As the public contact persons and "front line" judicial officers in criminal proceedings, magistrates attract the negative feedback that might otherwise adversely affect the judicial system itself.

The concept of maintaining a system by dispersing decision-making responsibilities has been developed and applied in regard to various state and federal judicial systems. For example, the involvement of prosecutors and defense attorneys in plea bargaining serves to spread responsibility for convictions and sentencing decisions away from the trial judge. The involvement of juries in making determinations in both civil and criminal cases serves to spread responsibility for decisions from the judicial system to the citizenry itself. In the federal judicial system, as the aforementioned examples illustrate, the magistrates serve this same function, common to other judicial contexts, of spreading decision-making responsibility and dispersing the foci of adverse feedback from the political environment.

The Dysfunction of Magistrates as a Judicial Interest Group

As new judicial officers who have been forced to struggle for recognition, status, and authority, the magistrates have built group solidarity within districts and nationally, because of common concerns and interests. Within districts such as District A, magistrates' common status problems and concerns about limited authority have led them to meet and act collectively to encourage the judges to grant them more authority and recognition. At the national level, the status disputes and basic financial concerns about keeping up with the district judges and bankruptcy judges in salary and pension benefits have led the National Council of Magistrates to secure the services of a lobbyist and spend $30,000 in 1986 alone trying to influence Congress on the issues of pay and benefits. In addition, the magistrates work strategically to influence policy determinations within the Judicial Conference and the Administrative Office. Although not all magistrates agree that judicial officers should act as an interest group and many magistrates do not participate in the national organization, the magistrates generally manifest many characteristics of any occupational interest group that undertakes planned, political actions on behalf of the group's collective interests.

The magistrates' formation of an active interest group is understandable in terms of their shared interests and collective disappointment in regard to expectations about status, authority, and material benefits. The activities of such a group, however, can generate problems within the judicial system. Interest group thinking and behavior can exacerbate conflicts with the district judges and thereby reduce cooperation and communication within federal courthouses. It is possible that the interest group has functional benefits for the judicial system if the magistrates can obtain additional resources for the system. But in an era of limited resources, it seems just as likely that the interest group behavior also has dysfunctional consequences by forcing segments of the judiciary to compete against each other for the limited pool of resources to be allocated to the Third Branch by Congress.

The existence of the magistrates' interest group activities is also understandable in terms of customary political behavior within the American political system. Although their activities have not had clearly identifiable adverse effects for the system, except for further alienating some resentful district judges, the existence of the magistrates as an interest group creates the potential for dysfunctional consequences within a system that needs shared goals and cooperation among internal authoritative actors for effective input processing and system maintenance.

MAGISTRATES AND THEIR FUNCTIONS

The discussion of magistrates and their functional consequences for the federal judicial system provides a conceptual context in which to understand the importance of the magistrates as actors within American government and politics. The magistrates' functions are comparable to those of specific judicial actors within the federal and state judicial systems. For example, prosecutors are involved in filtering processes and defense attorneys act as agent-mediators within criminal justice systems. The range of magistrates' tasks and authority, however, enables these subordinate judicial actors to have a wide variety of functional consequences, both manifest and latent, upon the federal judicial system. One focus of some functional analyses is to determine whether particular actors or phenomena are essential to or merely contribute to the maintenance of a particular system. It seems clear that if magistrates were abolished tomorrow, after a period of adjustment and turmoil, the federal courts could increase the number of district judges, law clerks, and other actors within the system in order to replace most the magistrates' functions. Because of the magistrates' broad array of activities, it seems unlikely that the magistrates' unique roles as subordinate judicial officers, which permit functions as authoritative decision makers, innovators, and agent-mediators, could be precisely replicated. Thus, as one would expect, without the magistrates, the federal judicial system would continue to exist, but in an altered form which would lack the previous flexibility for case-processing resources and system-maintaining mechanisms.

NOTES

1. Robert K. Merton, *Social Theory and Social Structure*, (New York: The Free Press, 1968).
2. Ibid., 114.
3. Ibid., 117.
4. Ibid., 86.
5. Ibid., 75.
6. Sheldon Goldman and Thomas P. Jahnige, *The Federal Courts as a Political System*, 3d ed. (New York: Harper & Row, 1985), 1–13.
7. Ibid., 3.
8. Ibid., 2.
9. Ibid.
10. Ibid.
11. Ibid., 3–6.
12. Donald Matthews, *U.S. Senators and Their World* (New York: Vintage Books, 1960), 116.
13. The "Switch" is associated with the Supreme Court's decision upholding state minimum wage laws in *West Coast Hotel Co. v. Parrish*, 300 U.S. 379 (1937) after rejecting such regulations for several decades.
14. Roosevelt, unhappy with the Supreme Court for striking his New Deal program legislation, proposed that the president be permitted to appoint additional members of the Court for each current member over the age of seventy. The plan would have allowed Roosevelt to appoint six new members to the Court. Robert G. McCloskey, *The American Supreme Court* (Chicago: University of Chicago Press, 1960), 169–179.
15. Goldman and Jahnige, *The Federal Courts*, 6–7.
16. Robert A. Dahl, "Decision-Making in a Democracy: The Supreme Court as a National Policy-Maker," *Journal of Public Law* 6 (1957): 279–295.
17. Richard Kluger, *Simple Justice* (New York: Vintage Books, 1975), 693–699.
18. David Easton, *A Systems Analysis of Political Life* (New York: John Wiley, 1965), 32.
19. Ibid.
20. Goldman and Jahnige, *The Federal Courts*, 91.
21. Administrative Office of the U.S. Courts, *Annual Report of the Director of the Administrative Office of the United States Courts* (Washington, D.C.: U.S. Government Printing Office, 1987), 37.

22. Steven Puro and Roger Goldman, "U.S. Magistrates: Changing Dimensions of First-Echelon Federal Judicial Officers," in *The Politics of Judicial Reform*, ed. Philip L. DuBois (Lexington, MA: Lexington Books, 1982), 145.

23. Lawrence Baum, "The Judicial Gatekeeping Function: A General Analysis," in *American Court Systems: Readings in Judicial Process and Behavior*, ed. Sheldon Goldman and Austin Sarat, 2d ed. (New York: Longman, 1989), 153.

24. Goldman and Jahnige, *The Federal Courts*, 94.

25. Ibid.

26. Administrative Office, *Annual Report*, 34.

27. William Bennett Turner, "When Prisoners Sue: A Study of Prisoner Section 1983 Suits in the Federal Courts," *Harvard Law Review* 92 (1979): 618.

28. Under Rule 12(b), defendants may make motions for dismissal by claiming: (1) lack of jurisdiction over subject matter; (2) lack of jurisdiction over the person; (3) improper venue; (4) insufficiency of process; (5) insufficiency of service of process; (6) failure to state a claim upon which relief can be granted; or (7) failure to join a party.

29. Administrative Office, *Annual Report*, 34.

30. Steven Puro, "Two Studies of Federal Magistrates," *The Justice System Journal* 11 (1986): 104.

31. U.S. Congress, House Report No. 1629, Federal Magistrates Act, *U.S. Code Congressional and Administrative News*, 1968, 4262.

32. 418 U.S. 461 (1974).

33. George F. Cole, *The American System of Criminal Justice*, 4th ed. (Monterey, CA: Brooks/Cole, 1986), 363.

34. Ibid.

35. Robert Carp and Russell Wheeler, "Sink or Swim: The Socialization of a Federal District Judge," *Journal of Public Law* 21 (1972): 359–393.

36. Linda J. Silberman, "Masters and Magistrates Part II: The American Analogue," *New York University Law Review* 50 (1975): 1363, 1363 n. 380.

37. Ibid., 1371.

38. Goldman has noted that we would not have a wholesale adoption of procedures for training professional judges, because "[a] career, civil service-type judiciary such as that found in Europe would be contrary to our political tradition and would be specially inapposite at a point when there is widespread recognition of the policymaking role of our courts." Sheldon Goldman, "Judicial Selection and the Qualities that Make a 'Good' Judge," *The Annals of the American Academy of Political and Social Science* 462 (1982): 123.

39. Robert P. Davidow, "Beyond Merit Selection: Judicial Careers Through Merit Promotion," *Texas Tech Law Review* 12 (1981): 886–907.

40. Statement of the Hon. Arthur Burnett, U.S. Magistrate, District of the District of Columbia, U.S. Congress, Senate Committee on the Judiciary, *Federal Magistrates Act: Hearings Before Subcommittee on Improvements in Judicial Machinery*, 95th Cong., 1st Sess., 1977, 223.

41. Letter from Glen K. Palman, Magistrates Division of the Administrative Office of the U.S. Courts, to the author (Dec. 10, 1986).

42. W. Gary Fowler, "Judicial Selection under Reagan and Carter: a Comparison of their Initial Recommendation Procedures," *Judicature* 67 (1984): 265–283.

43. E. M. Gunderson, "'Merit Selection': The Report and Appraisal of a Participant Observer," *Pacific Law Journal* 10 (1979): 683–706.

44. Administrative Office of the U.S. Courts, *The Federal Magistrates System: Report to the Congress by the Judicial Conference of the United States*, (Washington, D.C.: Government Printing Office, 1981), 3, citing U.S. Congress, Senate Report No. 371, 90th Cong., 1st Sess. (1967), 26–27.

45. U.S. Congress, House Report No. 1364, Magistrates Act of 1978, 95th Cong., 2d Sess. (1978), 6.

46. Thomas E. Willging, *Partial Payment of Filing Fees in Prisoner In Forma Pauperis Cases in the Federal Courts: A Preliminary Report* (Washington, D.C.: Federal Judicial Center, 1984).

47. *Recommended Procedures for Handling Prisoner Civil Rights Cases in the Federal Courts* (Washington, D.C.: Federal Judicial Center, 1980).

48. Merton, *Social Theory and Social Structure*, 117.

49. *Black's Law Dictionary* defines *stare decisis* as "to abide by, or adhere to, decided cases." *Black's Law Dictionary*, 5th ed. (St. Paul, MN: West Publishing, 1971), 1261.

50. Note, "Article III Constraints and the Expanding Civil Jurisdiction of Federal Magistrates: A Dissenting View," *Yale Law Journal* 88 (1979): 1053.

51. Ibid., 1053 n.170.

52. For example, Alexander v. Yale University, 459 F.Supp 1 (D.Conn. 1978).

53. For example, Williams v. Keenan, 106 F.R.D. 565 (D. Mass. 1985).

54. Abraham S. Blumberg, "The Practice of Law as a Confidence Game: Organizational Cooptation of a Profession," *Law and Society Review* 1 (1967): 15–39.

55. Carroll Seron, *The Roles of Magistrates: Nine Case Studies* (Washington, D.C.: Federal Judicial Center, 1985), 61–62.

56. Arthur Rosett and Donald Cressey, *Justice By Consent* (Philadelphia: Lippincott, 1976), 157.

57. Cole, *The American System of Criminal Justice*, 19–22.

58. United States v. Salerno and Cafaro, 107 S.Ct. 2095 (1987).

59. "First Jail, Then a Trial," *Newsweek*, 8 June 1987, p. 19.

10

Conclusion

The creation of a new, subordinate judicial office within the courts represents a particular kind of reform intended both to increase judicial resources and to insure the flexible development and utilization of those resources. In the case of the U.S. magistrates, concerns about the constitutionality of implementing an authoritative judicial office dictated that Congress grant to the Article III based district judges the formal power to define precisely the tasks and roles of the newly created subordinate judges. Although the district judges possess the formal authority to define the magistrates' roles, the ambiguous guidance from statutory sources and the judges' lack of experience with authoritative judicial subordinates created opportunities for other factors, such as magistrates' expectations and established practices within districts, to influence the development of the subordinates' roles within each courthouse.

Some magistrates may be locked into specific roles because their supervising judges have firm opinions about how subordinate judicial officers ought to be utilized. As the example of District A illustrates, however, magistrates' roles can change, sometimes in ways that directly contradict the district judges' stated intentions, if there are shifts in the composition or quantity of case-processing demands upon the district court. Thus, the broad authority possessed by the magistrates makes them especially flexible resources whose responsibilities can adjust with sensitivity to changing judicial needs, regardless of whether district court officials have formally or rationally planned changes in the subordinates' roles. This adaptive quality of these broadly authoritative, subordinate judges creates the possibility that federal courts can respond flexibly to a variety of pressures without the infusion of resources necessary when the judiciary is composed only of actors (e.g., judges and law clerks) whose responsibilities and authority, although somewhat flexible, are more precisely defined. For example, expectations about the proper judicial behavior and demeanor for district judges, possessed by both the incumbents and the public, may limit or at least hinder judges' ability to facilitate case processing through informal mechanisms or other nontraditional means. By contrast, because the precise definition of the magistrates' roles is not mandated by statute, these subordinate judges can more easily assume independent case-processing responsibilities, assist the district judges, or initiate innovations in response to the courts' needs without clashing with firmly settled expectations. These benefits of flexibility are accompanied, however, by risks that the same adaptive qualities of these subordinate judicial officers will lead to roles and activities which slip beyond the control of the court or otherwise have detrimental consequences for the judiciary's intended purposes.

As the discussion of the functional consequences for magistrates illustrated, there are particular risks from the introduction of a subordinate judicial officer that require continued scrutiny. Of particular importance is the risk of bureaucratization in which a hierarchy of judicial officers, making decisions beyond public scrutiny, changes the character of decision making from the expected ideal of individually considered judgments in each case to routinized, administrative processing of entire categories of cases. In addition, the risk from magistrates' latent functional consequence of coercing attorneys and litigants to consent to have cases heard by subordinate judicial officers, rather than constitutionally based district judges, contradicts congressional intent to protect litigants from undue pressure.

MAGISTRATES AND SPECIFIC CATEGORIES OF LITIGANTS

As Seron documented with her Specialist characterization for one model magistrates' role, magistrates are often the judicial officers exclusively responsible for reviewing specific categories of cases, primarily prisoner and Social Security cases. There has long been a fear that specialization in the judiciary carries unwarranted risks. Members of Congress feared that the implementation of a lower tier of judicial officers, namely the magistrates, would "create a dual system of justice" in which poor litigants would be deprived of their opportunities to have access to Article III judges.[1] Moreover, it was feared that the routine nature of repetitive decision making in categories of cases will lead to less careful judgments. As one commentator has written, "[d]iligent and conscientious review of magistrates' reports . . . must be emphasized, however, in order to avoid the danger that judges will simply 'rubber stamp' the recommendations, especially since these cases tend to be rather routine."[2]

Alternatively, some have urged specialization as a means to more effective case processing. Magistrates, as experts on prison and Social Security law, for example, can presumably give faster, more accurate review to cases than judges or nonspecialist magistrates who must start anew with each case. In a study of prisoners' habeas corpus cases, magistrates received a vote of confidence for fairness and effectiveness:

> And the use of magistrates has some clear advantages. In many instances, habeas corpus applications appear to receive fuller and more careful consideration than they did before the magistrates came into office. District judges, in turn, are relieved of a large share of a burden which they tend to regard as weary, stale, flat, and unprofitable, and are able to focus on those few cases that raise important and difficult questions.[3]

The question remains, however, whether specialization and the wholesale delegation of categories of cases have adverse or beneficial consequences for the application of appropriate review to claimants' petitions.

The evidence gathered through interviews and observations in this study's courthouses led to mixed conclusions. Overall, the evidence indicated that specialization has potentially harmful effects that must be monitored through special recognition and attention by the federal judicial officers.

Several magistrates had a special interest in the law governing either Social Security or prisoners' cases, and therefore indicated that they gave consistently detailed attention to the cases because of their own personal interest. Several other magistrates placed a heavy emphasis upon Social Security cases because such claims are so important to the arguably disabled claimants, who need money to support themselves and their families. One magistrate asserted that each Social Security case is more important than any corporate litigation involving millions of dollars, because corporations write off some losses, but disabled people may need the few hundred dollars each month from Social Security in order to survive.

These magistrates who indicated that they gave particular attention to each Social Security or prisoner case were in the minority. The general impression conveyed by most magistrates was that Social Security and prisoner cases are routine and burdensome, but unavoidable. When one reads prisoners' files, in particular, it is hard not to see that the assertions are often exaggerated, frequently not based upon appropriate constitutional claims, and usually in violation of some jurisdictional requirement such as exhausting remedies for habeas corpus or suing the appropriate defendant in civil rights cases. The usual response to continuing caseloads of routine, unsuccessful complaints seems to be a degree of cynicism about all cases in that category. Magistrates and their law clerks (and some judges) in different districts said such things as: "no one has any sympathy for prisoners"; "virtually all Social Security appeals are from people who should never qualify"; "I can usually judge a Social Security case just by looking to see which lawyer is representing the claimant"; "I can dispose of a dozen Social Security cases at home in an evening"; and "prisoners will claim anything to try to get released or win some money." As a purely empirical matter, all of these statements may be perfectly true. There are, however, inevitably some cases that present legitimate claims. Because so many cases are presented by inexperienced and uneducated pro se litigants, there is a continuing need for careful scrutiny to find the "grain" of meritorious cases amid the abundant "chaff." The risk from routinization of case categories is that the attitudes and experiences embodied in the statements mentioned above may have begun to cloud judgments, even in a slight way, so that claims may not receive the review that they deserve.

Prisoners' cases provide a very good example. William Turner's study of prisoners' civil rights cases documented the high dismissal rates for such suits. Sixty-eight percent of the suits were dismissed before the defendant even filed a responsive pleading and only 4 percent eventually went to trial.[4] Turner asserts that prisoners' cases often may be terminated by judicial officials even when they raise legitimate issues. According to Turner, "[i]t is possible that dismissal was justified in all the cases summarily disposed of. Yet there is no assurance that meritorious cases were sorted out from frivolous ones. There are many indications that cases were bureaucratically processed rather than adjudicated."[5] Roger Hanson studied prisoners' cases and took issue with Turner's assertions about the reasons that so many cases were dismissed. According to Hanson, "[the] data do not indicate that these decisions are made hastily or without a careful consideration of the facts and the law."[6]

These examples of careful empirical research present contradictory conclusions about the review of prisoners' cases, and the observations and interviews for this study provide no clear evidence supporting either side. However, just as one district judge warned the author that "I never let law clerks handle prisoners' cases for too long because they become cynical about them," several clues observed within the courthouses indicated that district courts must be cautious about assigning categories of cases exclusively to magistrates. In regard to prisoners' cases, there was a perceptible risk that magistrates and their law clerks, who are accustomed to dismissing such cases, approach the case files by first asking, "How can I dismiss this case?" rather than asking, "Does this case have any merit?" The magistrates have an interest in seeing prisoners' cases dismissed, not simply for their functional role as gatekeepers and filterers, but in a personal sense, because it permits them to avoid holding conferences and hearings with a class of potentially difficult and hostile litigants. This interest was not detectably manifested in any cases observed, because the magistrates always had legal grounds for dismissal, but the existence of institutional self-interest and concomitant negative attitudes about prisoners' cases must be recognized and held in check. Because prisoners are generally inexperienced and lacking legal resources as pro se litigants, it is especially difficult for them to contest effectively a magistrate's report and recommendations within the required ten-day period.

In regard to Social Security cases, similar concerns exist about complete and adequate reviews. For example, one magistrate was reported to have a checklist prepared that enabled law clerks to review Social Security cases without even reading the files completely. By contrast, Social Security claimants in another district enjoy special benefits from a magistrate's review, because in all decisions favoring claimants, the magistrate invites the claimants to consent to the subordinate judge's authority so that the favorable ruling will be a final decision. Social Security cases are generally difficult to monitor because of the low level of review that permits magistrates to uphold decisions by the administrative law judges if the decisions are supported by any evidence. Some magistrates have said that any Social Security decision can be upheld, because there is nearly always medical evidence supporting both parties upon which a decision could be based either way. Magistrates have the opportunity and therefore the risk of routinely approving decisions by administrative law judges. It is possible that magistrates, as well as judges, need to go through a continual self-examination process to ensure that their practices and procedures are designed to review each case completely. Magistrates must undertake assertive, careful reviews that are, to some degree, skeptical of the administrative law judges' determinations.

While the harms of specialization have not been systematically documented, observations and interviews in the district courts reveal that indicators of risk that may have adverse effects upon categories of litigants, such as prisoners and Social Security claimants, are clearly present. The fact that these litigants are generally less affluent than other litigants in the federal courts seems to be less important in their referral to the magistrates than the fact that their cases are more numerous and routine than other kinds of cases. The net effect is to make the magistrates the primary judges for two specific classes of claimants. The fact that the litigants are not given attention by Article III judges probably does not inherently affect their claims adversely, since the magistrates may provide as good or better review. The biggest difficulty is the continuing risk that high caseloads, cynical attitudes, and routinization of reviews may affect the results in some cases. Similar risks would exist if judges handled all cases themselves, except that judges would review the routine cases amid a varied menu of other cases. Thus, there can be particular risks of routinization for magistrates who are unable to control whether they are granted a diverse, interesting caseload. Several judges said that they always give their districts' magistrates an interesting variety of tasks so that the subordinate judges do not become bored, stultified, and ineffective from only working on prisoner and Social Security cases. Many judges, however, do not share that concern, so there is a continuing risk that reviews of certain categories of cases will be improperly routine and superficial.

MAGISTRATES' AUTHORITY OVER CONSENT TRIALS

The propriety of magistrates' consent authority has been the subject of detailed discussion and debate in Congress,[7] in the courts,[8] and in the law reviews.[9] This study cannot add anything to the legal arguments which have been litigated and decided, but a primary support relied upon to uphold the constitutionality of magistrates' authority is consent of the litigants—the voluntariness of which can be discussed as an empirical matter.

Voluntary consent was cited by Congress as one of the "three pillars" sustaining the constitutionality of magistrates' consent trial authority. The same argument was relied upon in the leading cases sustaining magistrates' authority, including *Pacemaker*[10] and *Wharton-Thomas*.[11] Congresswoman Elizabeth Holtzman had argued strenuously against magistrates' consent authority, because litigants would be coerced into consenting.[12] Representative Holtzman was correct in predicting that litigants would sometimes be improperly pressured to consent, but, according to observations in this study, she probably missed the mark in predicting that poor litigants in particular would be affected.

Although Seron's findings have been misinterpreted by some scholars to mean that "[parties show] little reluctance to allow[] a magistrate to handle [civil] case[s],"[13] there is no clear evidence about litigants' and lawyers' views on consenting to magistrates for trials. Seron did find clear evidence that consents in some districts are not entirely voluntary as required and assumed by the members of Con-

gress and judges who have supported the constitutionality of magistrates' consent trials:

> There was a clear consensus among [the California lawyers]
> interviewed that when a judge raises the question of consent to a
> magistrate—for whatever reason—lawyers feel that they have
> little choice but to go along with the suggestion. Attorneys con-
> sistently reported feeling some pressure to consent, particularly
> in a "smaller" case; when interviewees were asked to describe the
> reasons for consent, the overriding one given was that the judge
> had suggested it.[14]

In the observations and interviews conducted for this study, several
incidents were discovered which corroborated the view that judges
sometimes pressure litigants into consenting to the magistrates' authority. In one previously cited instance, a judge declared that a trial
would begin the following morning unless the litigants consented to
have the trial in front of a magistrate. Another judge stated in an
interview that he will not grant continuances in cases, but he tells
lawyers that they may consent and seek permission for a delay from
the magistrate. Magistrates in several districts stated that they knew
judges "encouraged" lawyers to consent. Because of the lawyers'
desire to avoid offending the district judges, this "encouragement"
worked as pressure on the lawyers to permit these cases to be heard
before subordinate judges.

Although these practices are apparently widespread, it did not
appear that most judges normally pressure litigants. Many judges are
so scrupulous about avoiding any mention of the consent option, that
the litigants in their districts do not seem to know that they have the
opportunity to consent to the magistrate. In other districts, it was
apparent that consents were not taking place even though the judges
were trying to educate the bar about the option. The lawyers in these
districts viewed consent as merely an option, and utilized magistrate-
supervised trials only when it fit with their strategies for a particular
case. Unfortunately, it is apparent that lawyers in some other districts
perceive the magistrate trial as required rather than optional.

During conferences and hearings, several magistrates told litigants
about their option of consenting. In all instances in front of the observer, the magistrates were very careful to indicate that they had no
interest in whether the litigants consented or not. Most magistrates
seemed sufficiently busy with a variety of tasks that they had no
interest in intentionally generating additional time-consuming work
for themselves by trying to encourage consents. The situation might
be different, however, if a magistrate finally gained an opportunity to

conduct trials after a long period of desiring such an opportunity. Such feelings exist among some magistrates in Districts A and B. If and when the opportunities for trials develop in those districts, the magistrates will need to be careful not to succumb to their personal desires to encourage consent trials.

Although the extent of improper pressures is not known, their existence alone is cause for concern. Because many judges have an interest in seeing trials diverted to the magistrates, it is apparent that the assumptions about the voluntariness of consents made by Congress and the courts were inaccurate. It is difficult to foresee how the situation can be corrected, other than through exhorting and reminding the judicial officers to avoid discussing the subject of consent with attorneys. It seems unlikely that any attorney would really wish to challenge the voluntariness of his or her own consent decision, unless a judge's coercive actions were obviously outrageous. Lawyers are not likely to admit publicly that they were weak in the face of improper conduct. They also would think twice about directly challenging the ethical conduct of a judge sitting in a court that provides a basis for their legal practice and livelihood. In the examples discovered during the course of this study, the judges' motivations were apparent and their actions clearly influenced the litigant, yet these particular actions were essentially immune from external scrutiny because scheduling trial dates and refusing continuances are part of a judge's prerogatives. Thus, the coercive actions were cloaked in the impenetrable discretionary authority of judges. The issue of consent remains a matter of concern that demands continued monitoring, because it is so important to the legitimacy of magistrates' authority. Unless magistrates' consent authority were to be abolished, which is highly unlikely since magistrates use it to perform important functions for the judicial system, it appears that the voluntariness underlying consents can only be policed from inside the judicial system.

MAGISTRATES AND OTHER BRANCHES OF GOVERNMENT

As judicial officers, magistrates are often placed in the position of undertaking judicial review of the actions of other branches of government. The magistrates' decisions can have implications for both separation of powers and federalism because the reviews may cover either federal or state government entities.

Serious concerns have been expressed by members of Congress, federal judges, and legal scholars that magistrates should not or would not exercise appropriate judicial action in regard to states and other federal branches of government. It has been argued that placing the authority to review acts of other branches in the hands of the magistrates will "greatly disturb" the "delicate balance [of separation of powers] upon which the decision in *Marbury*[15] so tenuously rests."[16] Furthermore, there is a potential barrier to independent action by the magistrates, because "a particular decision, though legally correct, might lead Congress to lower the pay of all magistrates."[17] In addition, because of their subordinate position, magistrates might evince a general reluctance to cause conflicts between governmental branches. As one observer noted:

whatever resentment may be felt in the state courts at having the [state] Supreme Judicial Court overturned by a district judge must be heightened if the overturning is, in substance, at the hands of a magistrate—an attitude to which magistrates are probably sensitive and which is likely to make them somewhat reluctant to grant relief to a [prisoner] even when circumstances require.[18]

During the course of the study, none of these problems surfaced in any manner that adversely affected the magistrates' actions. Magistrates regularly make determinations that affect other governmental institutions, but most of these decisions are in the form of reports and recommendations that receive a district judge's approval and are issued in the district judge's name—thus obviating the concerns outlined above. Magistrates can make decisions affecting other branches and state governments in consent cases, but the parties, including the government representatives, have voluntarily consented and assumed the risks of adverse decisions emanating from magistrates. In some districts, state governments refuse to consent to magistrates' authority as a matter of policy and in other districts such decisions depend upon the strategies of the state attorneys general.

Magistrates indicated no fears about salaries being reduced or tenure being affected because of court decisions adversely affecting the interests of the legislative and executive branches. Magistrates view themselves as judicial officers who are obligated to make whatever difficult decisions happen to come before them. Furthermore, they are confident that any attack on them would be construed by the judges as an attack on the judiciary. Thus, even in districts in which magistrates and judges disagree about the magistrates' roles, the judges' own interests dictate that they defend the magistrate system from external attack. It is possible, however, that judges intervene to prevent magistrates from making controversial decisions. Such intervention may either involve reversing the magistrate's decision or issuing the decision as an order from the Article III judge. Magistrates were observed exhibiting sensitivity to possible conflicts with other branches of government. Presumably this sensitivity was motivated by a desire to avoid the problem of an unknown judicial actor, whose authority and legitimacy are not clear to the public and state governments, making visible, controversial policy decisions. Thus, one magistrate was observed asking litigants not to consent in a case against a correctional institution, because the potential for a large-scale judicial intervention, as one magistrate put it, "really requires that a district judge's signature be on all orders."

Magistrates frequently reverse administrative determinations from the executive branch in Social Security cases. It is viewed as "common knowledge" to some magistrates that administrative law judges are under extreme pressure to limit the number of decisions approving disability claims. Thus, administrative law judges are reportedly limited to approving only ten percent of claims, no matter what the merits of the cases before them. Some magistrates with this perception of the administrative law judges view themselves as having been "passed the buck" to make the actual determination about benefits and undo the damage caused by the internal restrictions within the Department of Health and Human Services. In this instance, magistrates not only do not mind making decisions against the executive, they view some of the administrative law judges as practically asking them to issue reversals in the interests of justice.

In general, it appears that the judicial system has developed adequate means to protect the independence of magistrates' decisions which implicate federalism or separation of powers. The *Pacemaker* case established that magistrates are adjuncts of the Article III courts. As a practical matter, the district judges are available to back up any magistrates' decisions that will reach the outside world and bring the judiciary into conflict with other components of government. The real limitation upon magistrates' independence is not the other branches of government, but the district judges who wield such power over the magistrates' task assignments. The magistrates' independence may be curbed, but the outputs from the judicial system are preserved and protected in the cloak of Article III legitimacy, because the judges can control task assignments and decisions.

MAGISTRATES' STATUS: KEY TO ROLE CONGRUENCE AND CONFLICT

Concerns and disagreements about the status to be accorded to the subordinate federal judges as judicial officers have lingered in various districts throughout the history of the magistrate system. These conflicts over status, more than any other factor involving the magistrate system, distract judicial officers' attention from the courts' case-processing responsibilities and thereby detract from the operations of the judicial system. The magistrates have worked to ensure that they receive the appropriate prestige and benefits for their positions as federal judicial officers. At the same time, members of Congress and judges have expressed constitutional and personal concerns about differentiating district judges from magistrates. In many districts, it is the status of magistrates, rather than their task assignments, which really lie at the heart of conflicts between judges and magistrates. For example, the magistrates in District A were dissatisfied with their limited role and limited task assignments. Yet the magistrates in District A occasionally presided over trials, even though such practices are legally contrary to their lack of statutorily required designation by the district judges. By contrast, the magistrates in District B, who are addressed as "Judge" and are regarded with respect throughout the district, evinced higher levels of satisfaction, even though their task assignments were more limited than the duties in District A.

Members of Congress emphasized that magistrates should be clearly differentiated from judges:

Under this bill, the clear line between the functions of the magistrate and the functions of the district judge, underscored by Chief Justice Burger in *Weber*, is totally obliterated. Under S.1613, the magistrate cannot be distinguished from an Article III, life-tenured judge. The magistrate will be presiding over trials in a black robe behind a bench in the courtroom used by the district judges. The magistrate will be empaneling juries, examining witnesses, making evidentiary rulings, finding facts, and entering judgments, just as the district judge does. From the standpoint of appearance, procedure, and function, an impartial observer will not be able to tell the difference between a magistrate and an Article III judge. The magistrate will, under S.1613, look like a judge, act like a judge, and speak like a judge. Unfortunately, a magistrate is not a judge, at least not in an Article III sense. [19]

In response to this concern expressed on constitutional grounds that "the magistrate will . . . look like a judge," most magistrates would say, "So what?" The magistrates point to the *Pacemaker* decision, which the Supreme Court declined to review, to note that they have legitimate constitutional authority as Article III adjuncts. Moreover, they possess broad statutory authority, including the ability to preside over trials, through three legislative enactments by Congress. Therefore, according to these subordinate judges, in order to fulfill their duties as judicial officers effectively, magistrates both need and deserve to be accorded with status as judges. This status need not imply equality with district judges in terms of authority, since district judges clearly have broader authority, but it is in the best interests of the judiciary to have magistrates regarded and performing as acknowledged federal judges.

By contrast, many district judges, particularly those with a limited conceptualization of the magistrates' roles, emphasize clear differentiation between judges and magistrates. Several judges complained that magistrates "think that they are judges." As previously noted, one judge in District A became angry when a memo addressed to the district's judges was sent to the magistrates and when magistrates' names were included on a list of the district's judges. Another judge complained that magistrates "think they are free agents—acting like an independent judiciary."

The conflicting status expectations between magistrates and judges have been manifested in regard to several specific issues. For example, the issue of how magistrates are to be addressed has been a serious concern in a number of districts. Most magistrates are concerned with being addressed by an appropriate title, whether "Judge" or "Magistrate," if only because they are officers of the federal court and they represent the court in their actions both within and out of court. Many magistrates, on the other hand, view the title "Judge" not only as an entitlement, but also as a functional necessity if they are to perform effectively when presiding over trials. Many district judges, by contrast, insist that magistrates and judges be differentiated by title. In District A, some judges instructed staff members that magistrates were not to be addressed as "Judge."

Concerns about the appropriate title for the position that replaced the commissioners dates back to the first discussions of the legislation which subsequently became the 1968 Magistrates Act. In common parlance, "magistrate" is a generic term for judicial officer which can refer to judges at all levels of judicial systems, from lay judges responsible for minor matters to professional trial judges. The term "magistrate" is an honored and prestigious title in the English legal system, but it has less favorable connotations in the United States because it is commonly used for low-level lay judges or the stereotypical "justice of the peace" in rural areas.[20] As observed in District C and other districts in which low level state officials possess the title of "Magistrate," the U.S. magistrates feel that their image and exercise of authority suffers because their title creates confusion with the more familiar and better established state court title and position. A survey of the Federal Bar Association revealed that nearly half of the lawyers would prefer that magistrates be given a new title in order to avoid the detrimental confusion.[21] There has been a concern that the title of the position serves to deter attorneys and clients from consenting to have cases heard by magistrates, since they would prefer to have the case handled by a "judge." Thus, the potential flexibility and benefits of the magistrate system are diminished.[22]

A report to Congress by the Judicial Conference, prepared by the Administrative Office, minimized the difficulties with the magistrates' title by saying that the "best way to overcome any localized concerns as to the appropriateness of the title of United States magistrates is for the district courts to use their magistrates to the fullest and to inform the bar as to the importance attaching to the office."[23] Although observations in District D and elsewhere bear out the accuracy of the Administrative Office's analysis, this exhortation cannot influence those district judges who possess a narrow conceptualization of the magistrates' roles, insist on differentiating judges from magistrates, and therefore believe that the title, even with its detrimental implications, is appropriate for the magistrates.

Magistrates and their national organization have not been ambivalent about the title. When magistrates see their colleagues in places like District B called "Judge" as a matter of course by attorneys and district judges alike, they recognize the status that is possible for their office to attain. Therefore many magistrates feel frustrated by the relatively low status accorded to them by judges in their own districts. Recently, in what could be regarded as a minor symbol of rebellion, the magistrates in one circuit voted to recommend to the Judicial Conference that U.S. magistrates henceforth be known as "Associate Judges." The titles "Associate Judge" and "Deputy Judge" were among the alternatives to "Magistrate" that had been discussed when the office was created. Because many judges vigorously oppose any title change that might reduce the differentiation between district judges and magistrates and, moreover, because the magistrates also sought other goals related to pay and benefits, leaders of the magistrates' national organization persuaded the circuit group to rescind their resolution. Instead, the national leaders attempted to utilize less formal means to improve the status of magistrates, such as having friendly district and circuit judges attempt to persuade the Chief Justice of the United States to issue an internal memorandum to the federal judiciary permitting the use of the title "Judge" for magistrates. According to some magistrates, former Chief Justice Burger insisted on the title "Magistrate," but they hope that Chief Justice Rehnquist will be less rigid.

The form of address for magistrates has become an emotional issue for magistrates and judges alike in districts in which differing expectations exist. At a conference for magistrates from several circuits, one well-known magistrate addressed the assembled magistrates and other officials about the potential for obtaining consent trials through the use of the title "Judge." He concluded his remarks by shaking his head sadly and saying, "there are still judges out there who won't allow magistrates to be called judge," whereupon one magistrate from District A yelled out from the audience, "No kidding!" Although the assembled magistrates laughed in commiseration with their colleagues from District A and elsewhere, the emphasis given to the subject by the speaker and the abrupt interjection by the audience member were indicative of the heartfelt importance that title and other aspects of status have for magistrates. Because many judges are equally strong in their opposition to granting magistrates the status of full judicial officers, the Administrative Office, while desiring to encourage broader utilization of magistrates, seeks to downplay the title issue in order to avoid generating emotional opposition among district judges. Such opposition from Article III judges might ignite opposition to other aspects of the magistrate system.

The accoutrements of judicial office are also a source of conflicting status-related expectations between magistrates and some judges. The judicial robe is valuable to magistrates because their image and effectiveness as judicial officers are enhanced by their ability to rely upon and utilize the familiar symbols of the courts. As one magistrate commented in regard to magistrates' work at criminal detention hearings, "There is something nice about wearing a robe—you can talk [the government] out of [seeking in camera presentation of evidence]. The robe makes you more persuasive." Early observers of the magistrate system commented upon the desirability of magistrates wearing the traditional black robe of a judicial officer.[24] According to magistrates and officials at the Administrative Office, magistrates in a few districts are forbidden to wear robes. The number of districts in which magistrates are not permitted to wear judicial robes has not been established, but the continued existence of such districts has been documented by Seron.[25] An official at the Administrative Office stated that the biggest continuing problem within the magistrate system involves those districts in which judges will not permit the magistrates to wear a robe, park in the courthouse parking lot, eat in the judge's lunchroom, or other matters, which, although sometimes small in a practical sense, can loom large in symbolic meaning by conveying the magistrates' lowly status and role. In District B, in which the magistrates' respected status is clear, the wearing of judicial robes is taken for granted. In fact, at the installation ceremony for a new judge in District B, the chief judge instructed the magistrates to bring their robes and sit with the robed federal and state judges at the front of the auditorium. Such clear endorsements of the magistrates' status are unimaginable in some districts, in which judges take a narrow view of the magistrates' roles.

Magistrates relate their concerns about status not just to their relationship with district judges, but also within the context of the entire federal judicial branch. Magistrates' status and role can be affected by the judges' law clerks, often to an extent that magistrates themselves will never know. Because of their close and continual contact within chambers, law clerks are in a good position to develop strong personal relationships with the judges. In their clear and universal roles as personal assistants to the judges, law clerks can influence case decisions as well as the organization of case processing.[26] Several judges admitted that they permitted their law clerks to help determine which tasks would be sent to the magistrates. One judge said that his law clerks are permitted to keep the "sexy cases," with the clear implication that the routine, pedestrian, and boring tasks are reserved for the magistrates.

Several judges stated explicitly that they train their law clerks by having them review the magistrates' work. Thus magistrates can have reports and recommendations rejected and returned to them bearing all of the earmarks of a decision by a junior law clerk rather than the judge. For any magistrate, who inevitably has more experience than judges' law clerks and may even have previously been a law professor, state judge, or U.S. attorney, it can be a demeaning slap in the face to have recent law school graduates overrule carefully considered opinions on civil litigation, Social Security, or prisoner matters. Overall, the influence that law clerks are permitted to have over magistrates' tasks and roles within district courts can convey unintentional but stinging messages from the judges about the status of the magistrates within the judiciary.

These unresolved and continually brewing battles over magistrates' status are a consequence of the limited definition given to magistrates by Congress and the congressional deference to district judges in administering the magistrate system. The federal courts benefit from the flexible utilization of magistrates, but a price is paid in terms of internal conflict and job dissatisfaction, because the issue of magistrates' status has never been completely settled in the judiciary. Although Congress anticipated some practical problems in creating subordinate judges, the intangible accoutrements and status of judicial office have emerged as a primary source of festering problems.

THE IMPORTANCE OF MAGISTRATES: A CONCLUDING COMMENT

Magistrates are obviously important actors within the judiciary because of their decision-making authority and myriad functions for maintaining the judicial system. An understanding of the magistrates' roles and functions is especially important in light of their relative invisibility within the federal courts. Important discretionary decisions are made daily by a tier of subordinate judges who are not recognized or understood by the public. When political actors are beyond easy public scrutiny, there are always risks that their practices and actions will conflict with or have adverse consequences for the governmental principles, structures, and processes of the constitutional system. In the case of the magistrates, although their flexibility and adaptability create risks that their roles will evolve in unpredictable directions, these judicial officers have generally functioned within the limits of controllable expectations. Certain aspects of the magistrates' roles and functions, particularly decisions affecting categories of litigants (e.g., Social Security claimants and prisoners) and the coerced consents from litigants, deserve continued examination and monitoring. Overall, however, these anomalous judicial actors, who are subordinate yet authoritative judges, make valuable contributions to the operations of the judicial system. The magistrates have clearly become integrated as important functional components of the district courts whose influence and importance continue to develop and evolve.

NOTES

1. Dissenting Views of the Hon. Elizabeth Holtzman, U.S. Congress, House Report No. 1364, Magistrates Act of 1978, 95th Cong., 2d Sess., 1978, 42.

2. Comment, "An Expanding Civil Role For United States Magistrates," *American University Law Review* 26 (1976): 105.

3. David L. Shapiro, "Federal Habeas Corpus: A Study in Massachusetts," *Harvard Law Review* 87 (1973): 366.

4. William Bennett Turner, "When Prisoners Sue: A Study of Prisoner Section 1983 Suits in the Federal Courts," *Harvard Law Review* 92 (1979): 618.

5. Ibid., 625.

6. Roger A. Hanson, "What should be done when prisoners want to take the state to court?" *Judicature* 70 (1987): 224.

7. Dissenting Views of the Representative John F. Seiberling, U.S. Congress, House Report No. 1364, 40–41.

8. Wharton-Thomas v. United States, 721 F.2d 922 (3rd Cir. 1983); Pacemaker Diagnostic Clinic v. Instromedix Inc., 725 F.2d 537 (9th Cir. 1984) (en banc).

9. Peter G. McCabe, "The Federal Magistrate Act of 1979," *Harvard Journal on Legislation* 16 (1979): 343–401; Note, "Article III Constraints and the Expanding Civil Jurisdiction of Federal Magistrates: A Dissenting View," *Yale Law Journal* 88 (1979): 1023–1061.

10. 725 F.2d at 543.

11. 721 F.2d at 925.

12. Dissenting Views of the Hon. Elizabeth Holtzman, U.S. Congress, House Report No. 1364, 42.

13. Robert A. Carp and Ronald Stidham, *The Federal Courts*, (Washington, D.C.: CQ Press, 1985), 77. Carp and Stidham misinterpret Seron's tables to imply that parties are very frequently willing to consent to have magistrates hear their cases. In fact, Seron's data concerned magistrates' *perceptions* of parties' willingness to consent. Seron warned, even then, that the figures "must be interpreted with some caution," because some of the magistrates responding to the survey had misinterpreted the question being put to them. Carroll Seron, *The Roles of Magistrates in Federal District Courts* (Washington, D.C.: Federal Judicial Center, 1983), 65–66.

14. Carroll Seron, *The Roles of Magistrates: Nine Case Studies*, (Washington, D.C.: Federal Judicial Center, 1985), 61–62.

15. Marbury v. Madison, 2 L.Ed.60 (1803) (decision establishing concept of judicial review, which helped to form the judiciary's place in the constitutional system of checks and balances between the three separated branches of government).

16. Dissenting views of Representatives Robert F. Drinan and Thomas N. Kindness, U.S. Congress, House Report No. 1364, 38.

17. *Pacemaker Diagnostic Clinic v. Instromedix Inc.*, 725 F.2d 537, 552 (Schroeder, J., dissenting).

18. Shapiro, "Federal Habeas Corpus," 366–367.

19. Dissenting Views of Representatives Robert F. Drinan and Thomas N. Kindness, U.S. Congress, House Report No. 1364, 37.

20. *The Federal Magistrates System: Report to the Congress by the Judicial Conference of the United States* (Washington, D.C.: U.S. Government Printing Office, 1981), 60–61.

21. Ibid., 62.

22. Ibid.

23. Ibid.

24. Linda J. Silberman, "Masters and Magistrates Part II: The American Analogue," *New York University Law Review* 50 (1975): 1363, n. 379.

25. According to Seron's study, the magistrates in the Eastern District of Kentucky are not permitted to wear judicial robes. Seron, *The Roles of Magistrates: Nine Case Studies*, 63 n. 67.

26. For a description of the role of law clerks within the federal courts, see Carp and Stidham, *The Federal Courts*, 78–82.

Select Bibliography

Aug, J. Vincent. "The Magistrate Act of 1979: From a Magistrate's Perspective." *Cincinnati Law Review* 49 (1980): 363–376.

Baum, Lawrence. "The Judicial Gatekeeping Function: A General Analysis." In *American Court Systems: Readings in Judicial Process and Behavior*, 2d ed., edited by Sheldon Goldman and Austin Sarat, 153–157. New York: Longman, 1989.

Carp, Robert A., and Ronald Stidham. *The Federal Courts*. Washington, D.C.: Congressional Quarterly, 1985.

Carp, Robert A., and Russell Wheeler. "Sink or Swim: The Socialization of Federal District Judges." *Journal of Public Law* 21 (1972): 359–393.

Comment. "An Adjudicative Role for Federal Magistrates in Civil Cases." *University of Chicago Law Review* 40 (1973): 584–599.

Comment. "An Expanding Civil Role for United States Magistrates." *American University Law Review* 26 (1976): 66–108.

Cooley, John W. "Designing an Efficient Magistrate Referral System: The Key to Coping with Expanding Federal Caseloads in the 1980s." *Civil Justice Quarterly* 1 (1982): 124–150.

Davidow, Robert P. "Beyond Merit Selection: Judicial Careers Through Merit Promotion." *Texas Tech Law Review* 12 (1981): 886–907.

Easton, David. *A Systems Analysis of Political Life*. New York: John Wiley, 1965.

Feeley, Malcolm M. *Court Reform on Trial*. New York: Basic Books, 1983.

Fish, Peter G. *The Politics of Federal Judicial Administration*. Princeton: Princeton University Press, 1973.

———. "Merit Selection and Politics: Choosing a Judge of the United States Court of Appeals for the Fourth Circuit." *Wake Forest Law Review* 15 (1979): 635–654.

Fiss, Owen. "The Bureaucratization of the Judiciary." *Yale Law Journal*. 92 (1983): 1442–1468.

General Accounting Office. *Potential Benefits of Federal Magistrates System Can Be Better Realized*. Washington, D.C.: U.S. Government Printing Office, 1983.

———. *The U.S. Magistrates: How Their Services Have Assisted Administration of Several District Courts; More Improvements Needed*. Washington, D.C.: U.S. Government Printing Office, 1974.

Gibson, James L. "The Role Concept in Judicial Research." *Law and Policy Quarterly* 3 (1981): 291–311.

Goldman, Sheldon. "Judicial Selection and the Qualities that Make a 'Good' Judge." *The Annals of the American Academy of Political and Social Science* 462 (1982): 112-124.

Goldman, Sheldon, and Thomas P. Jahnige. *The Federal Courts as a Political System*, 3d ed. New York: Harper & Row, 1985.

Hanson, Roger A. "What should be done when prisoners want to take the state to court?" *Judicature* 70 (1987): 223-227.

Howard, J. Woodford. *Courts of Appeals in the Federal Judicial System.* Princeton: Princeton University Press, 1981.

McCabe, Peter G. "The Federal Magistrates Act of 1979." *Harvard Journal on Legislation* 16 (1979): 343-401.

McCree, Wade H., Jr. "Bureaucratic Justice: An Early Warning." *University of Pennsylvania Law Review* 129 (1981): 777-797.

Merton, Robert K. *Social Theory and Social Structure.* New York: The Free Press, 1968.

Note. "Article III Constraints and the Expanding Civil Jurisdiction of Federal Magistrates: A Dissenting View." *Yale Law Journal* 88 (1979): 1023-1061.

Note. "Federal Magistrates and the Principles of Article III." *Harvard Law Review* 97 (1984): 1947-1963.

Peterson, Richard W. "The Federal Magistrates Act: A New Dimension in the Implementation of Justice." *Iowa Law Review* 56 (1970): 62-99.

Posner, Richard A. *The Federal Courts: Crisis and Reform.* Cambridge, Mass.: Harvard University Press, 1985.

Puro, Steven. "Two Studies of Federal Magistrates." *The Justice System Journal* 11 (1986): 102-105.

———. "United States Magistrates: A New Federal Judicial Officer." *The Justice System Journal* 2 (1976): 141-156.

Puro, Steven, Roger A. Goldman, and Alice M. Padawer-Singer. "The Evolving Role of U.S. Magistrates in the District Courts." *Judicature* 64 (1981): 437-449.

Resnik, Judith. "Managerial Judges." *Harvard Law Review* 96 (1982): 376-448.

———. "The Mythic Meaning of Article III Courts." *University of Colorado Law Review* 56 (1985): 581-617.

Ryan, John Paul, Allan Ashman, Bruce D. Sales, and Sandra Shane-DuBow. *American Trial Judges.* New York: The Free Press, 1980.

Seron, Carroll. *The Roles of Magistrates in the Federal District Courts.* Washington, D.C.: Federal Judicial Center, 1983.

———. *The Roles of Magistrates: Nine Case Studies.* Washington, D.C.: Federal Judicial Center, 1985.

———. "Magistrates and the work of federal courts: a new division of labor." *Judicature* 69 (1986): 353-359.

———. "The Professional Project of Parajudges: The Case of the U.S. Magistrates." *Law and Society Review* 22 (1988): 557-574.

Shapiro, David L. "Federal Habeas Corpus: A Study in Massachusetts." *Harvard Law Review* 87 (1973): 321-372.

Sheldon, Charles H. *The American Judicial Process: Models and Approaches.* New York: Dodd, Mead & Co., 1974.

Silberman, Linda J. "Masters and Magistrates Part II: The American Analogue." *New York University Law Review* 50 (1975): 1297–1372.

Sinclair, Kent, Jr. *Practice Before Federal Magistrates*. New York: Matthew Bender, 1987.

Stumpf, Harry P. *American Judicial Politics*. New York: Harcourt Brace Jovanovich, 1988.

Turner, William Bennett. "When Prisoners Sue: A Study of Prisoner Section 1983 Suits in the Federal Courts." *Harvard Law Review* 92 (1979): 610–663.

Index

ABOUT THE AUTHOR

CHRISTOPHER E. SMITH is Assistant Professor of Political Science at the University of Akron. He earned degrees at Harvard University, the University of Bristol (England), and the University of Tennessee College of Law. He received his Ph.D. from the University of Connecticut. He has contributed articles to *Judicature, The Justice System Journal, Howard Law Journal, Wayne Law Review*, and other scholarly journals.